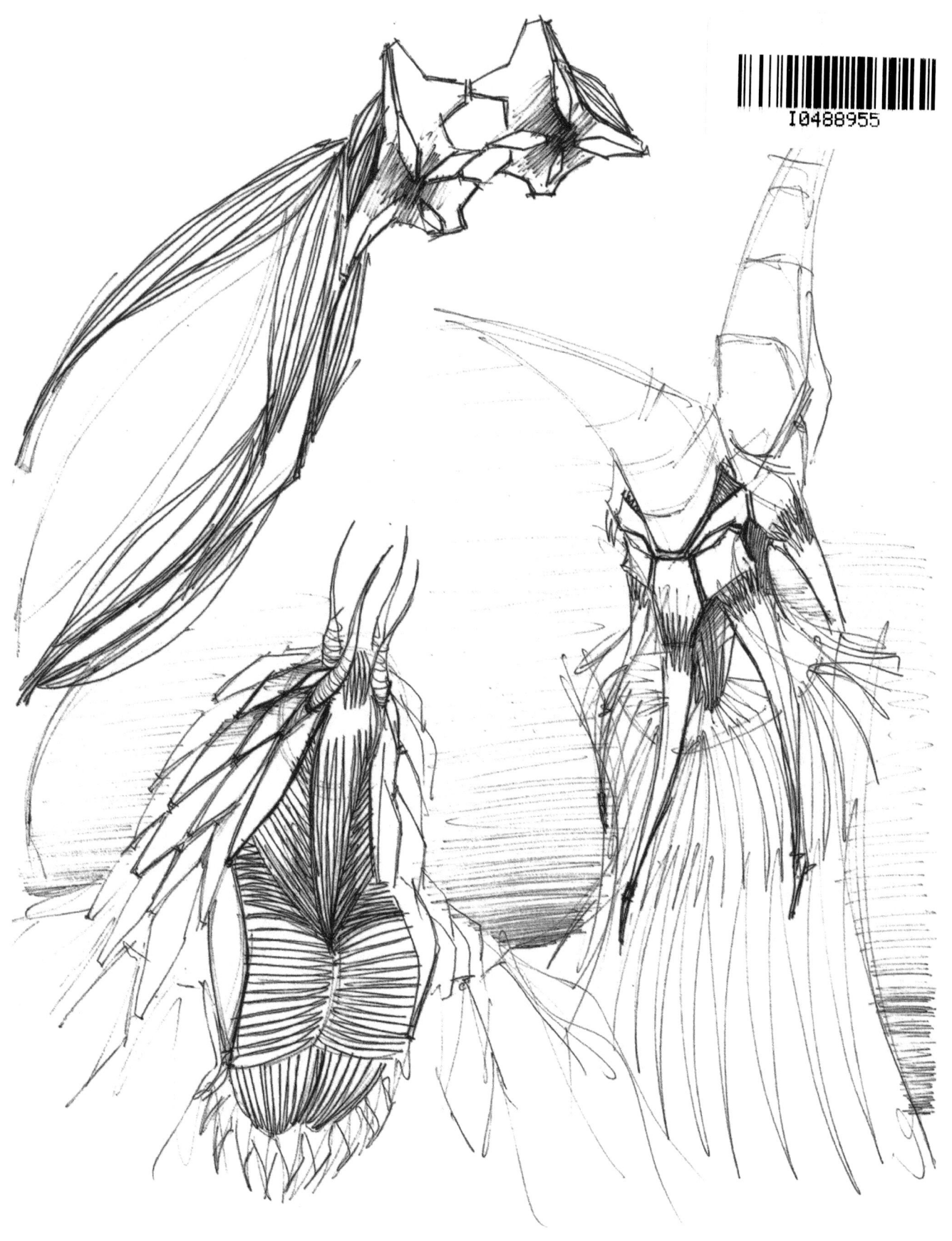

ISHTAR GATES

MARCO AURELIO GALAN HENRIQUEZ

I0488955

Copyright © 2013 Marco Aurelio Galan Henriquez

All rights reserved.

ISBN: 1492975605
ISBN-13: 978-1492975601

DEDICATION

To Hieronymus Bosch

The untold vision has frozen in dark bleeding lines

The ancient ghosts of Babylon emerge through the abyssal voice
of a dying mind

A mask of dust has broken

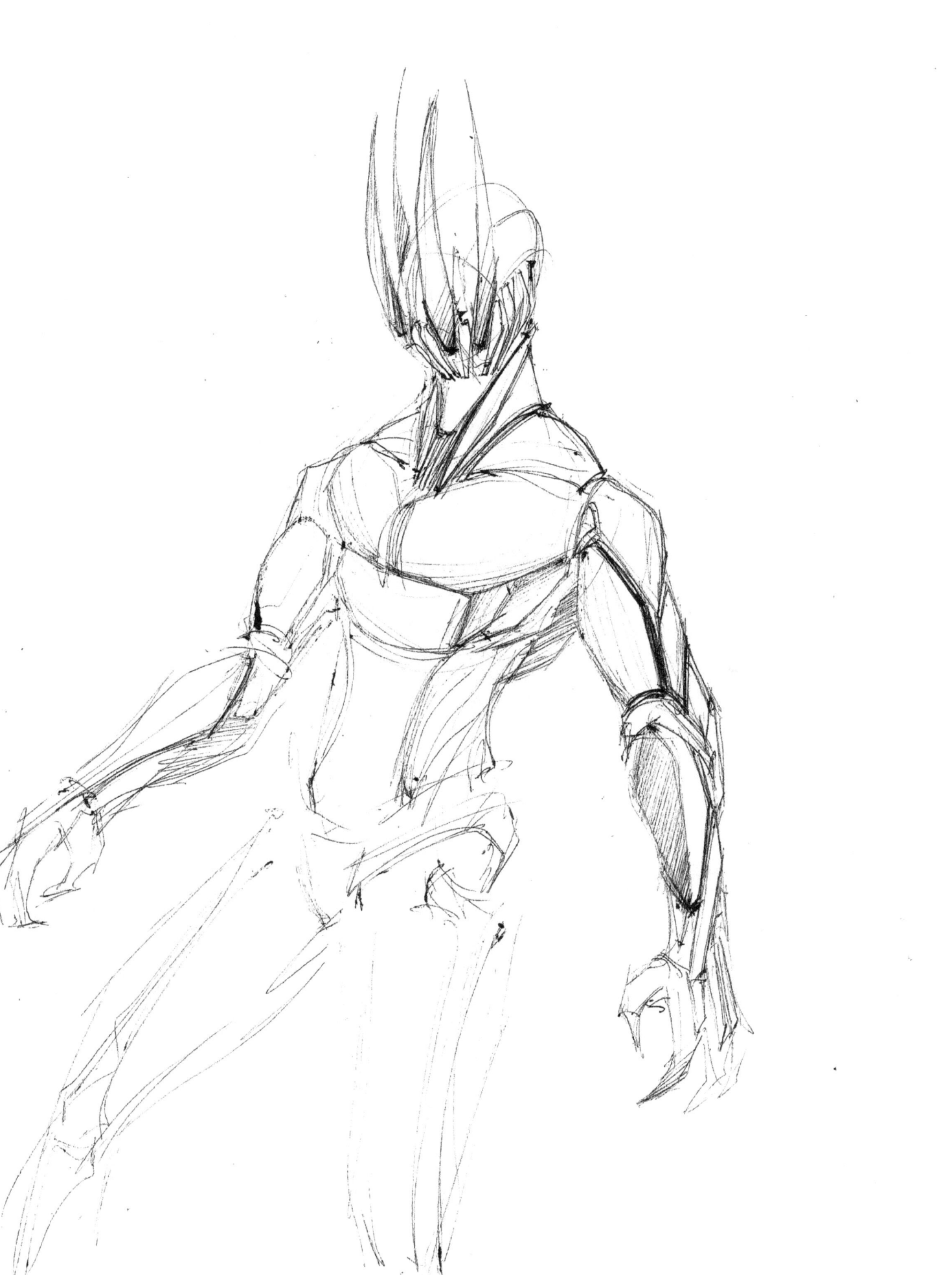

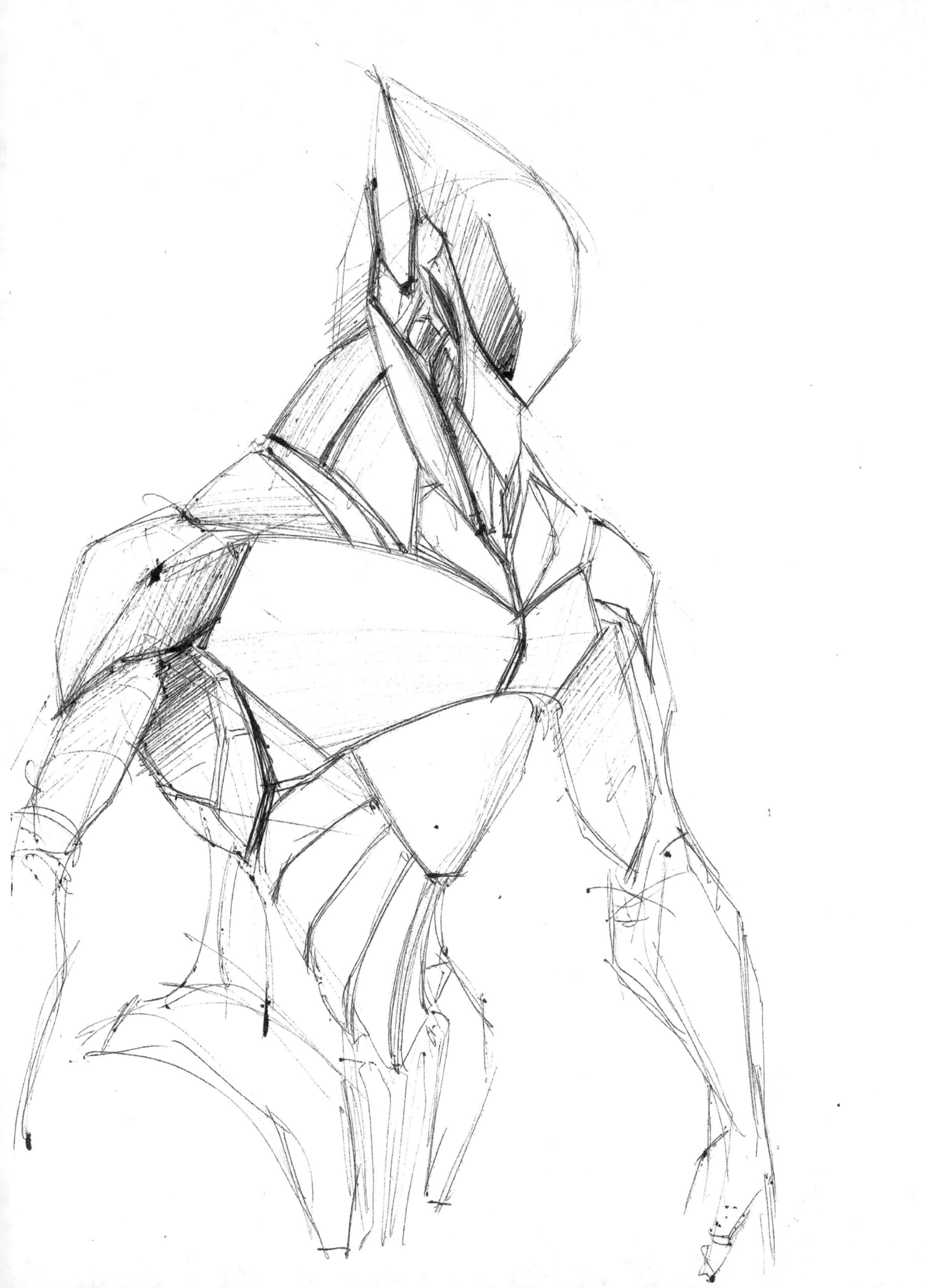

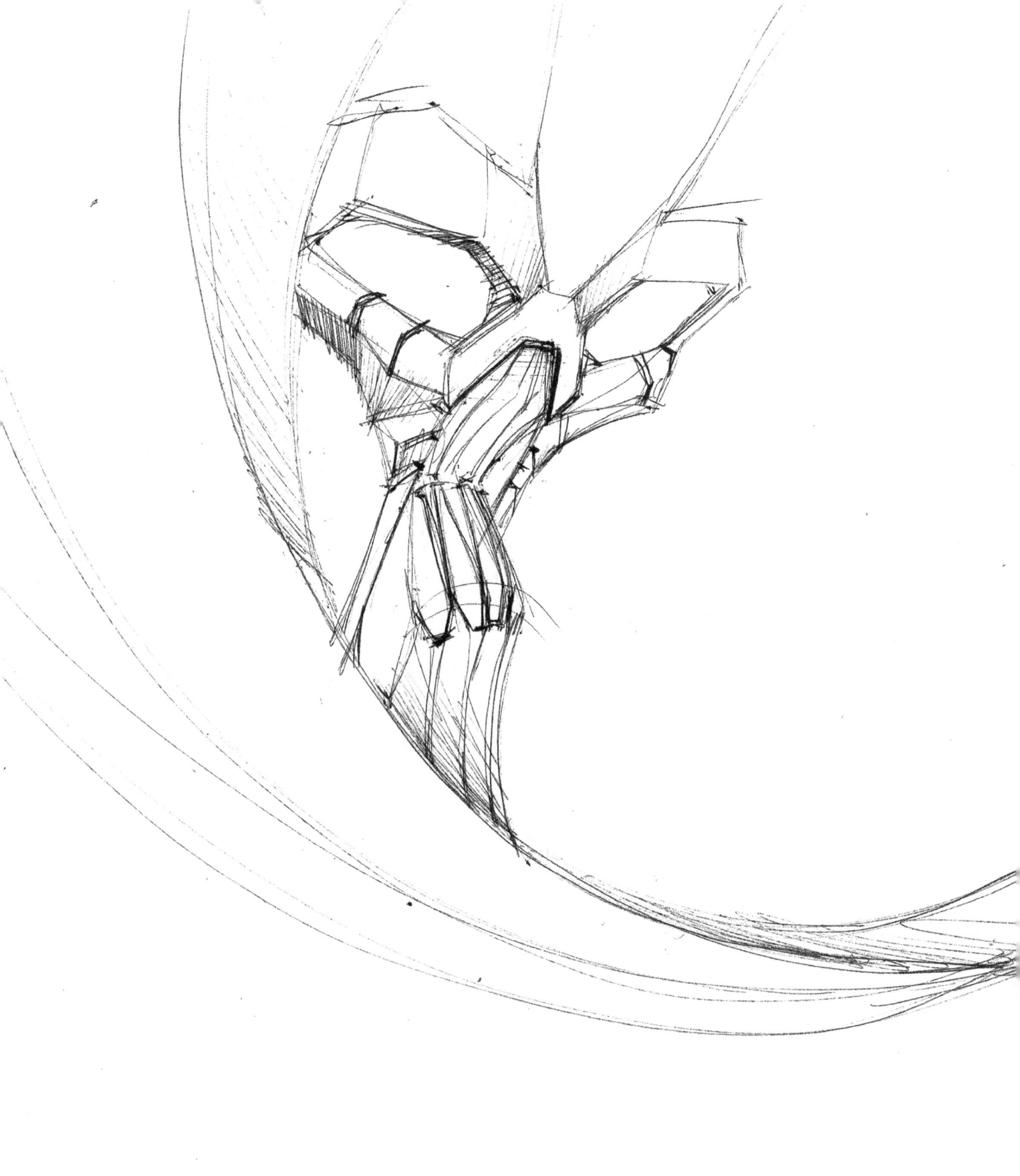

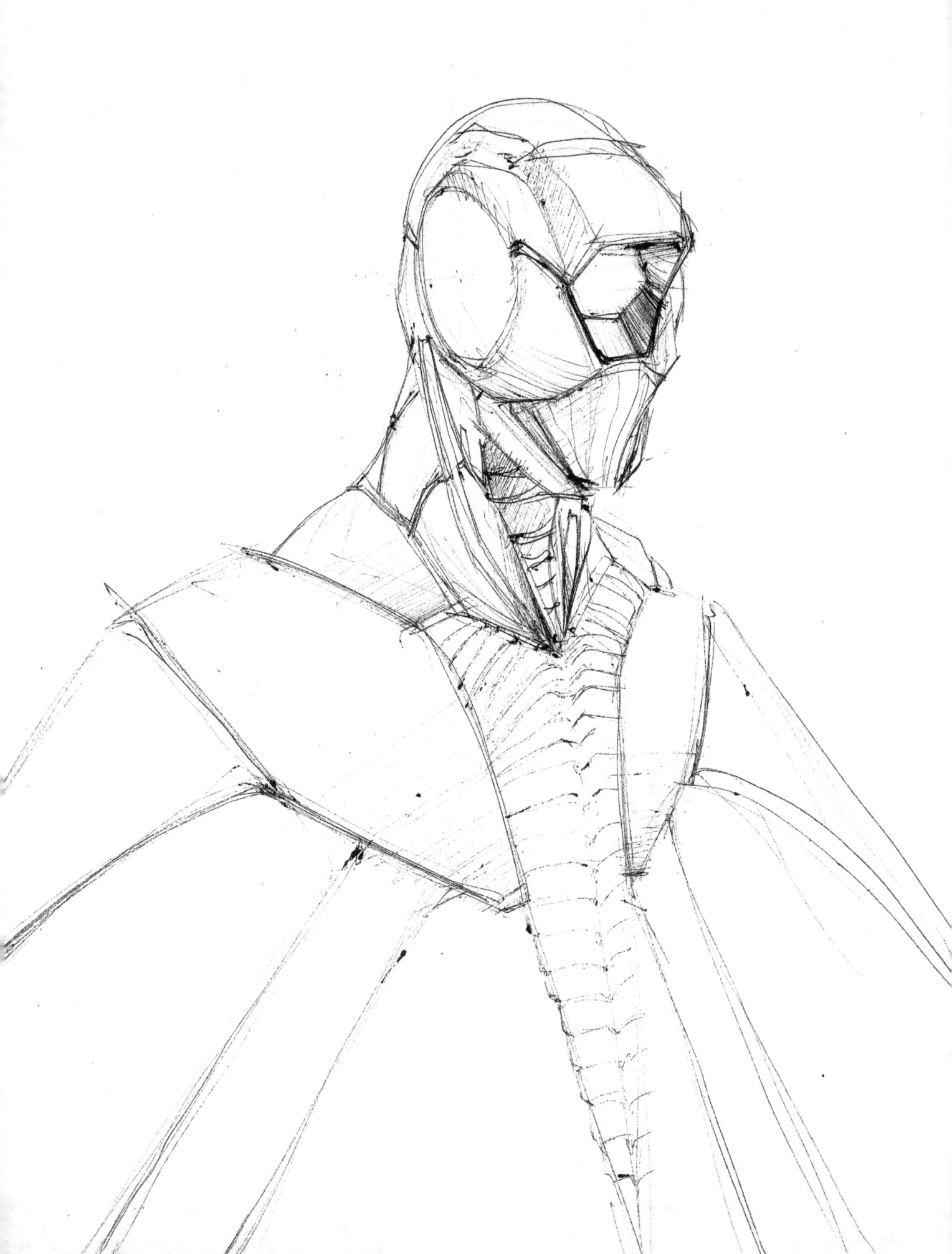

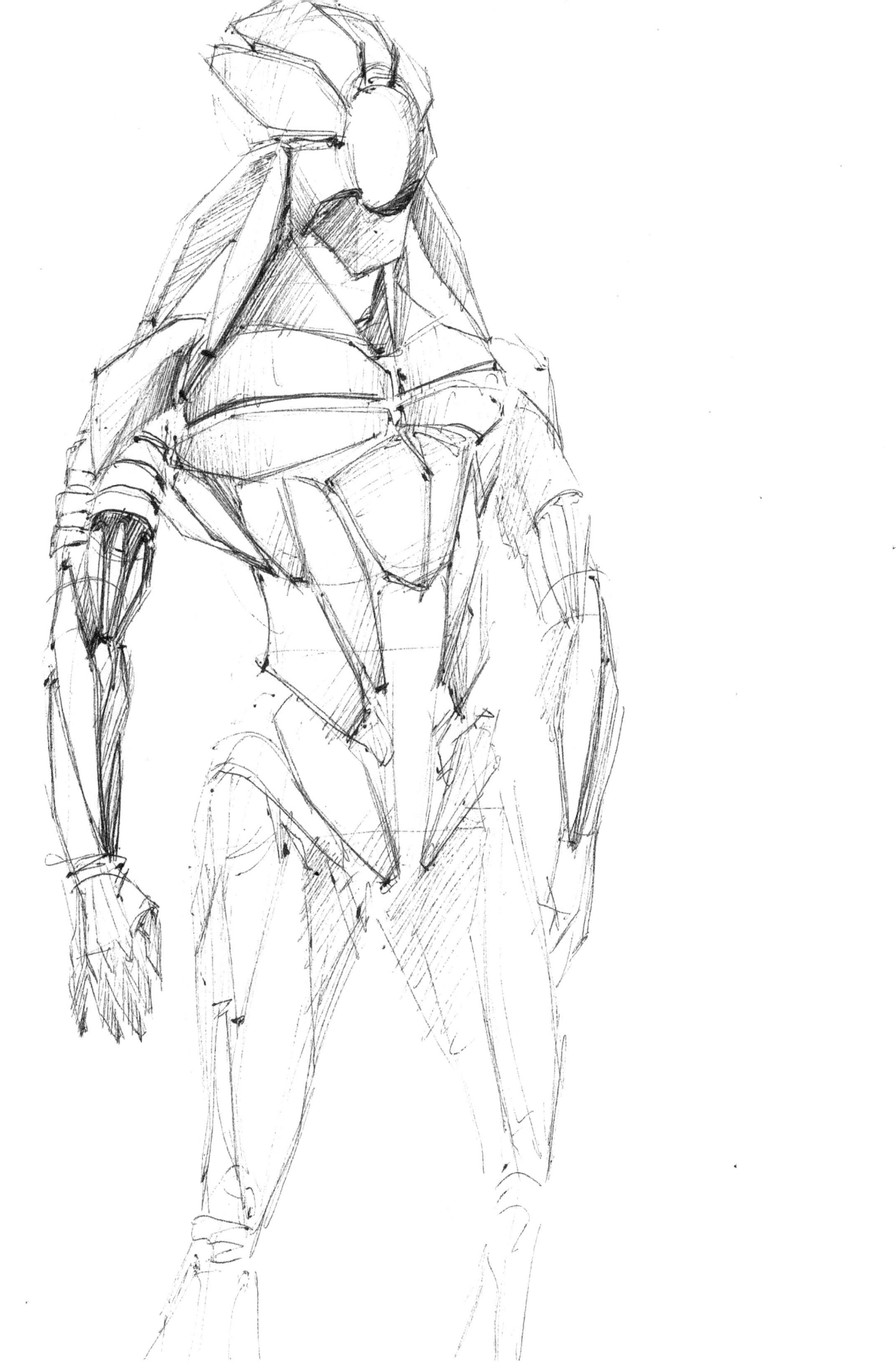

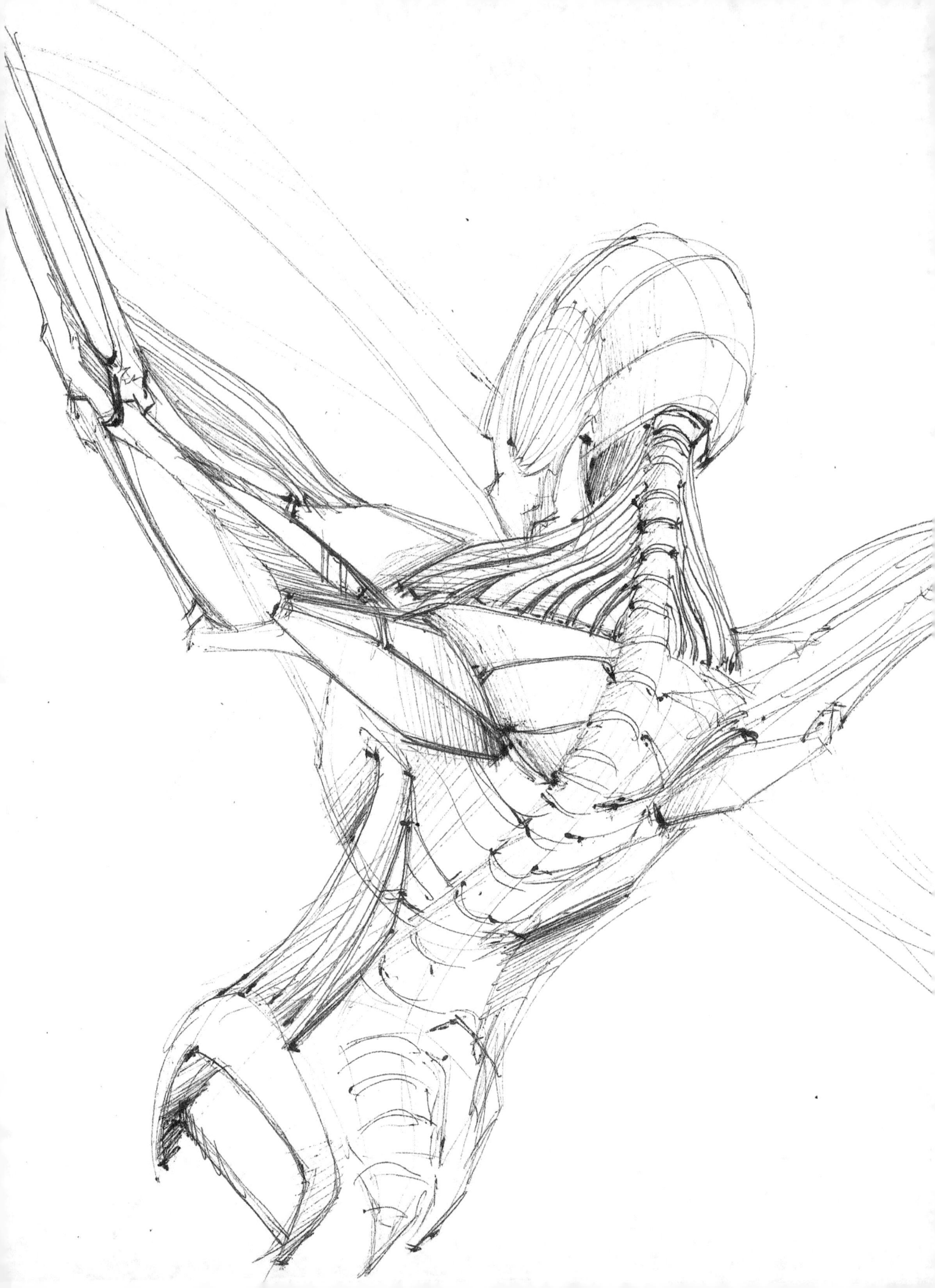

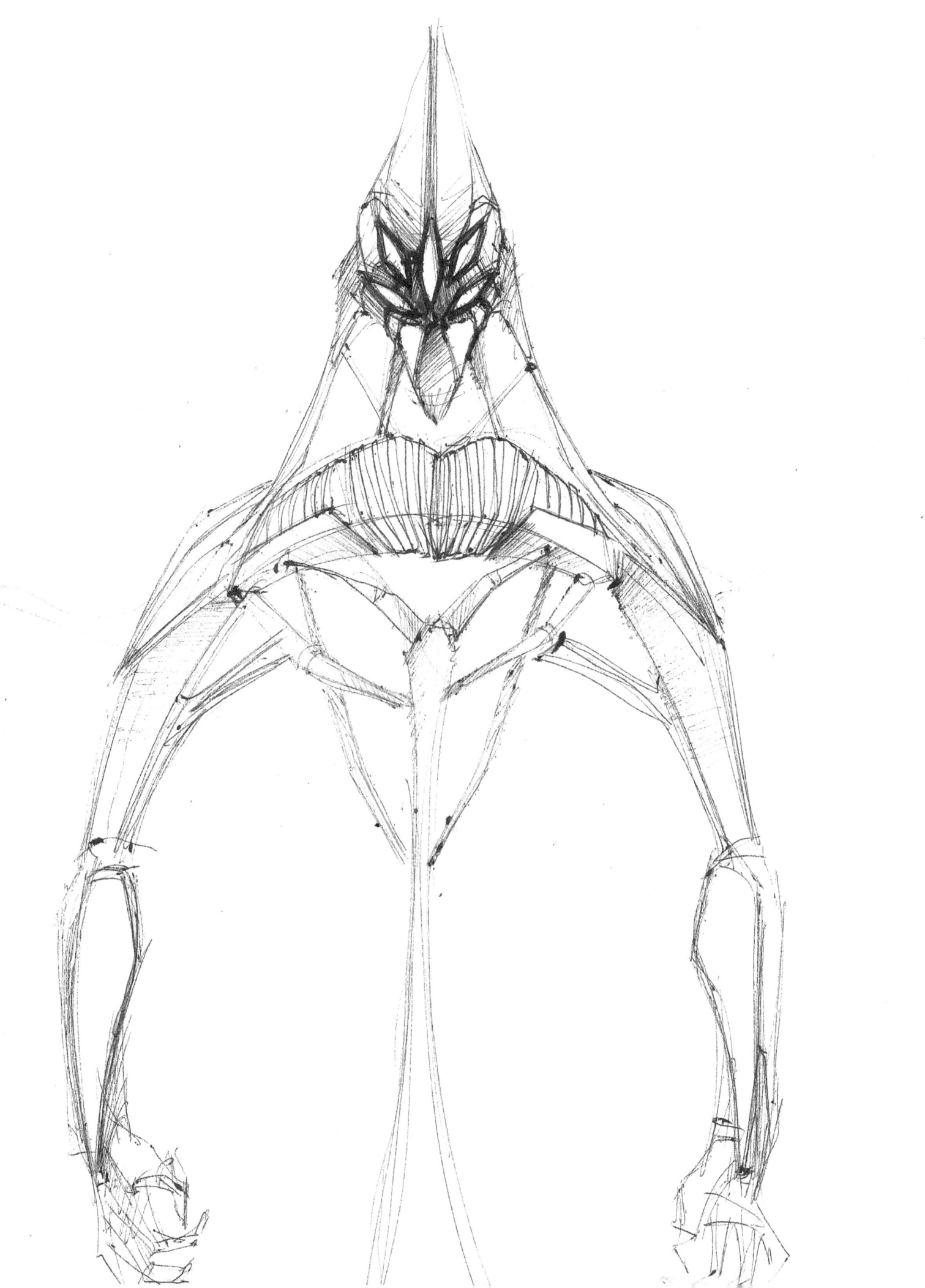

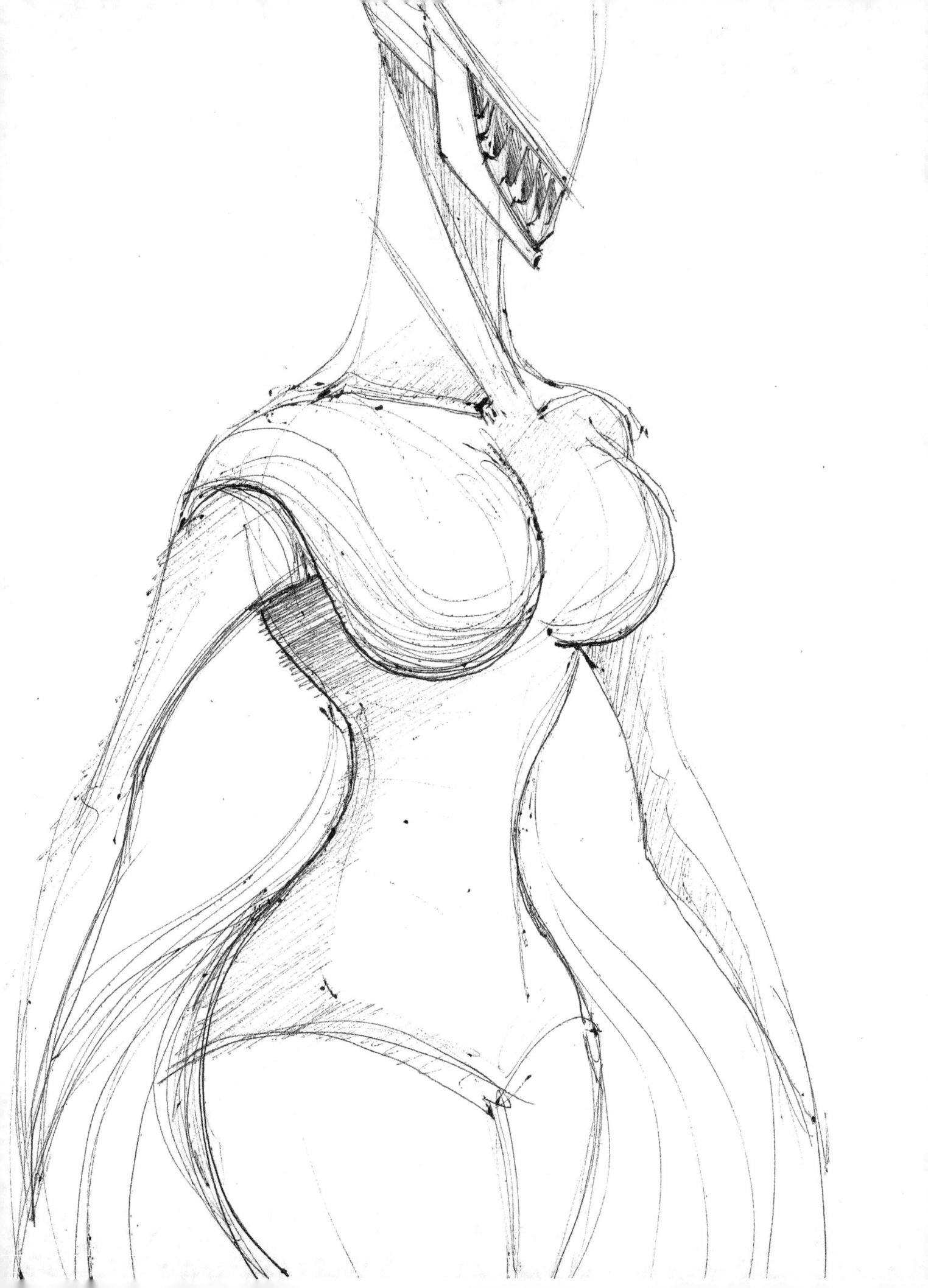

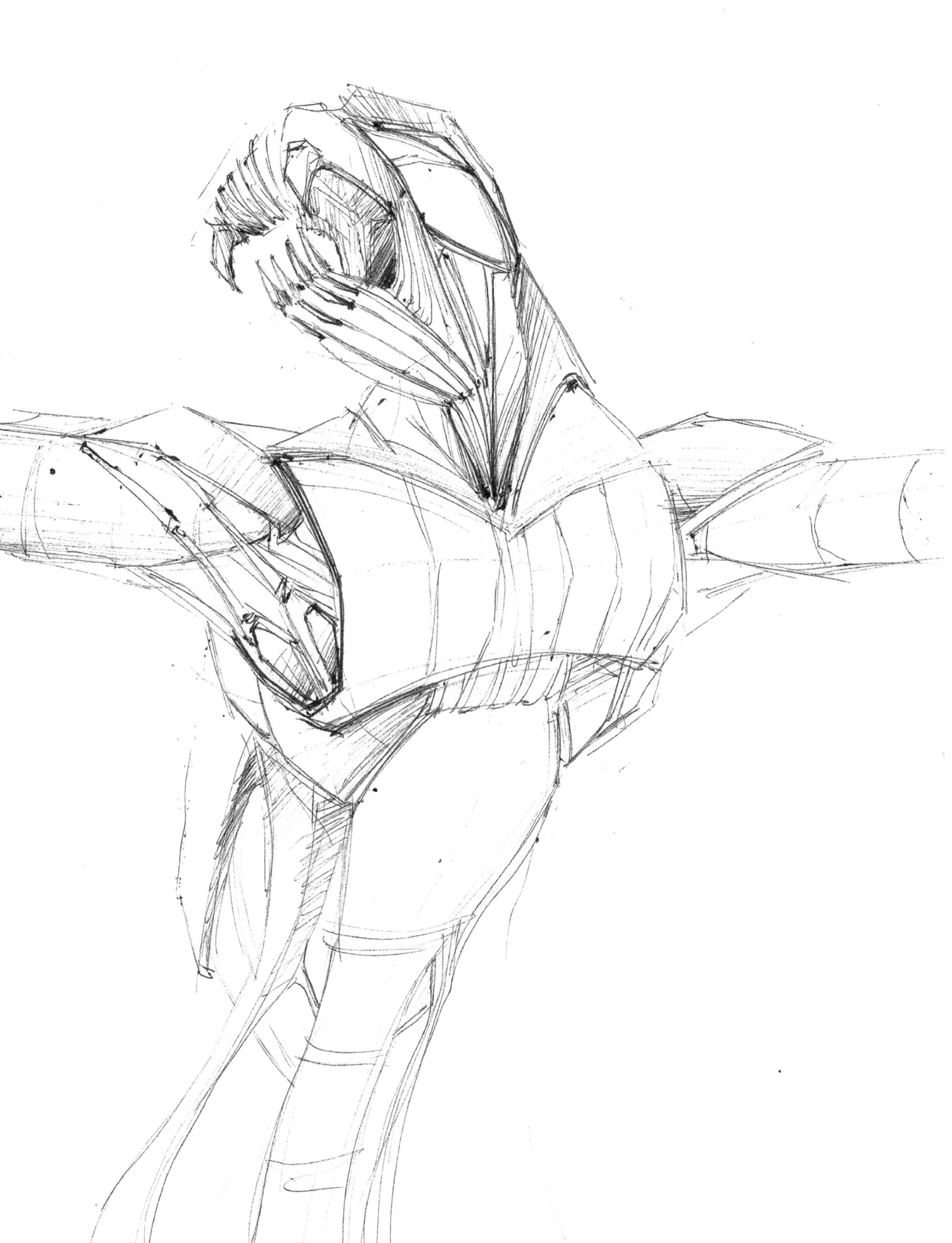

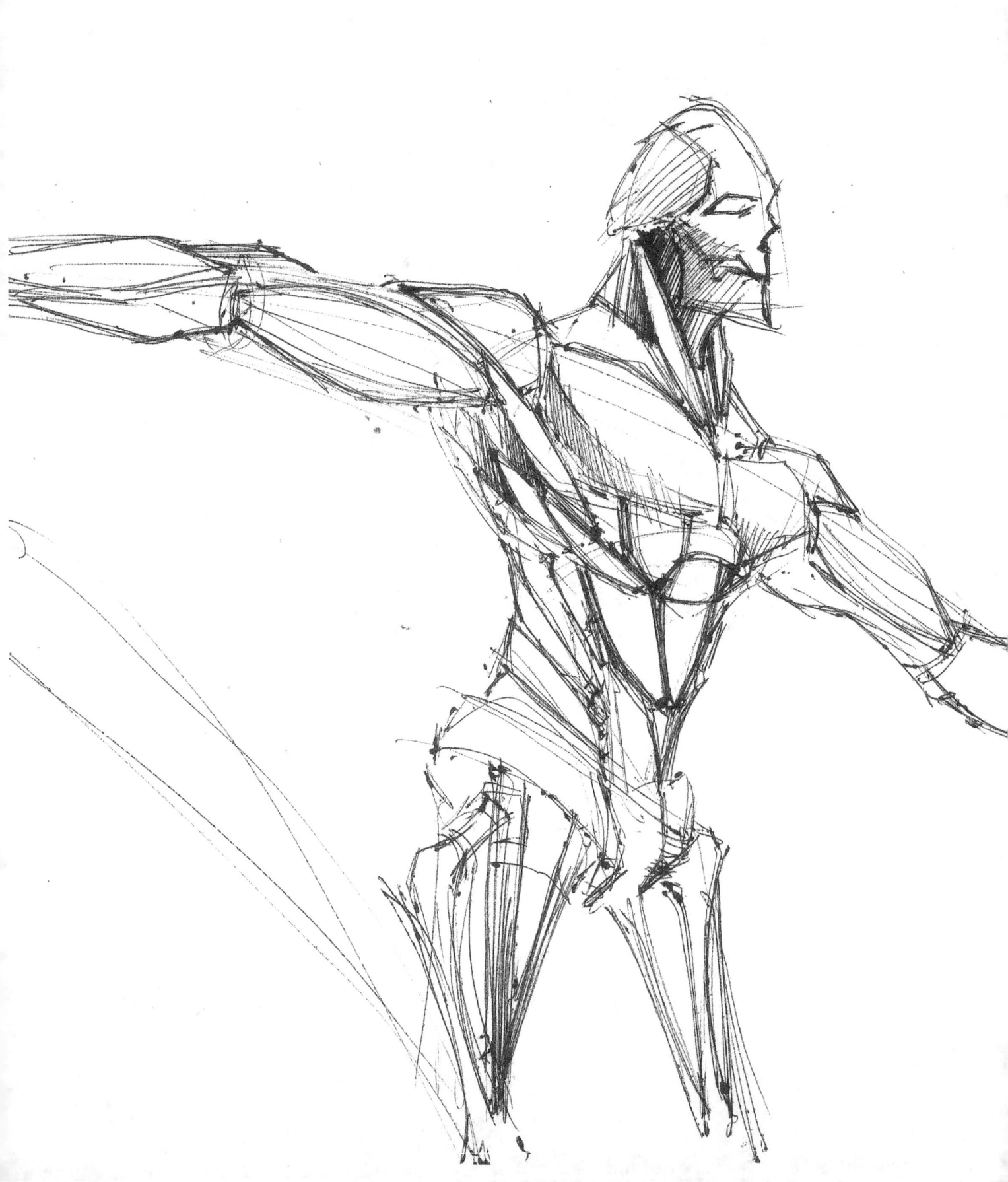

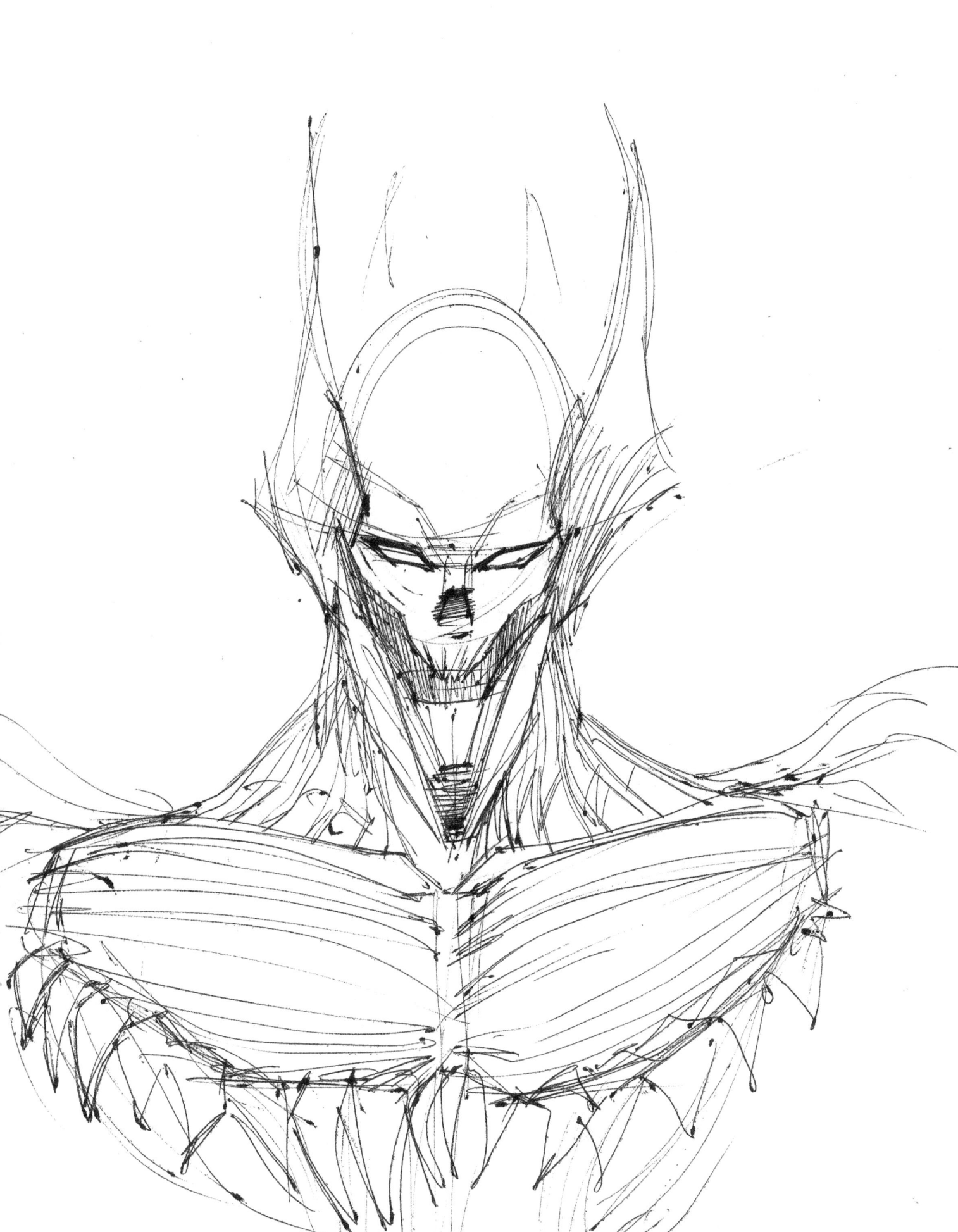

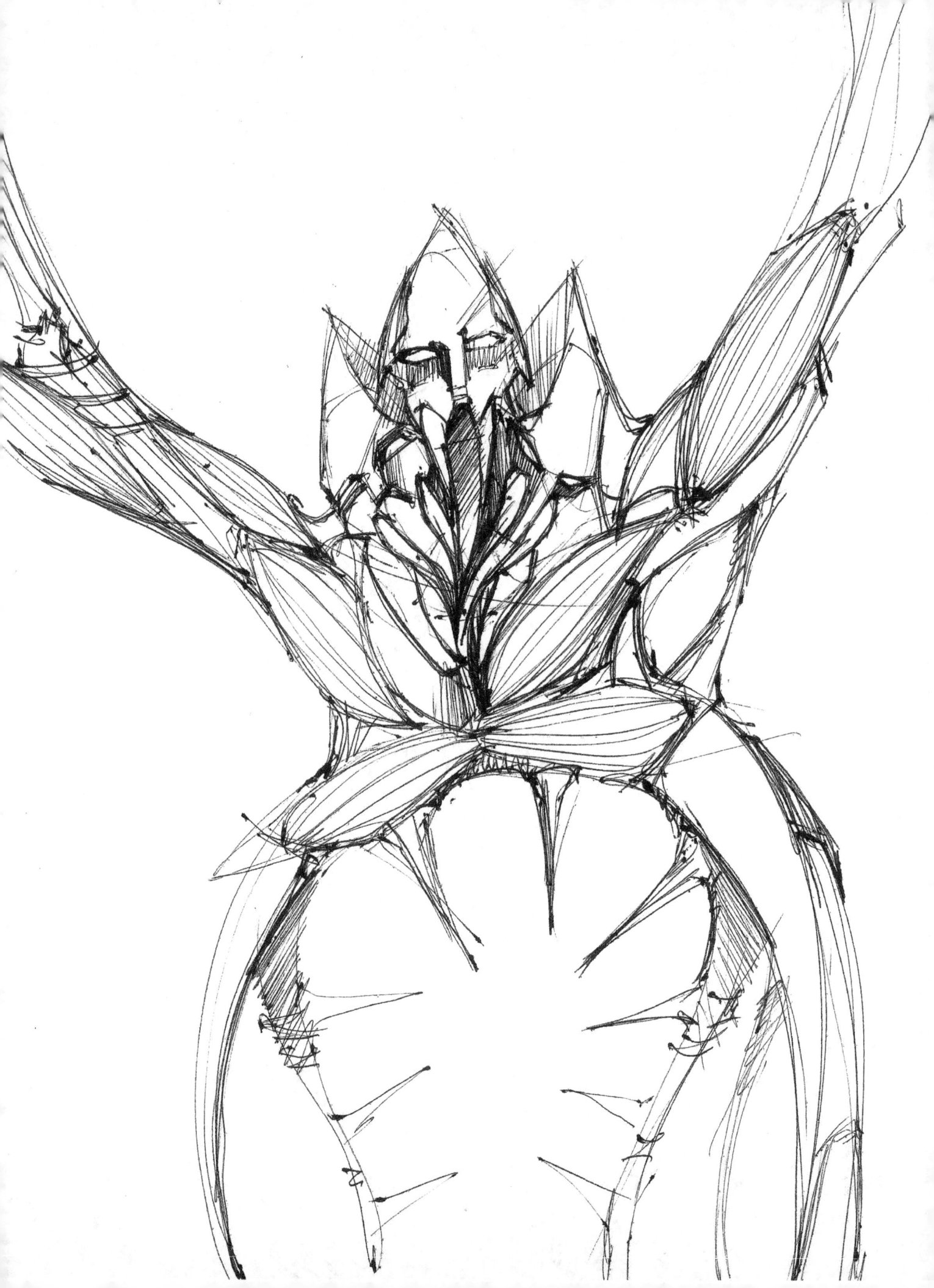

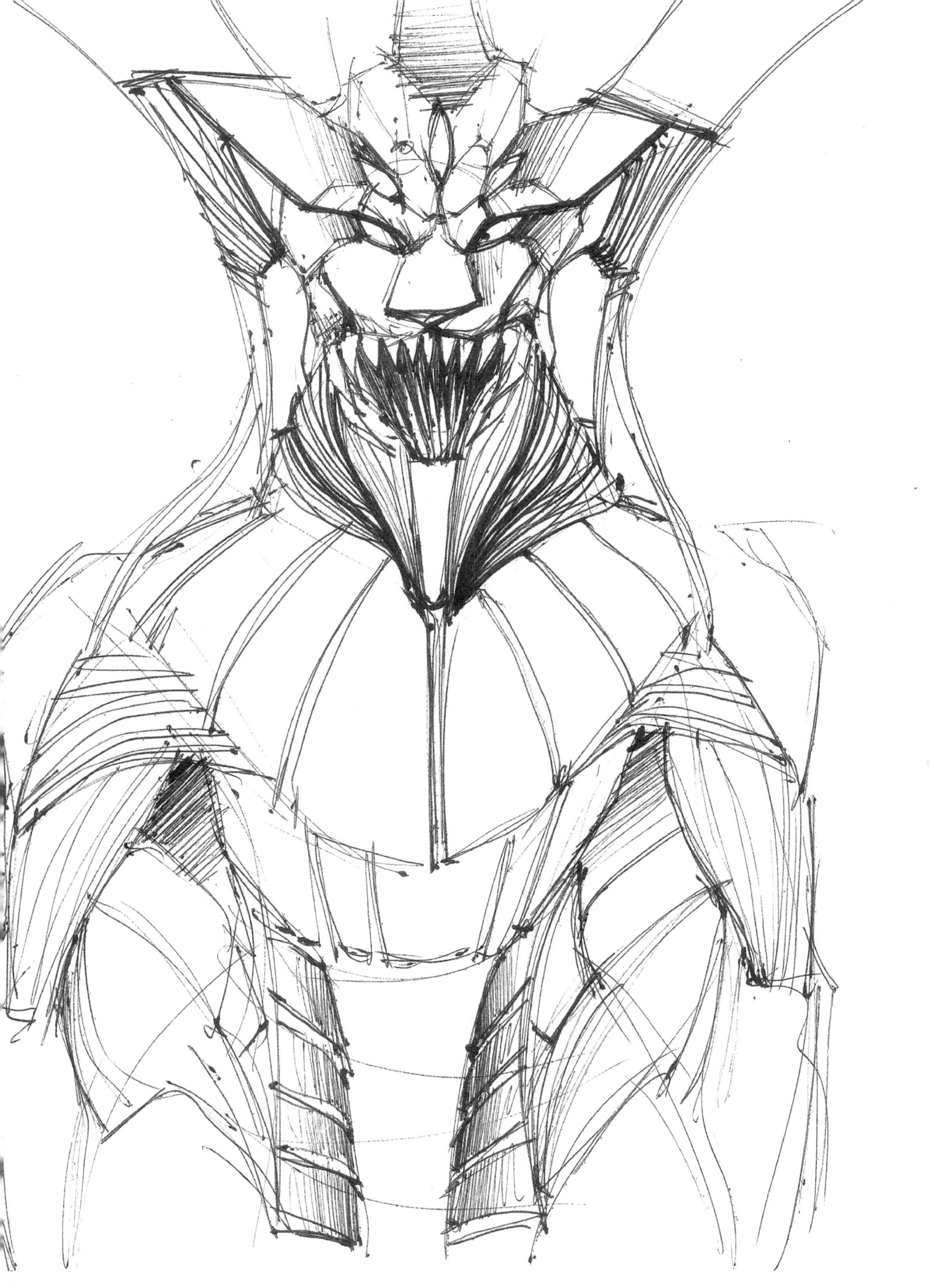

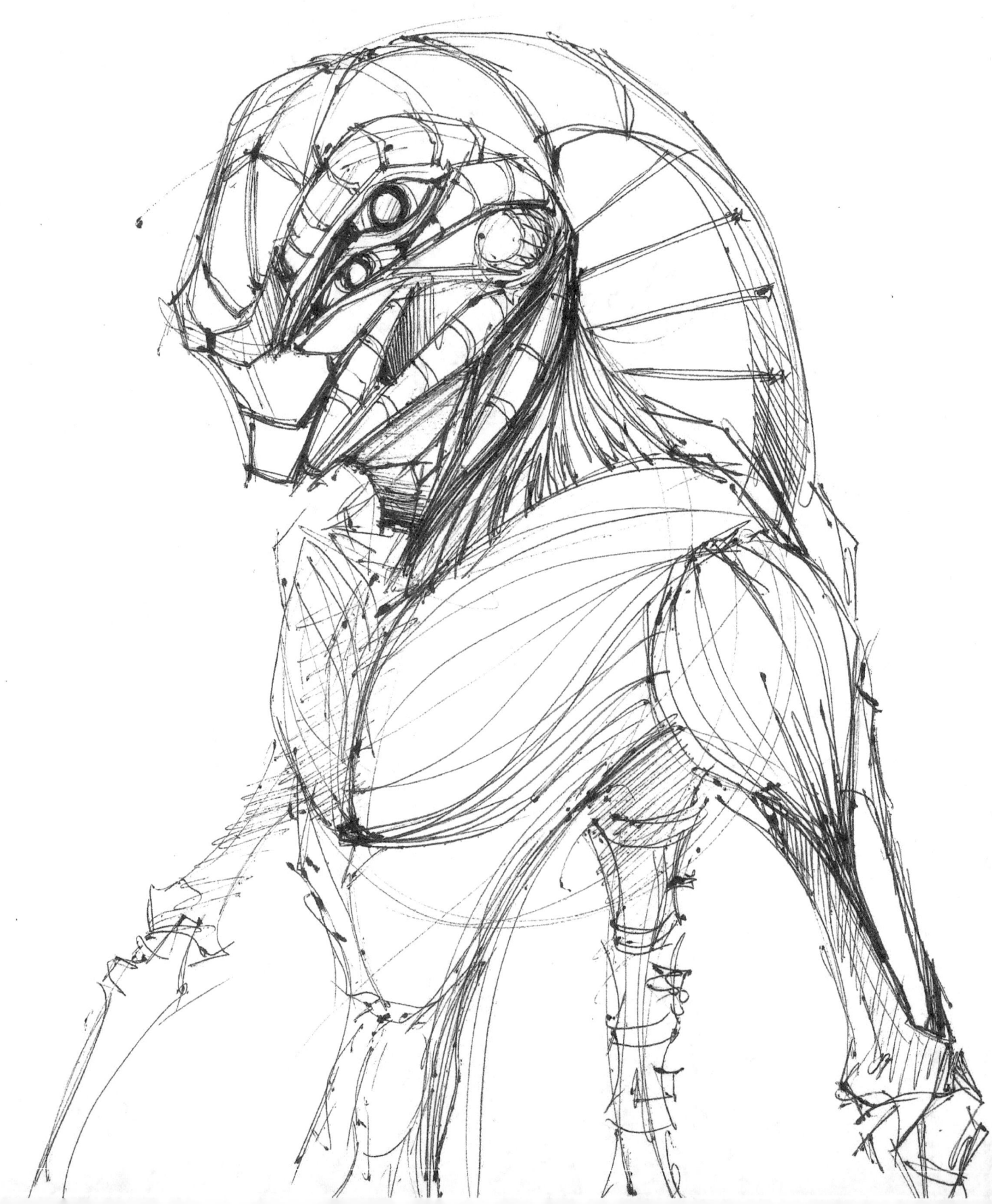

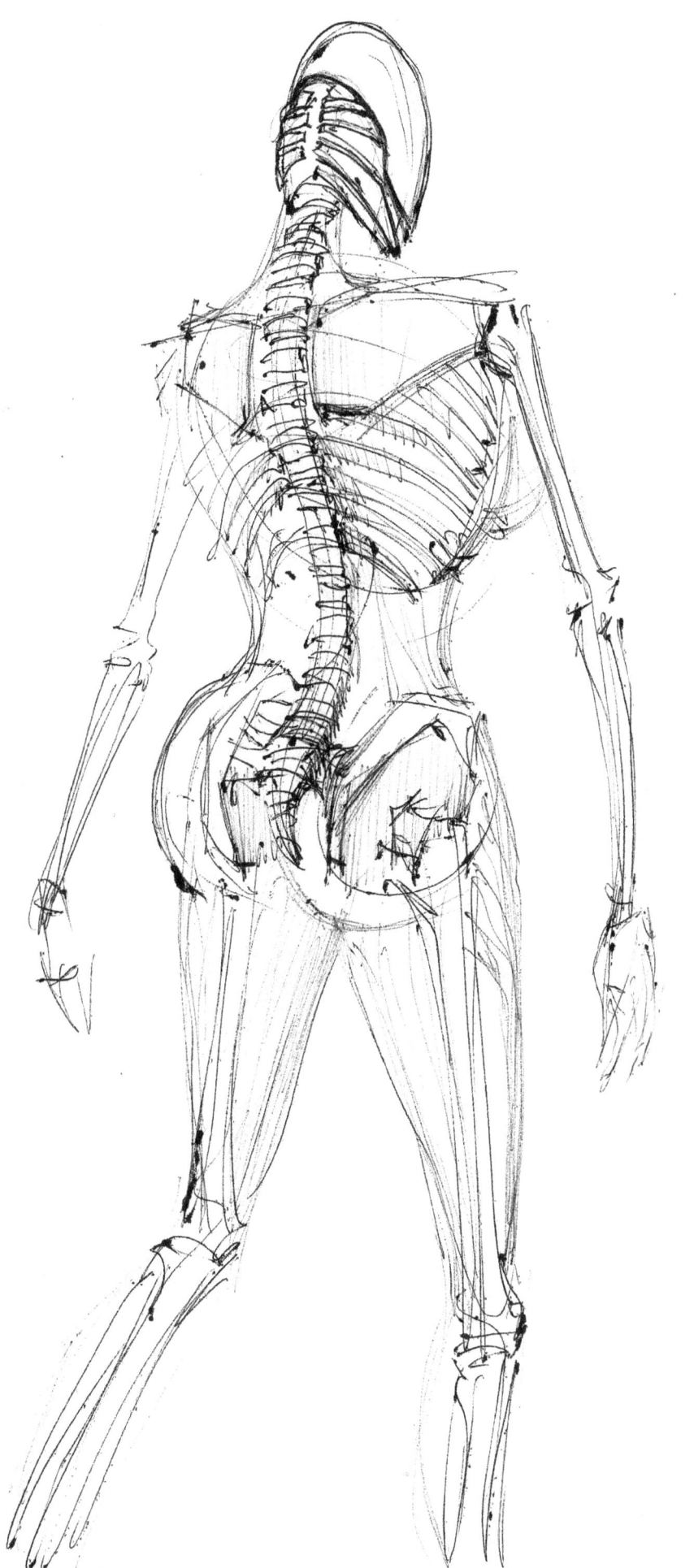

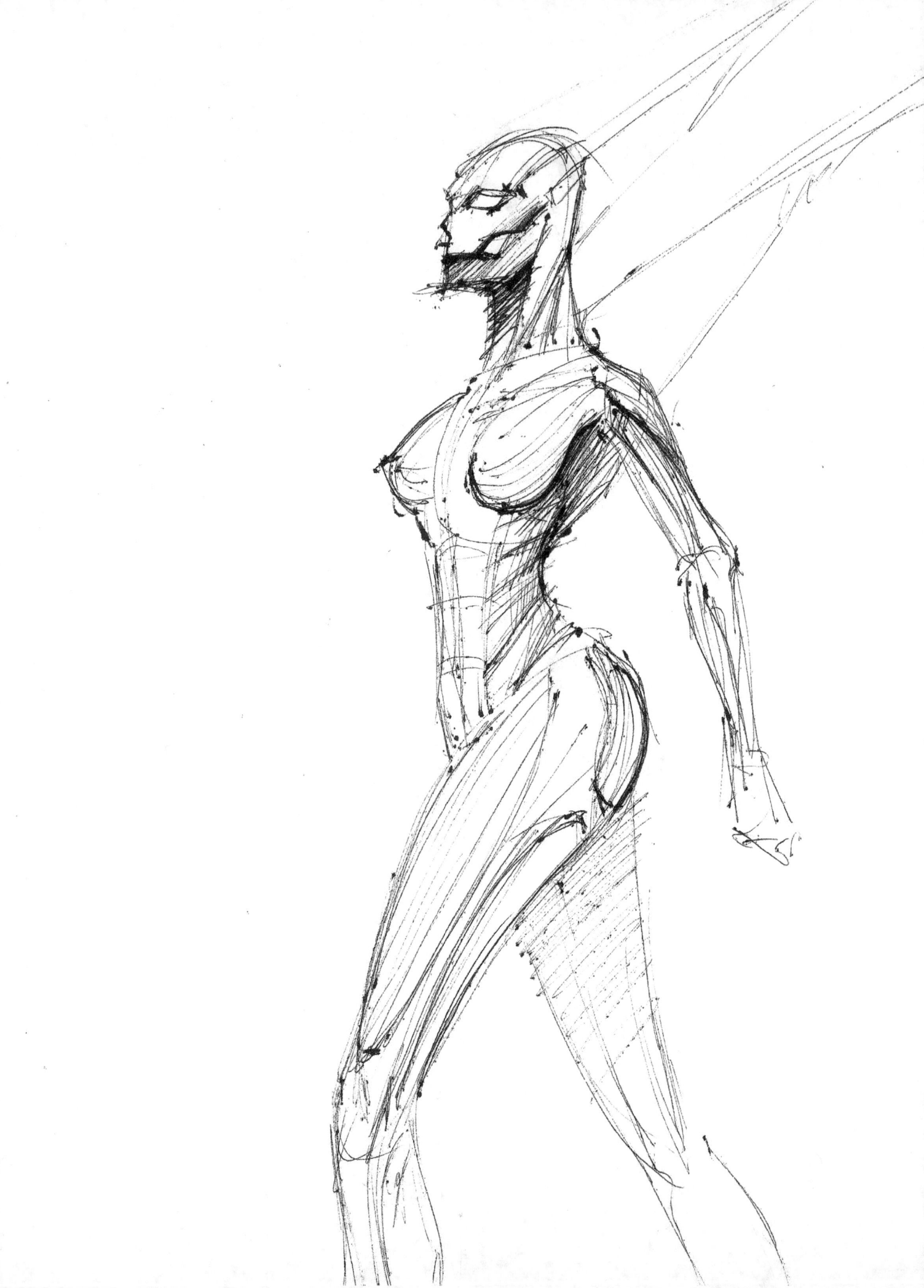

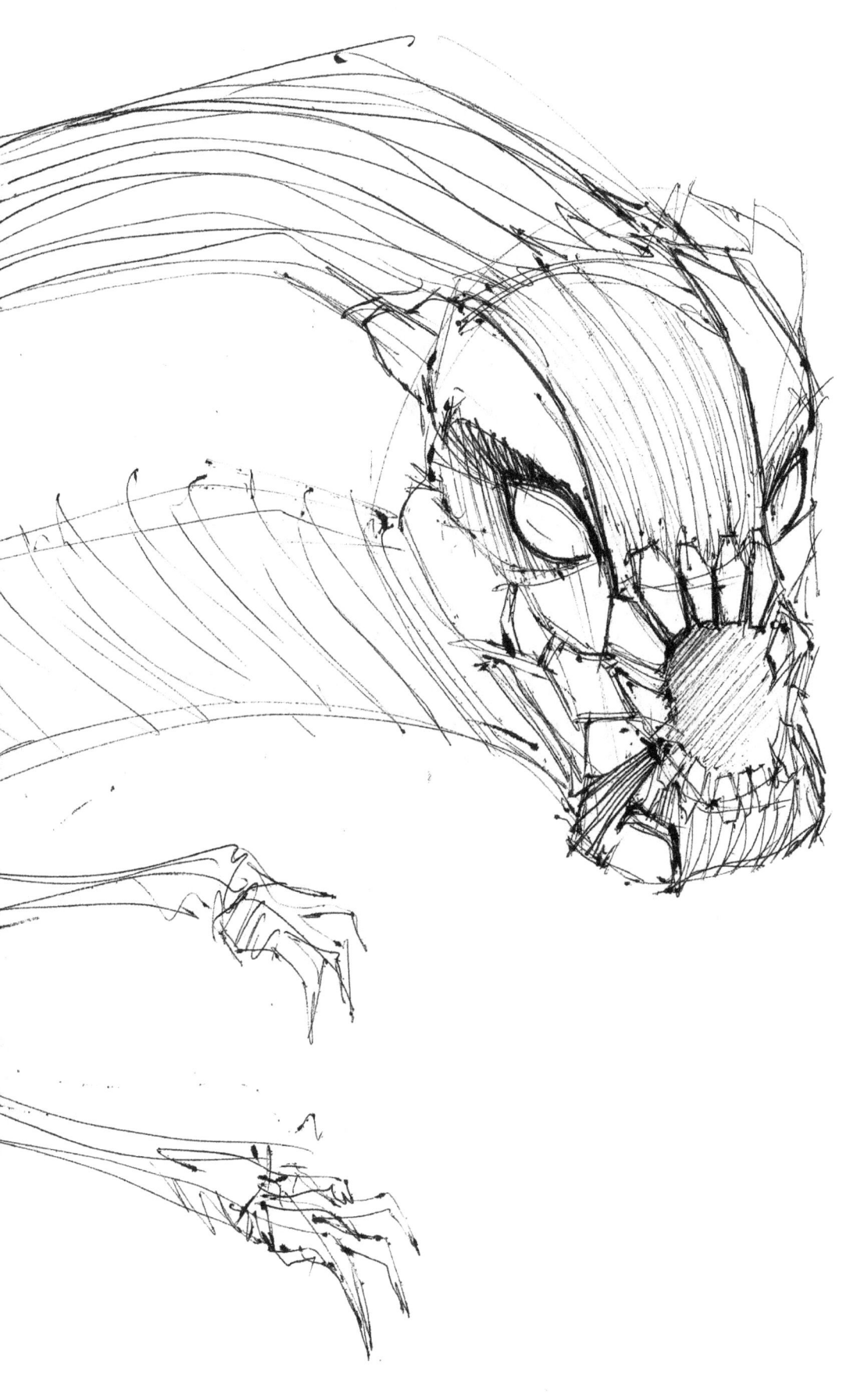

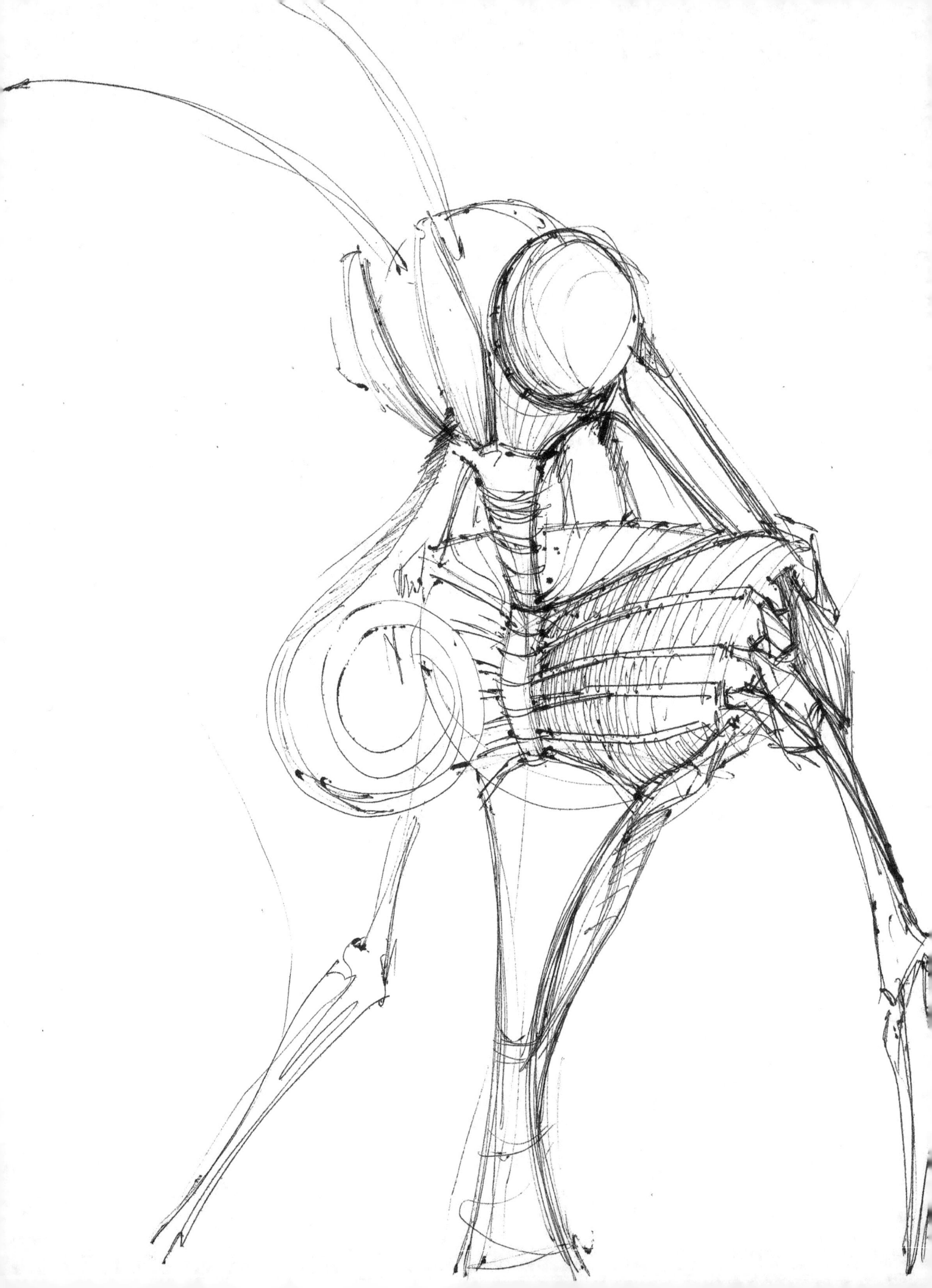

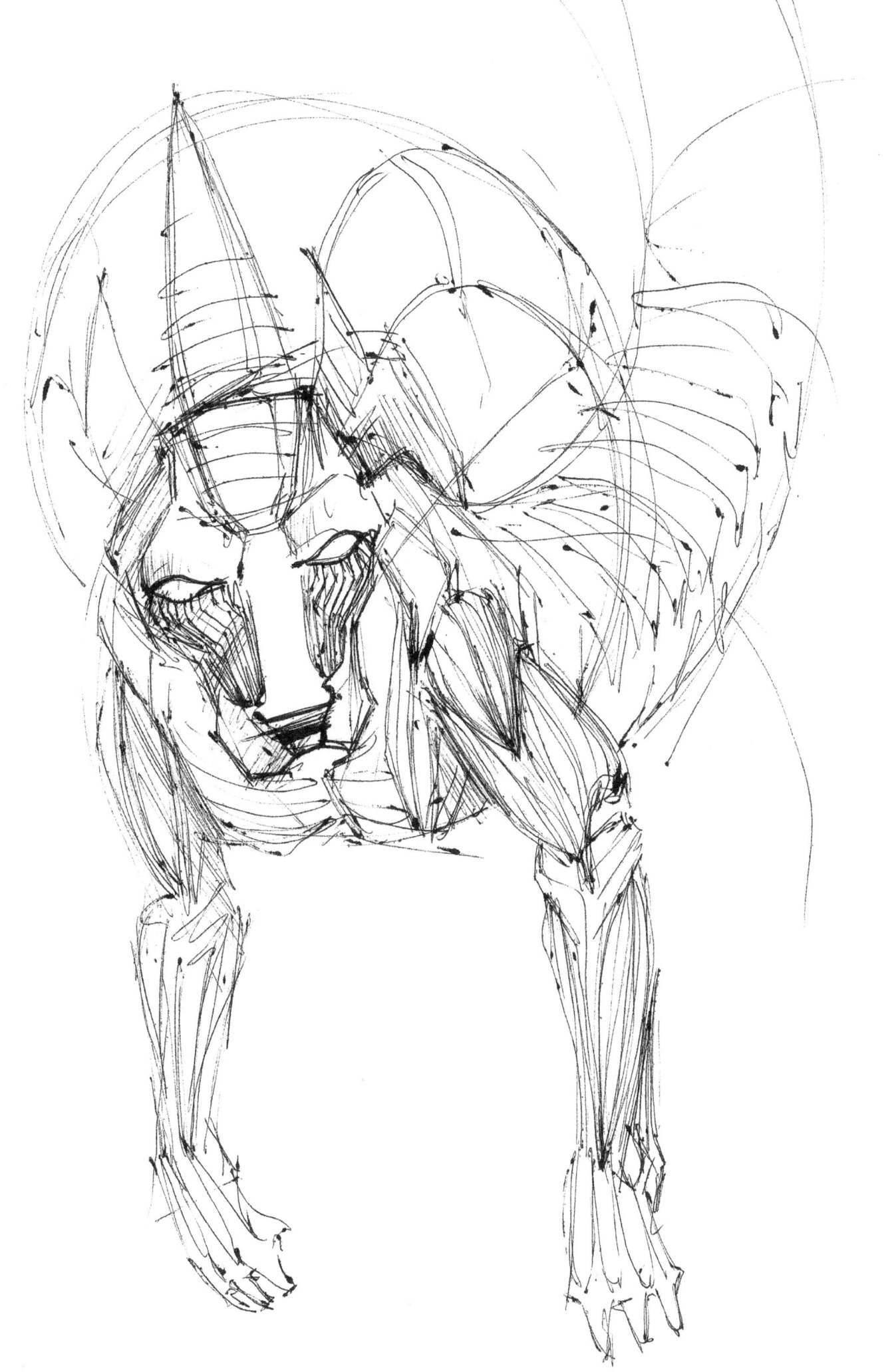

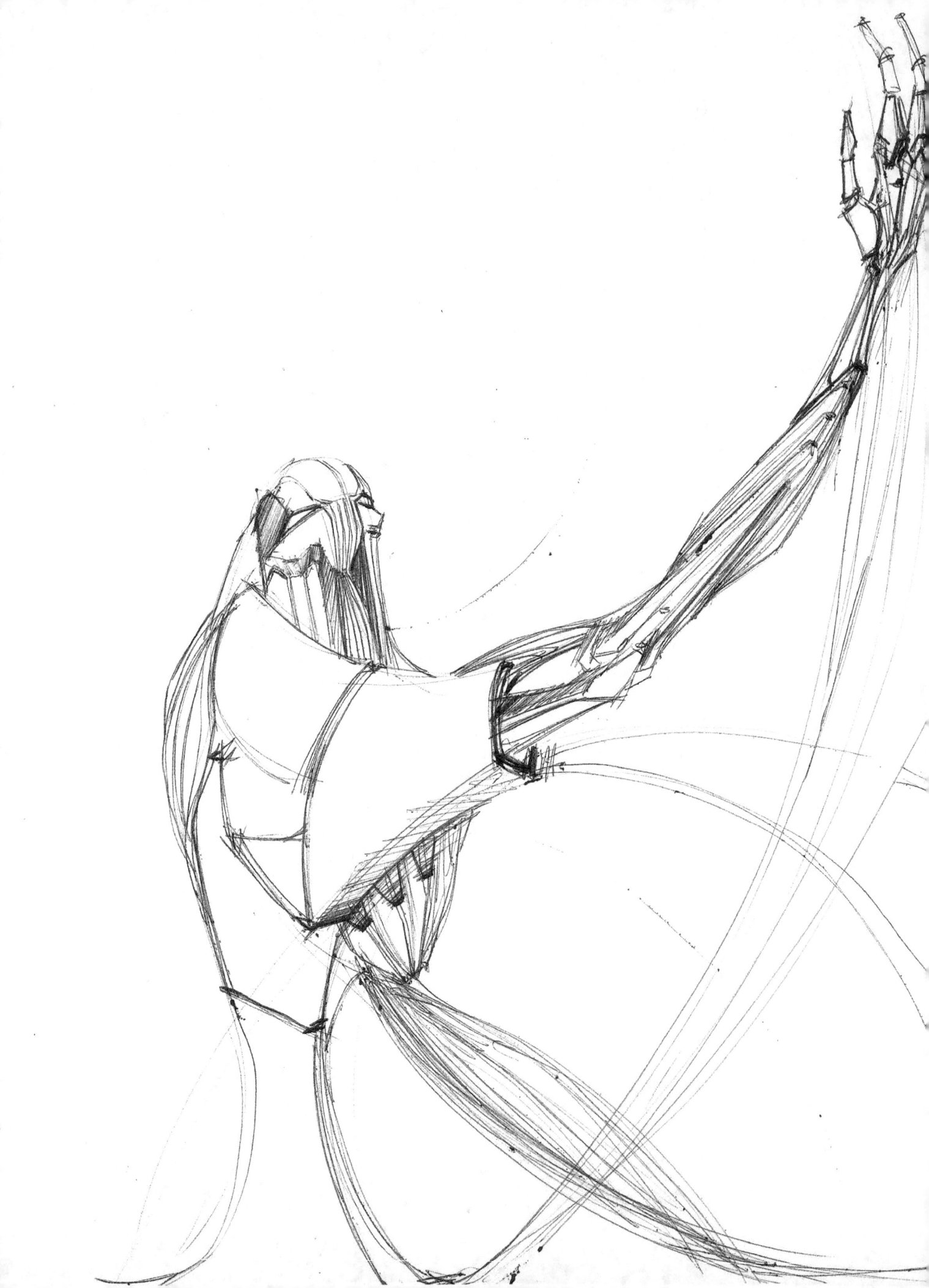

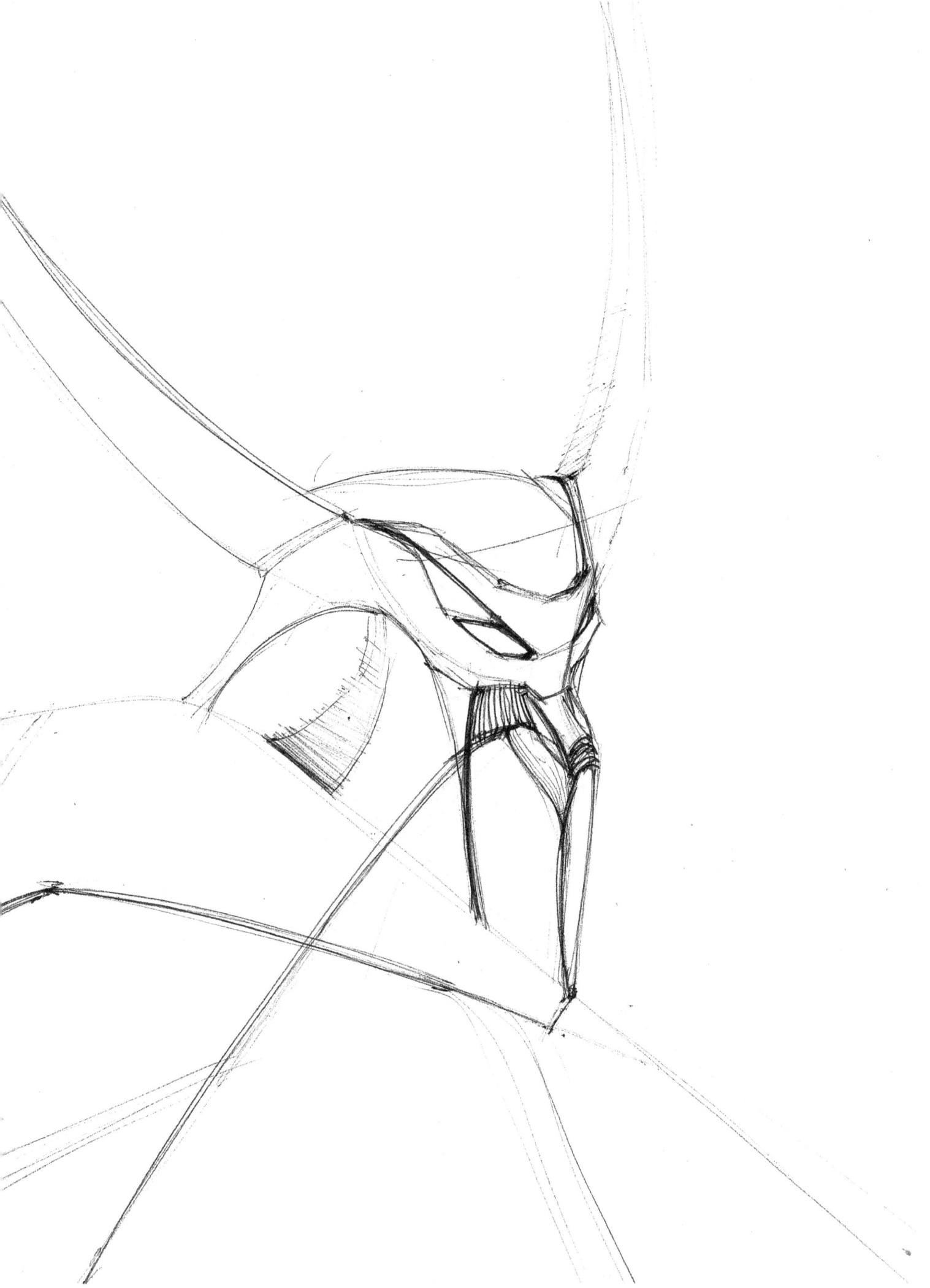

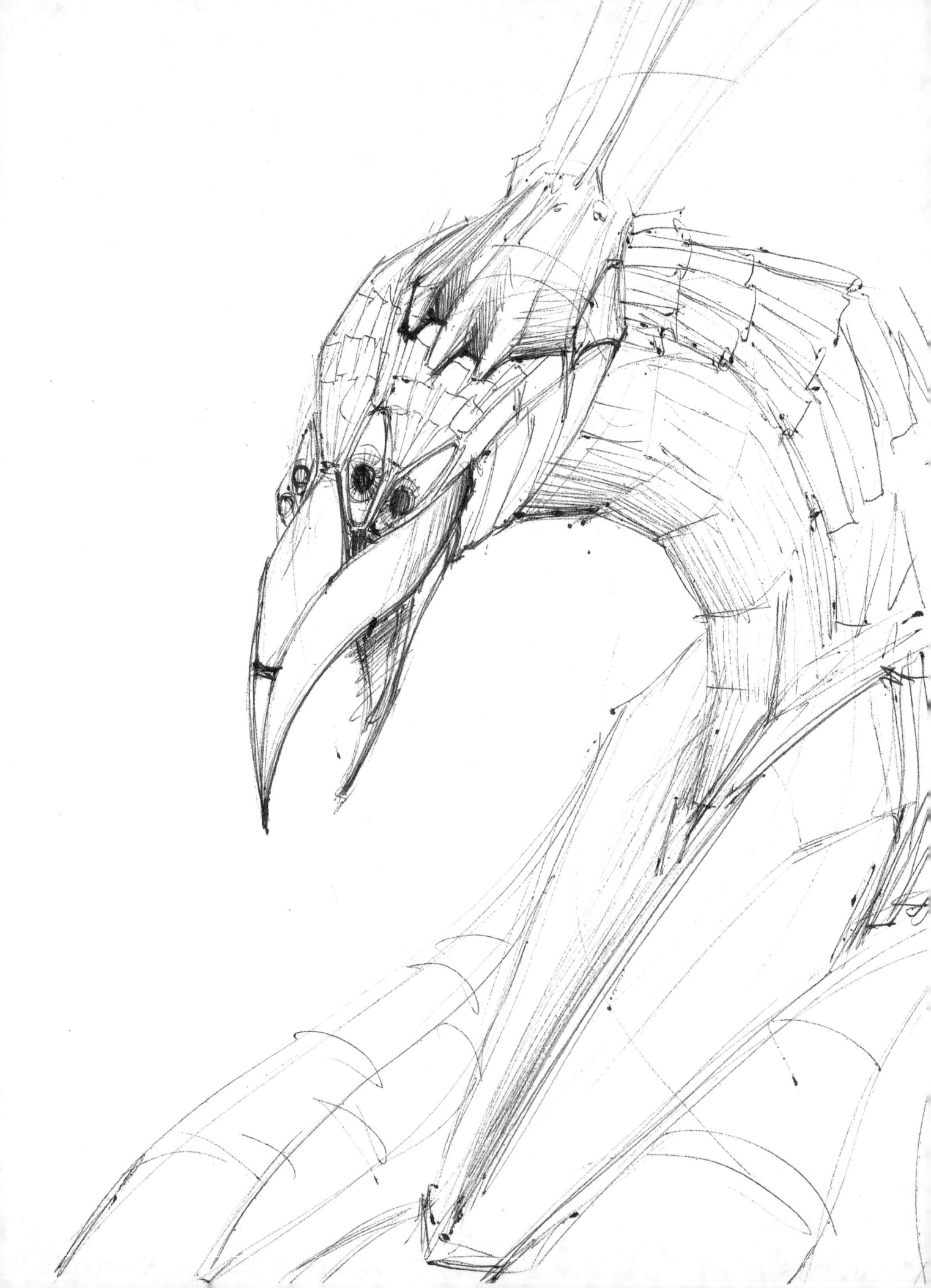

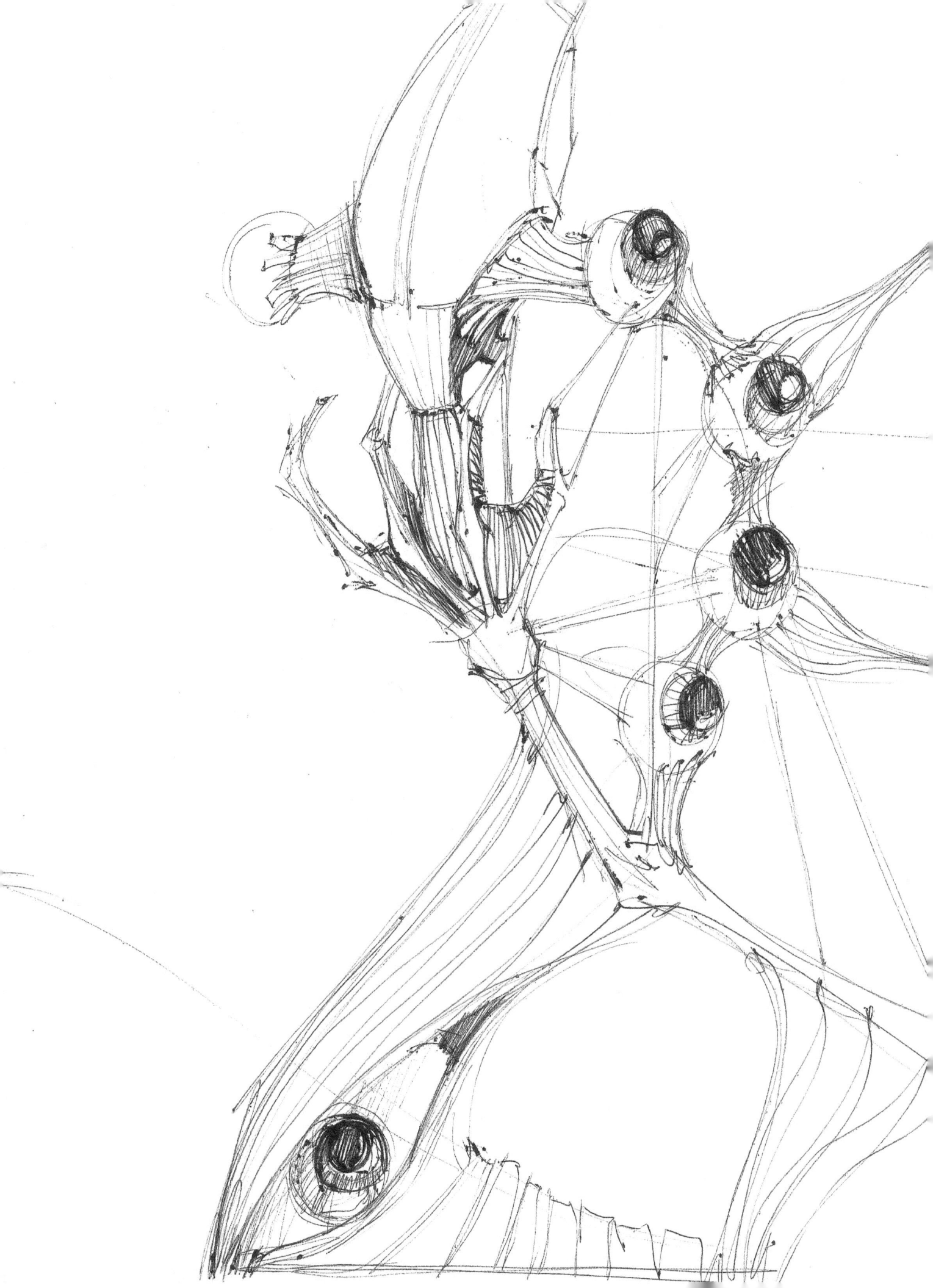

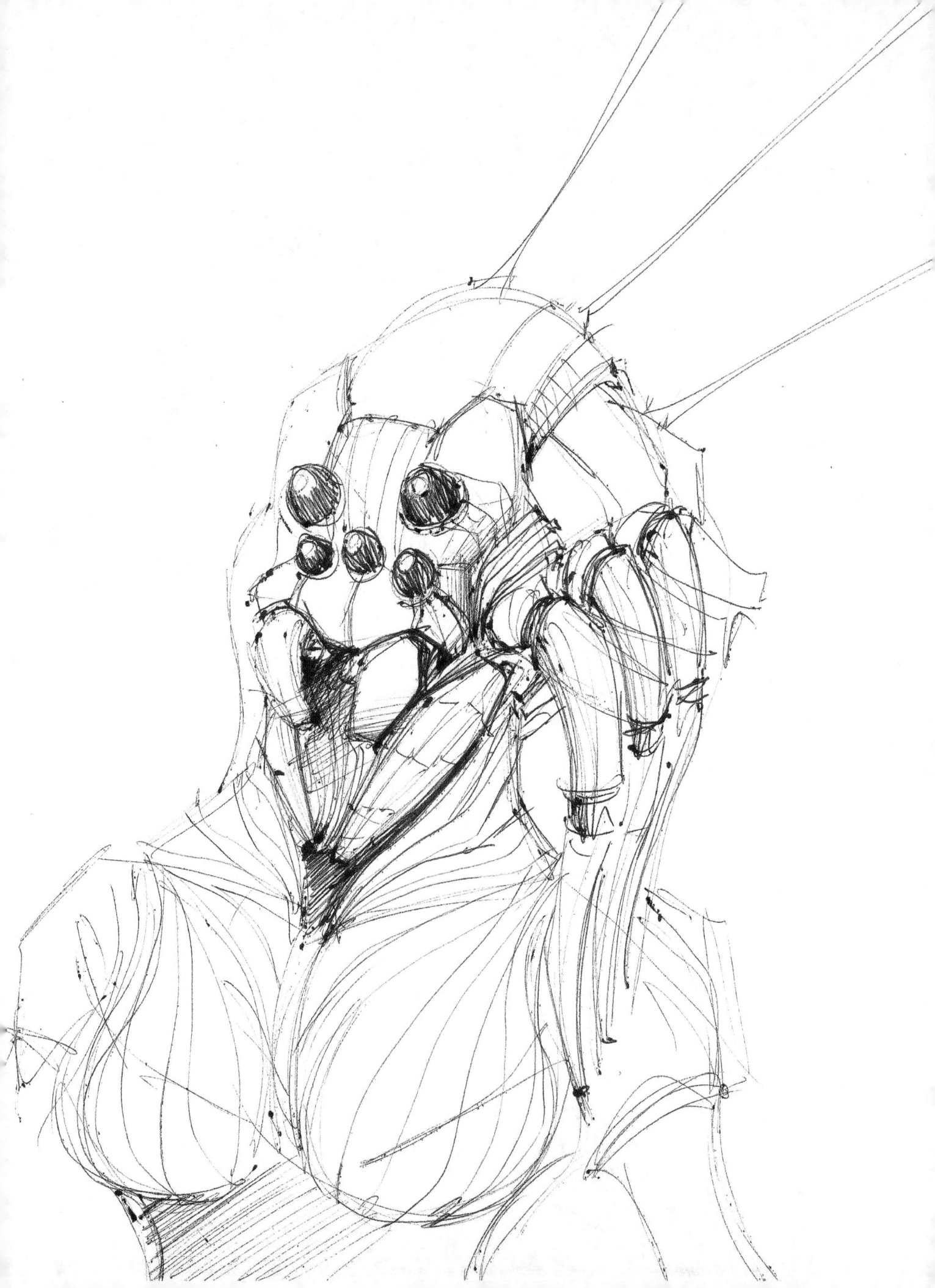

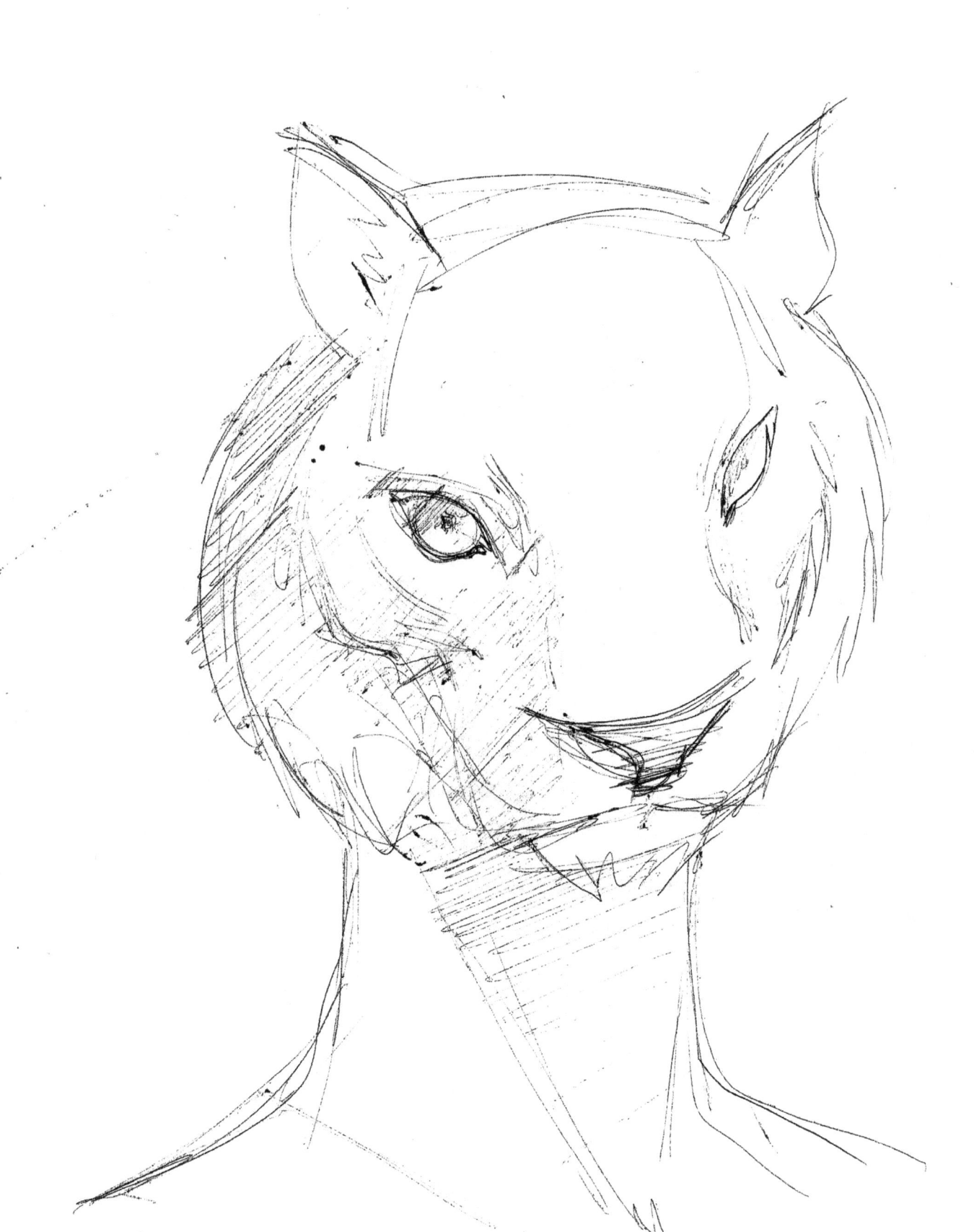

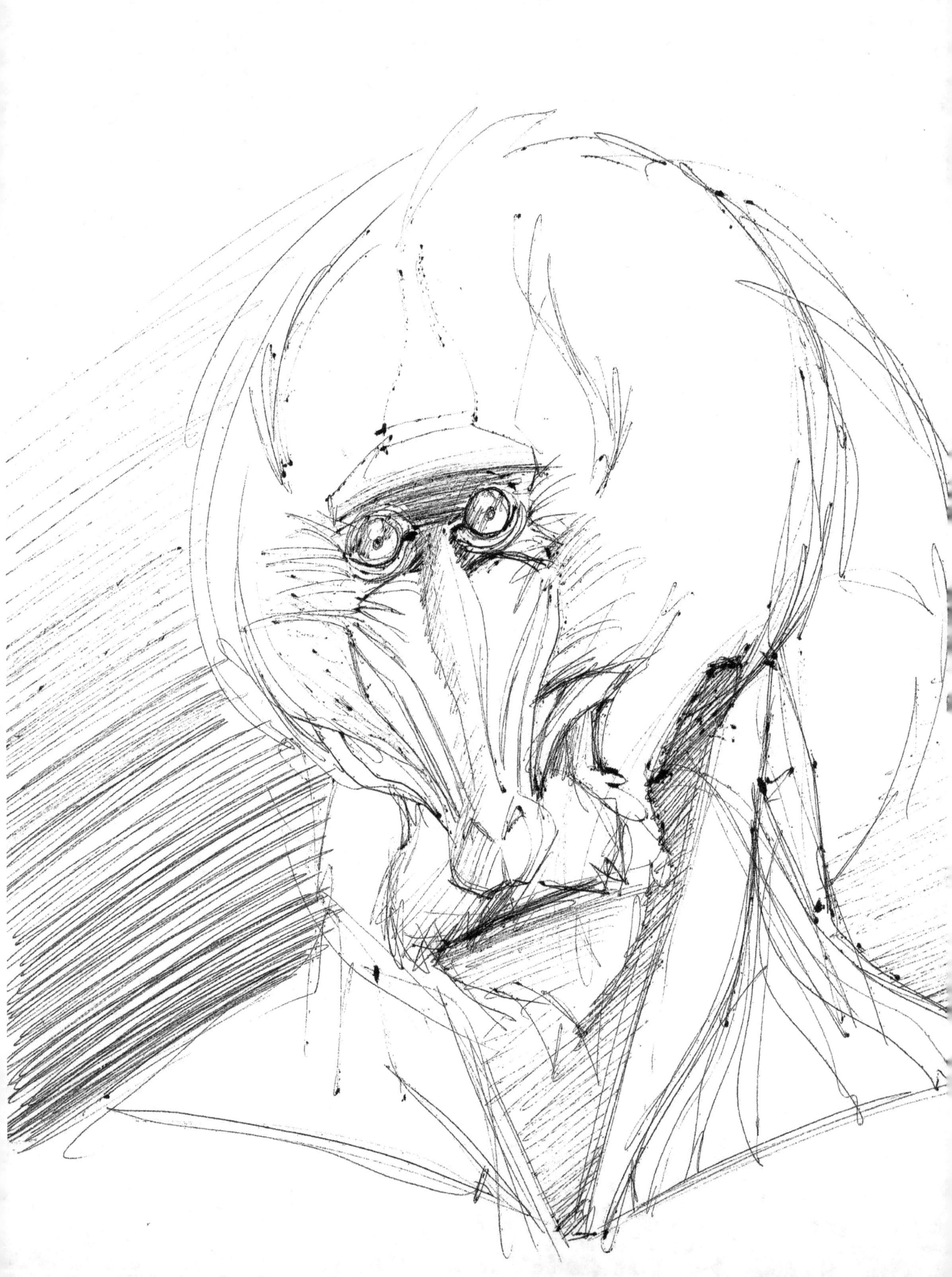

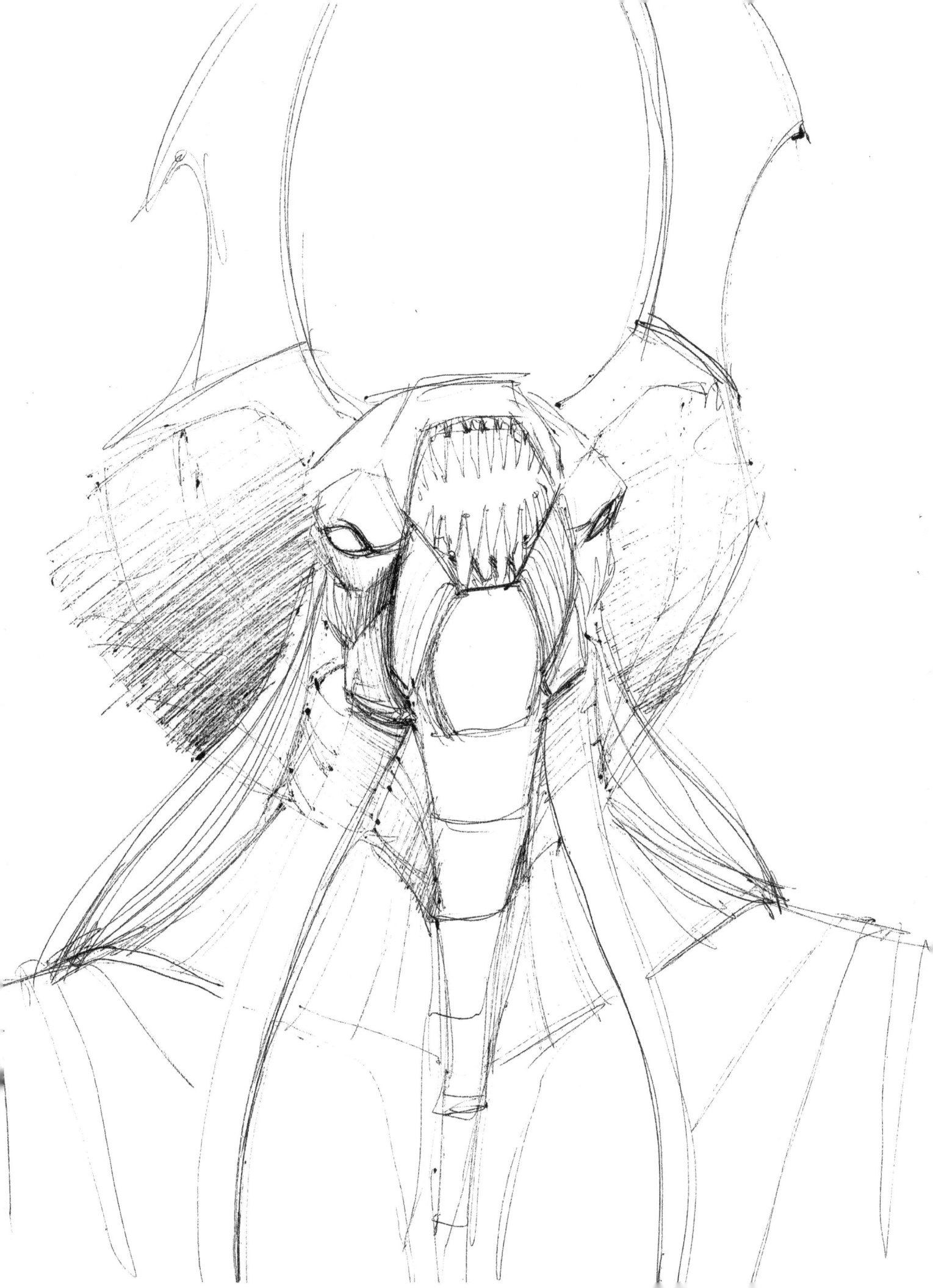

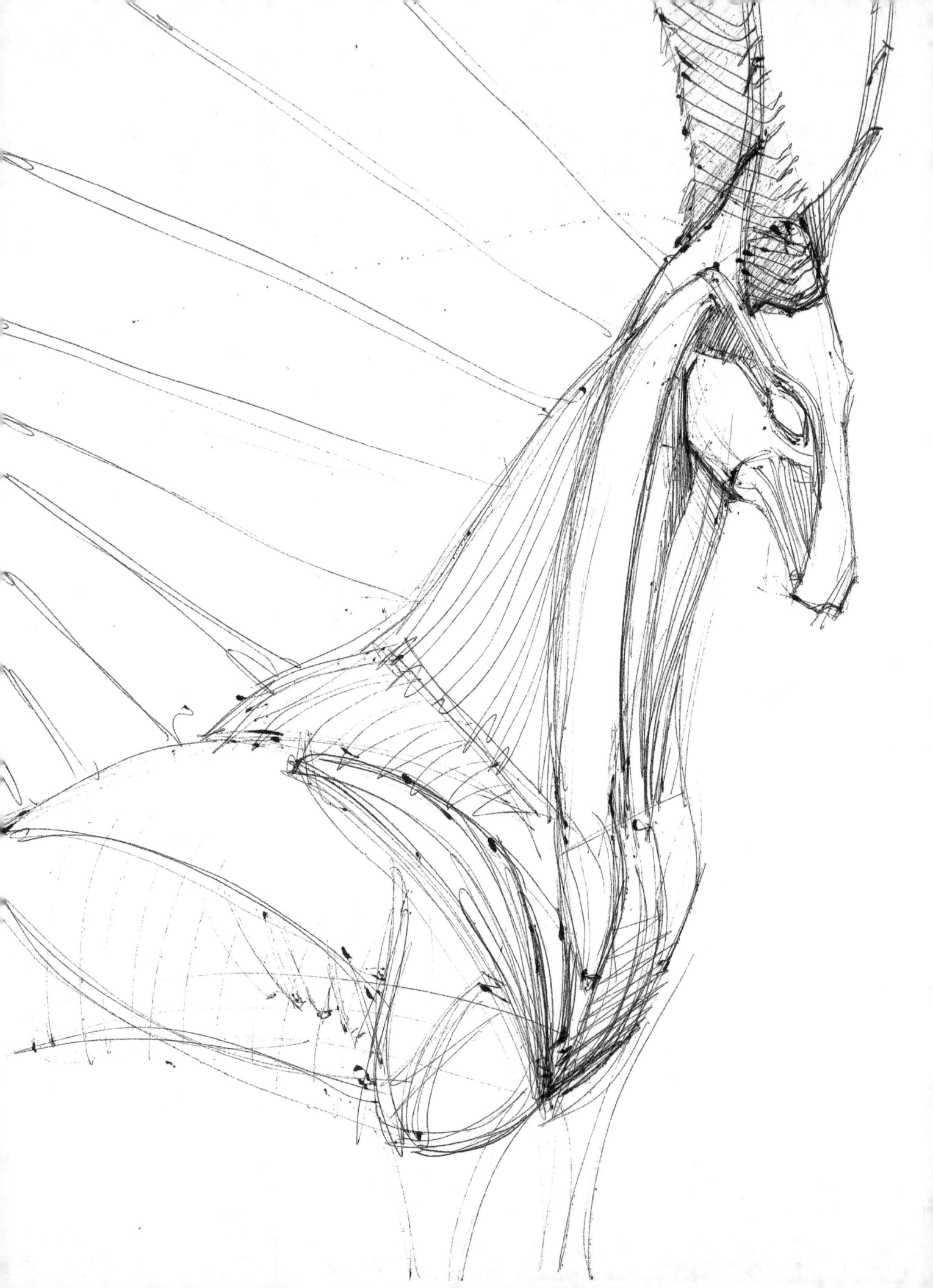

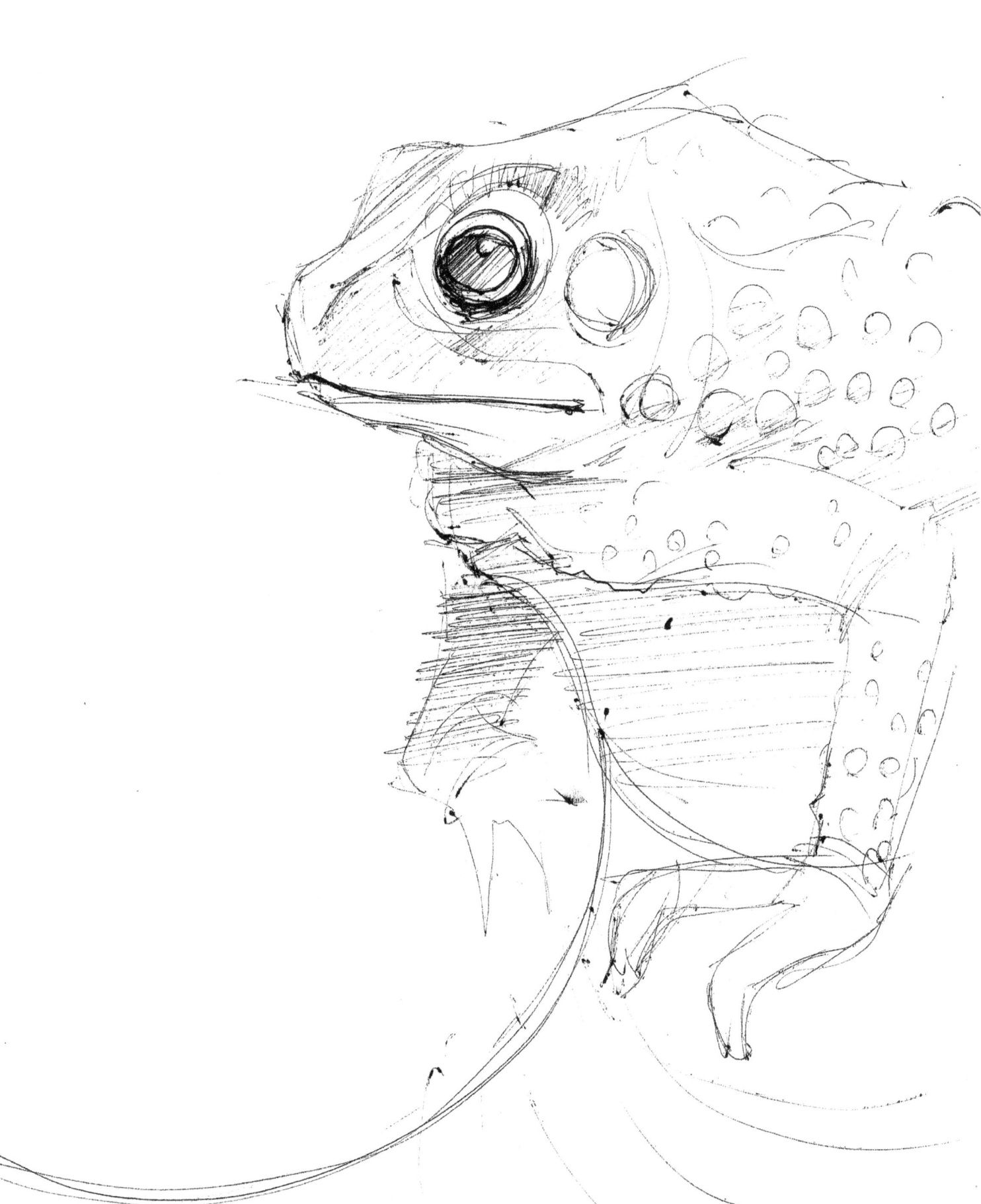

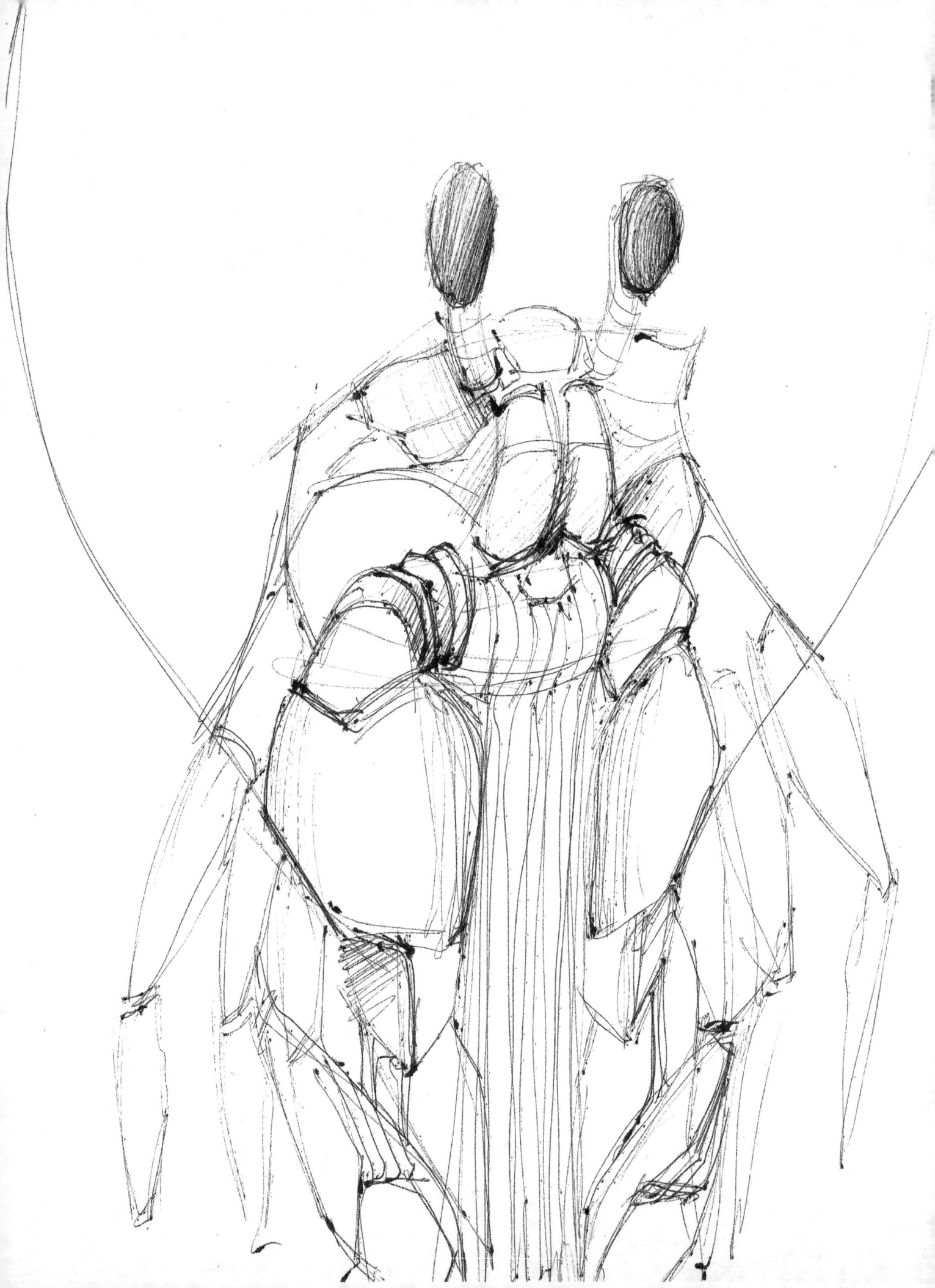

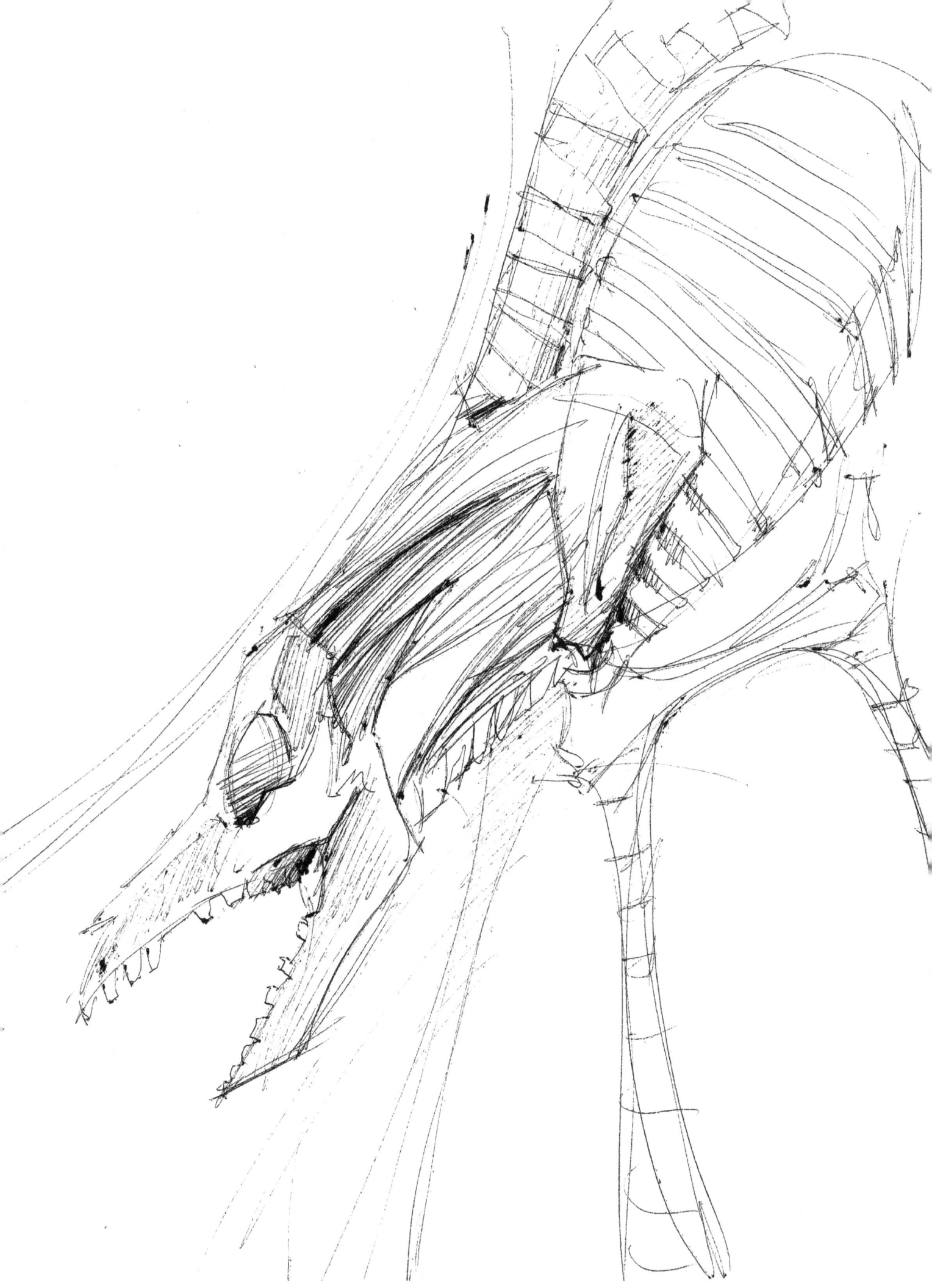

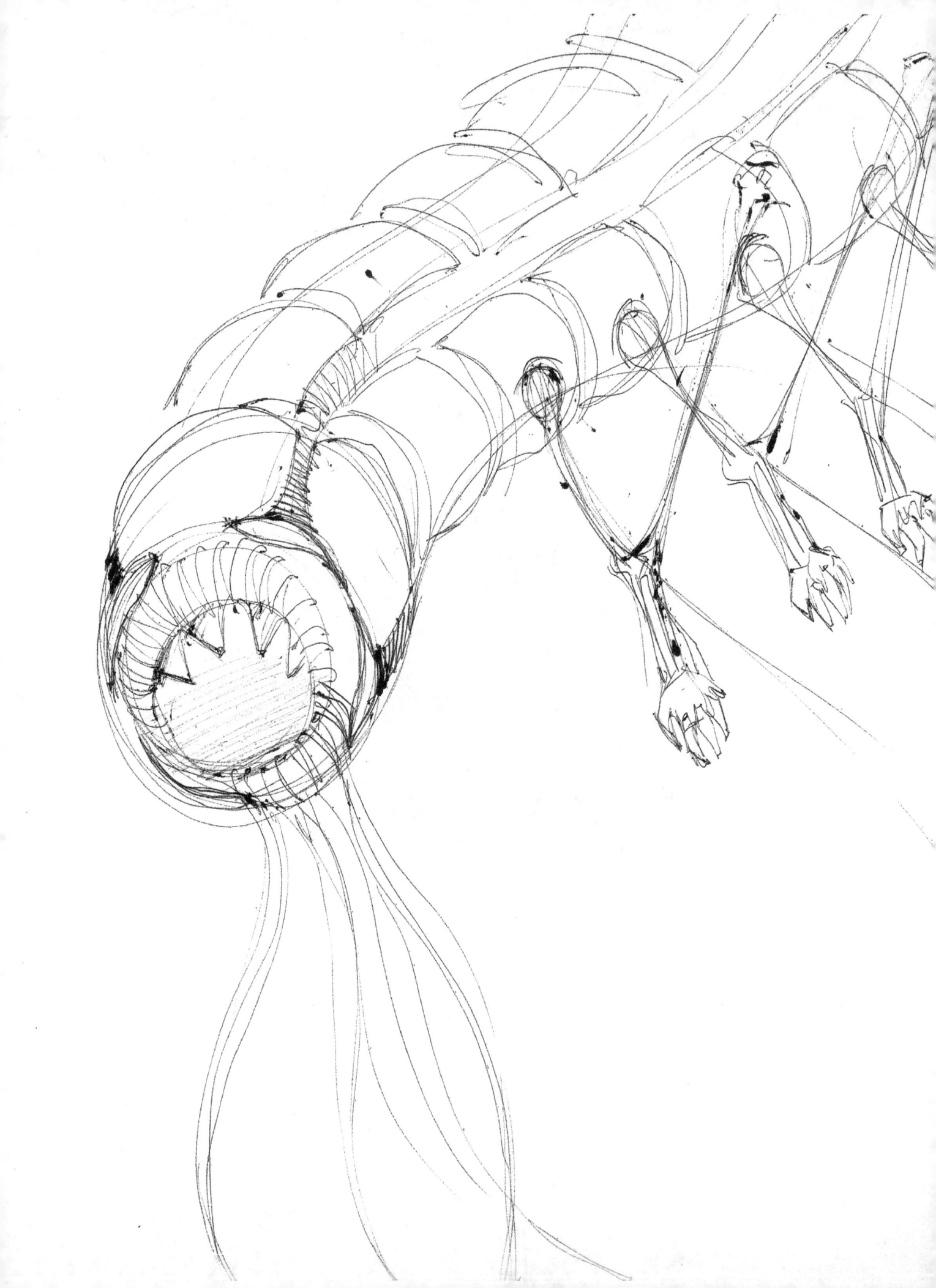

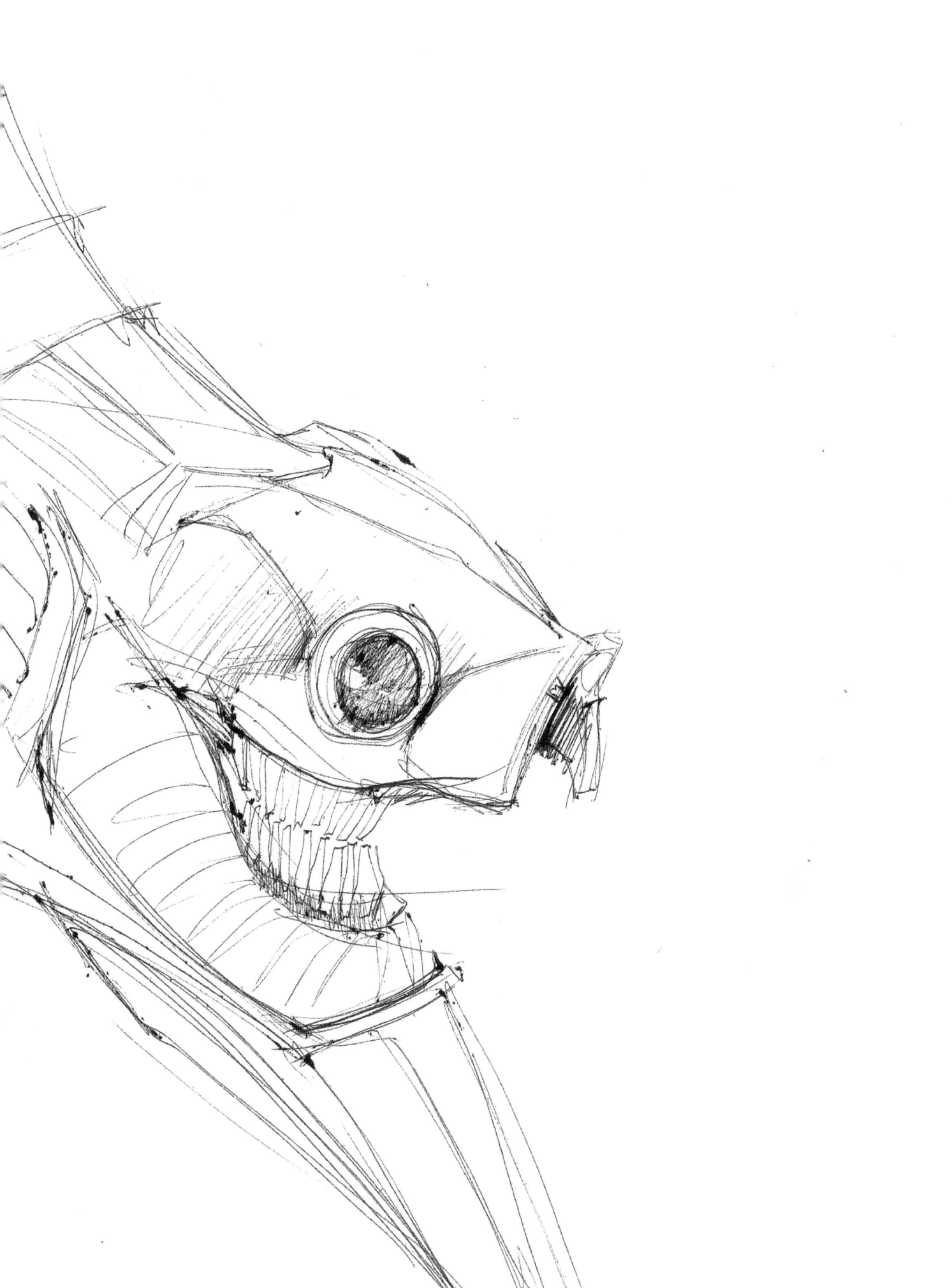

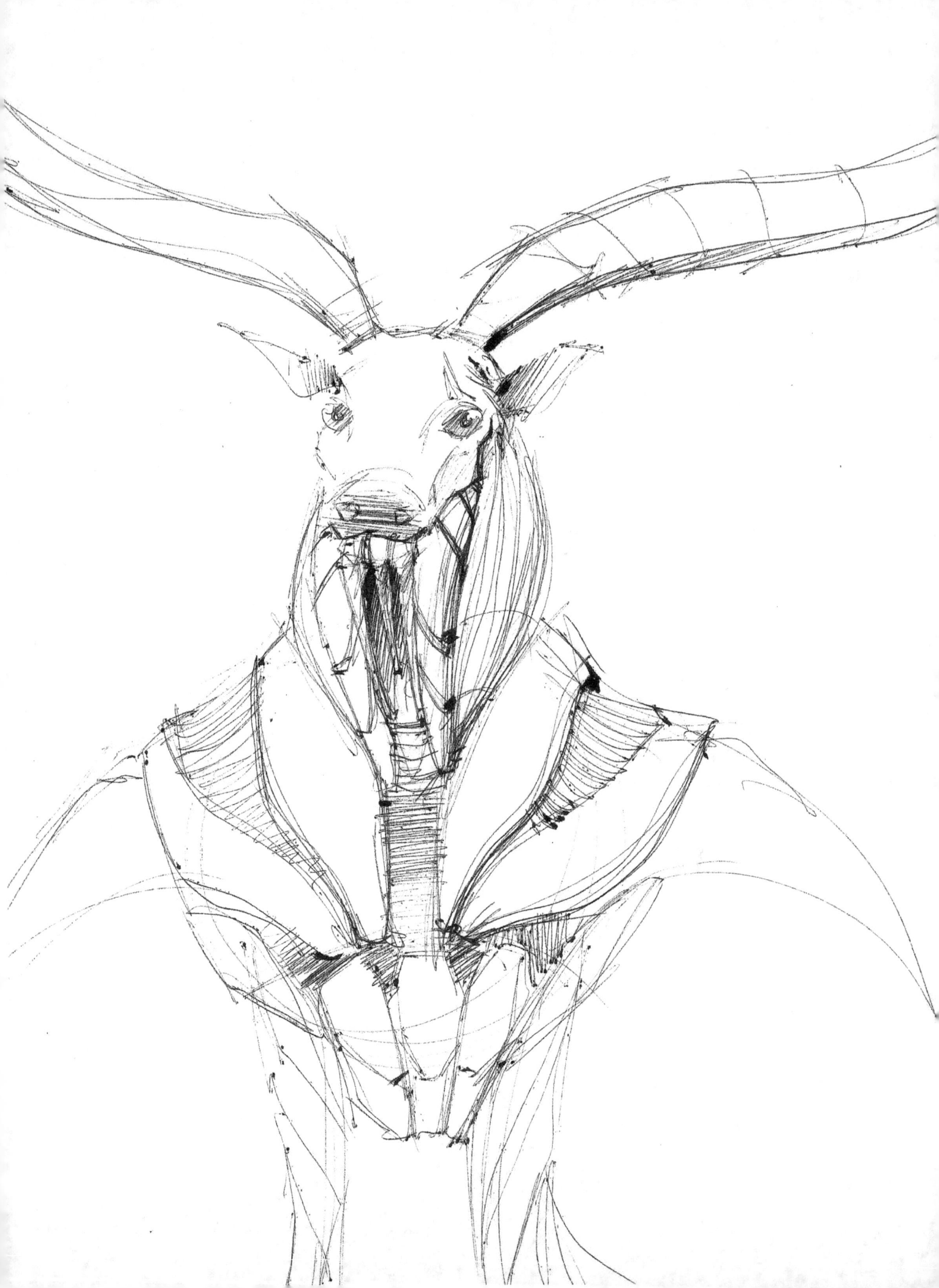

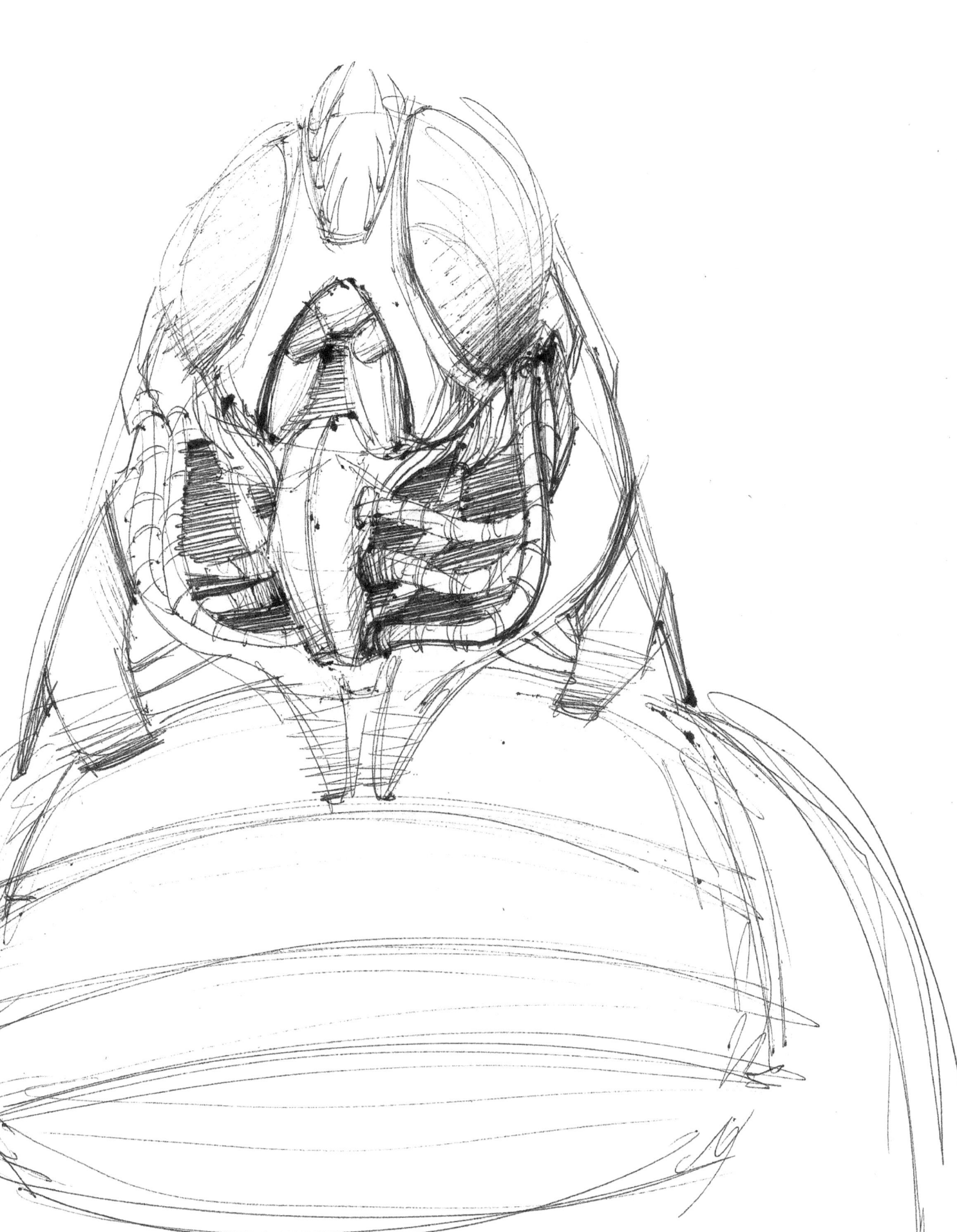

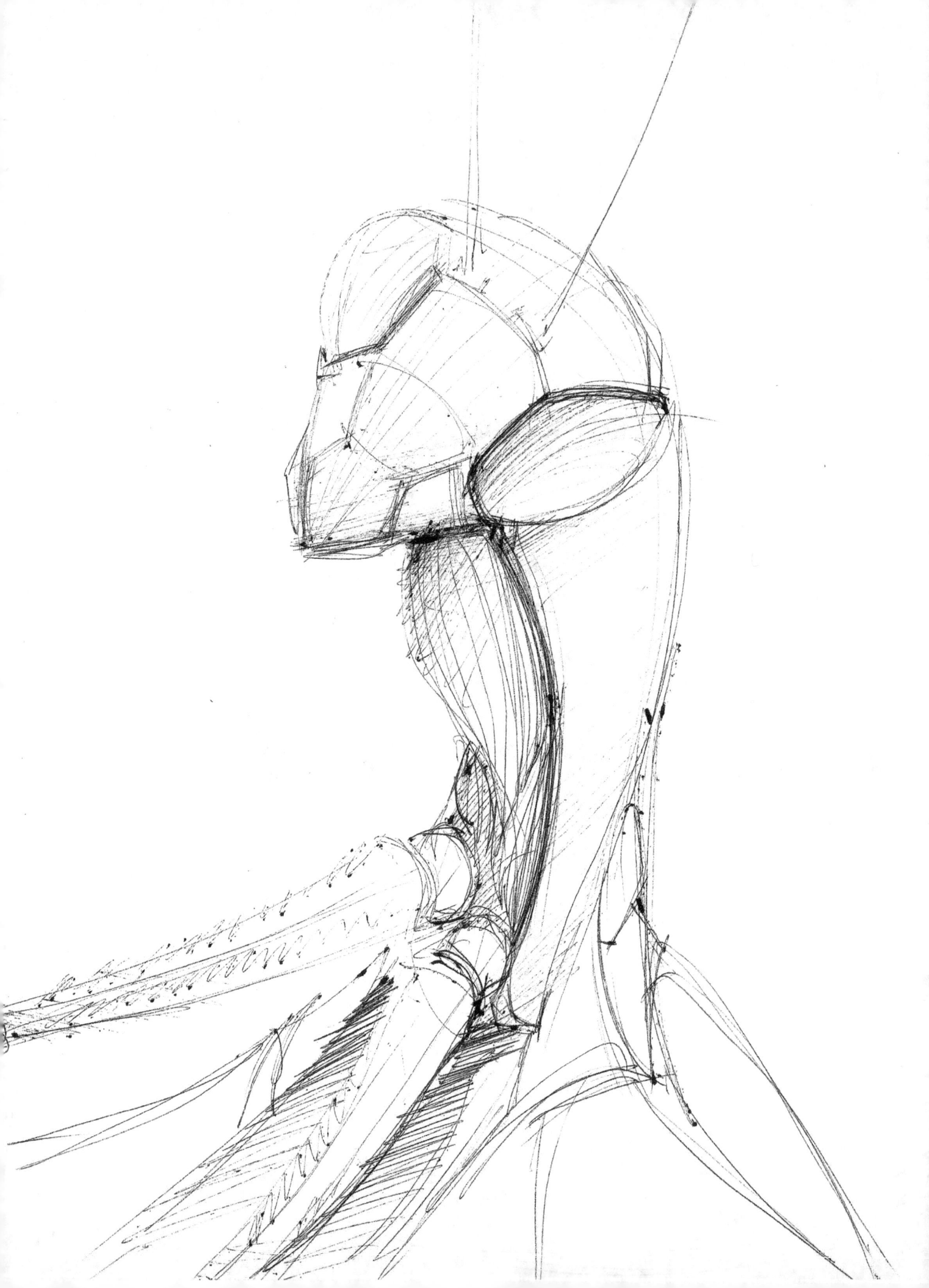

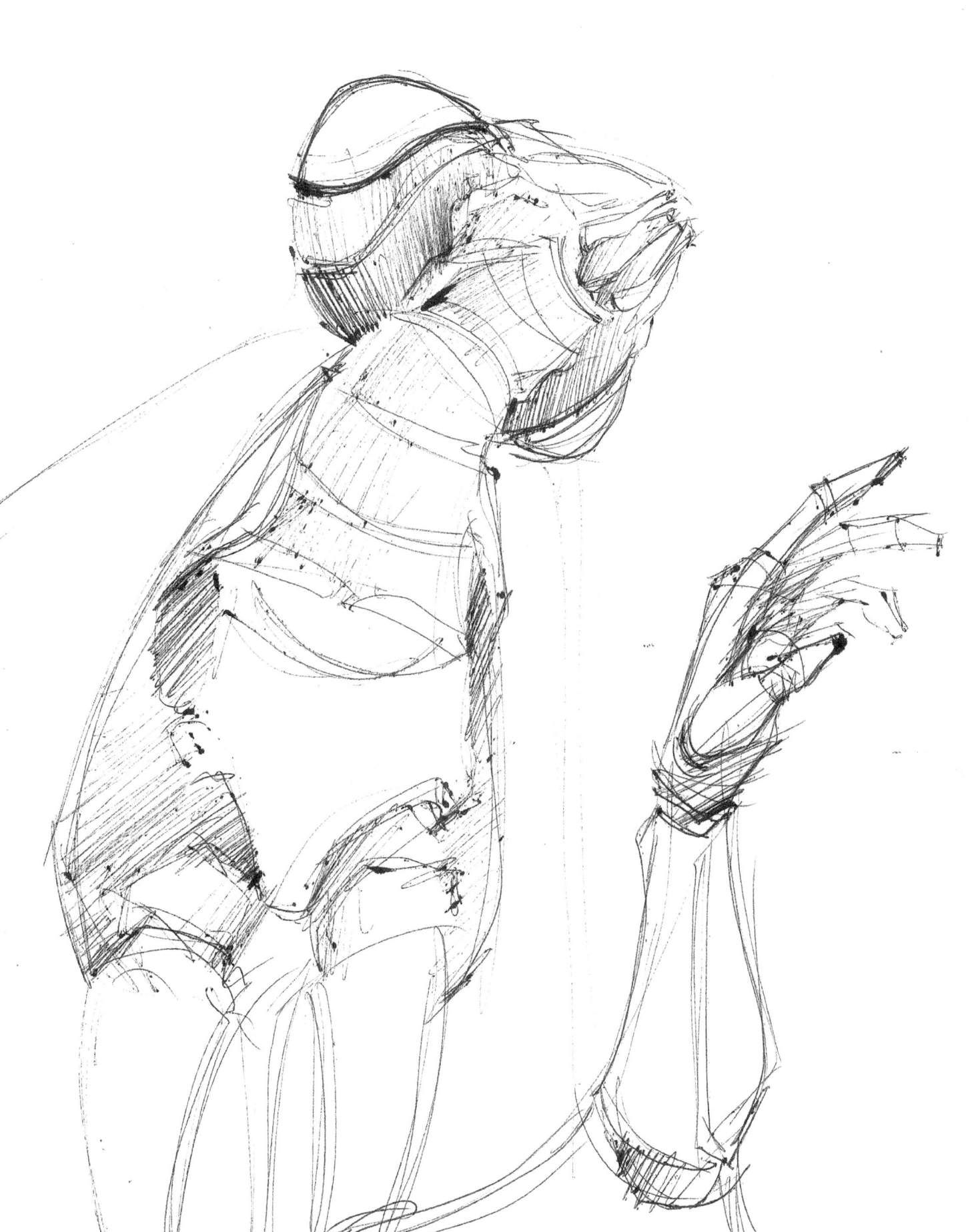

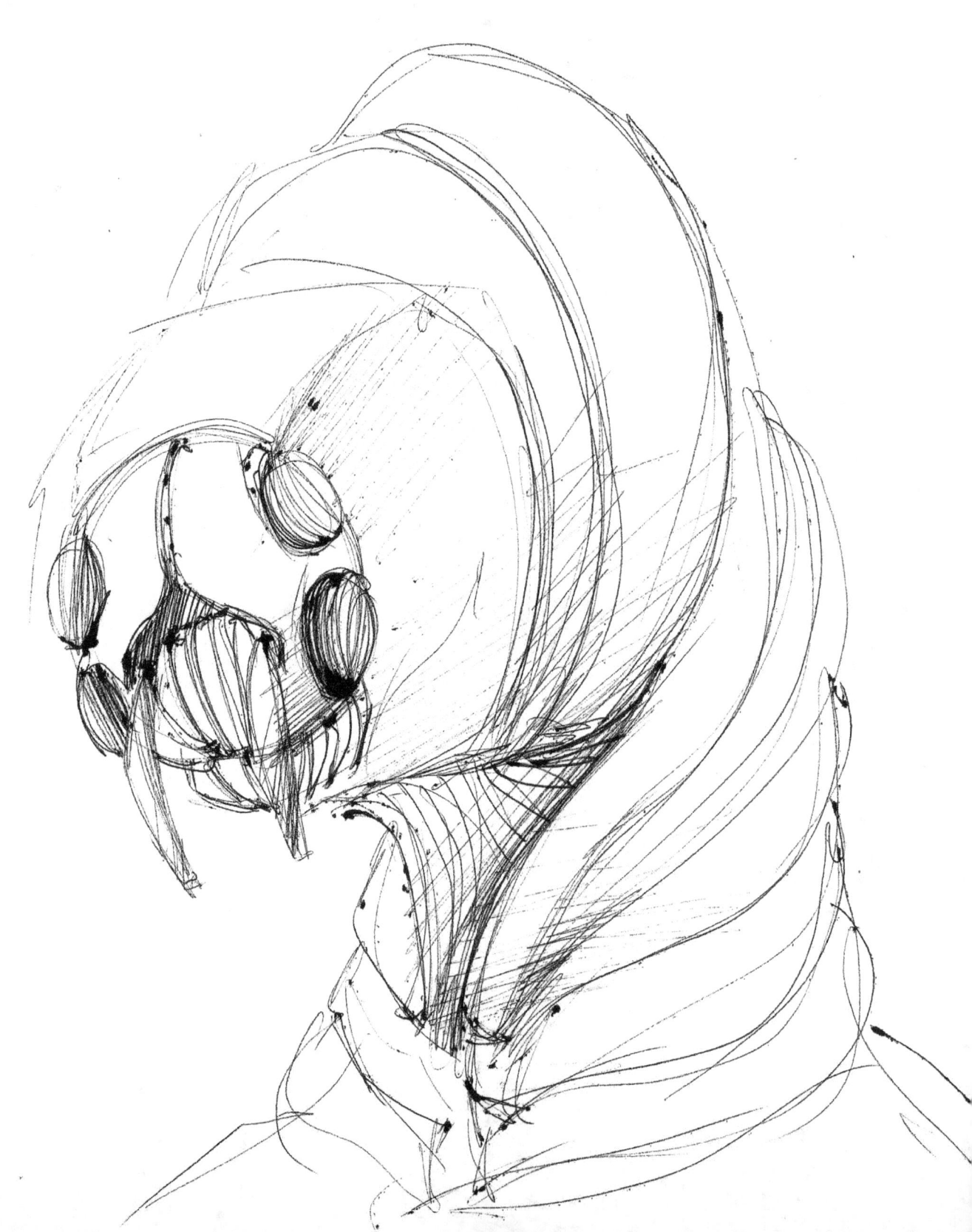

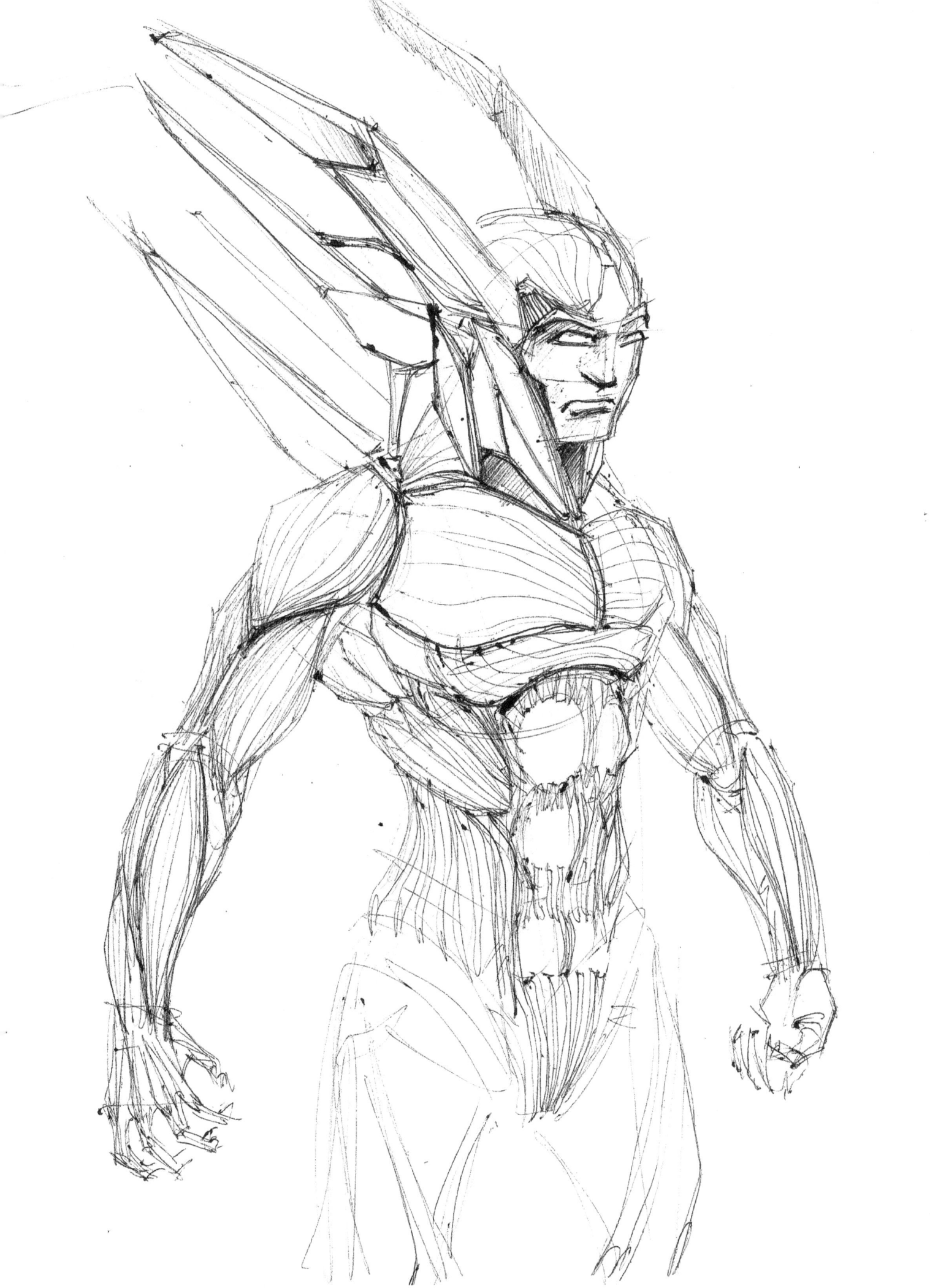

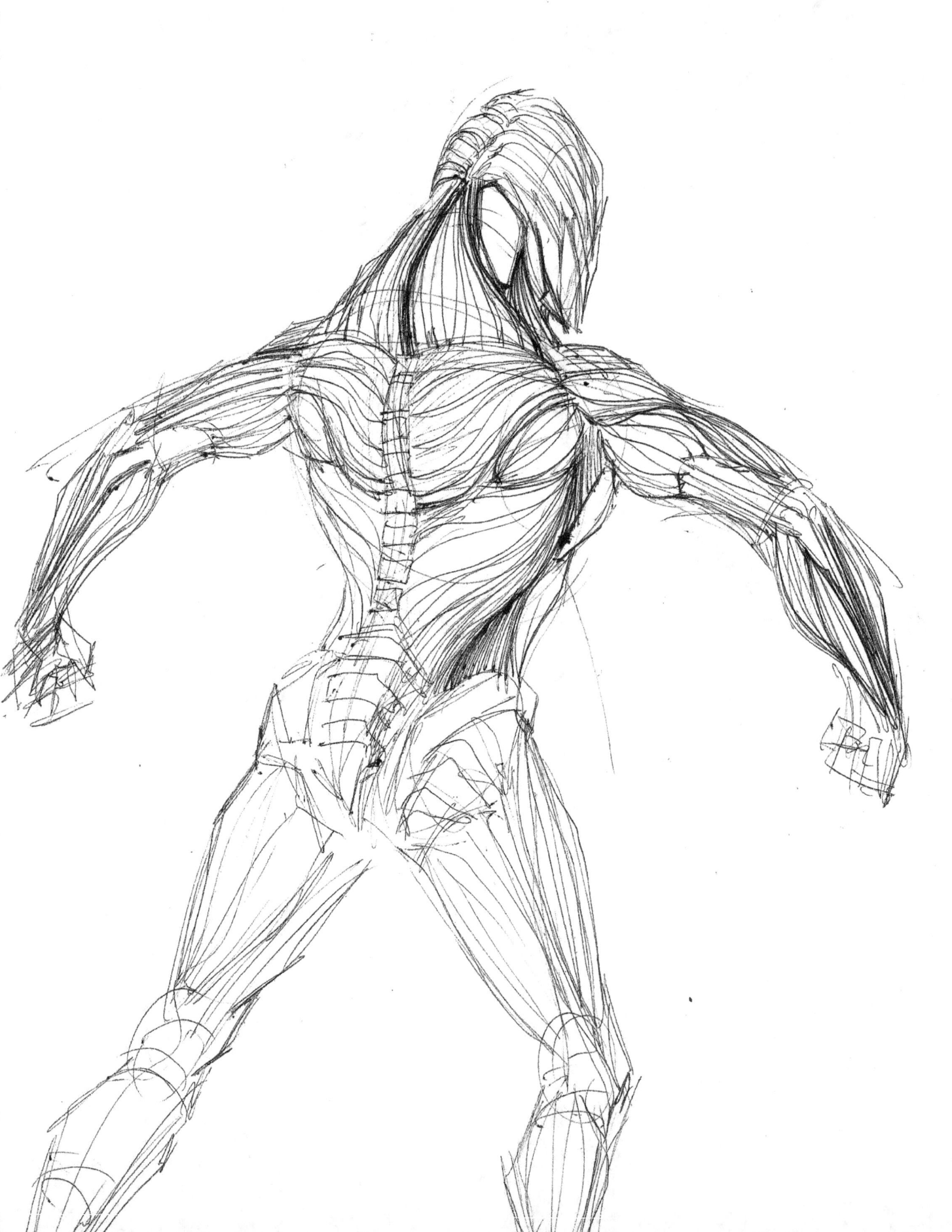

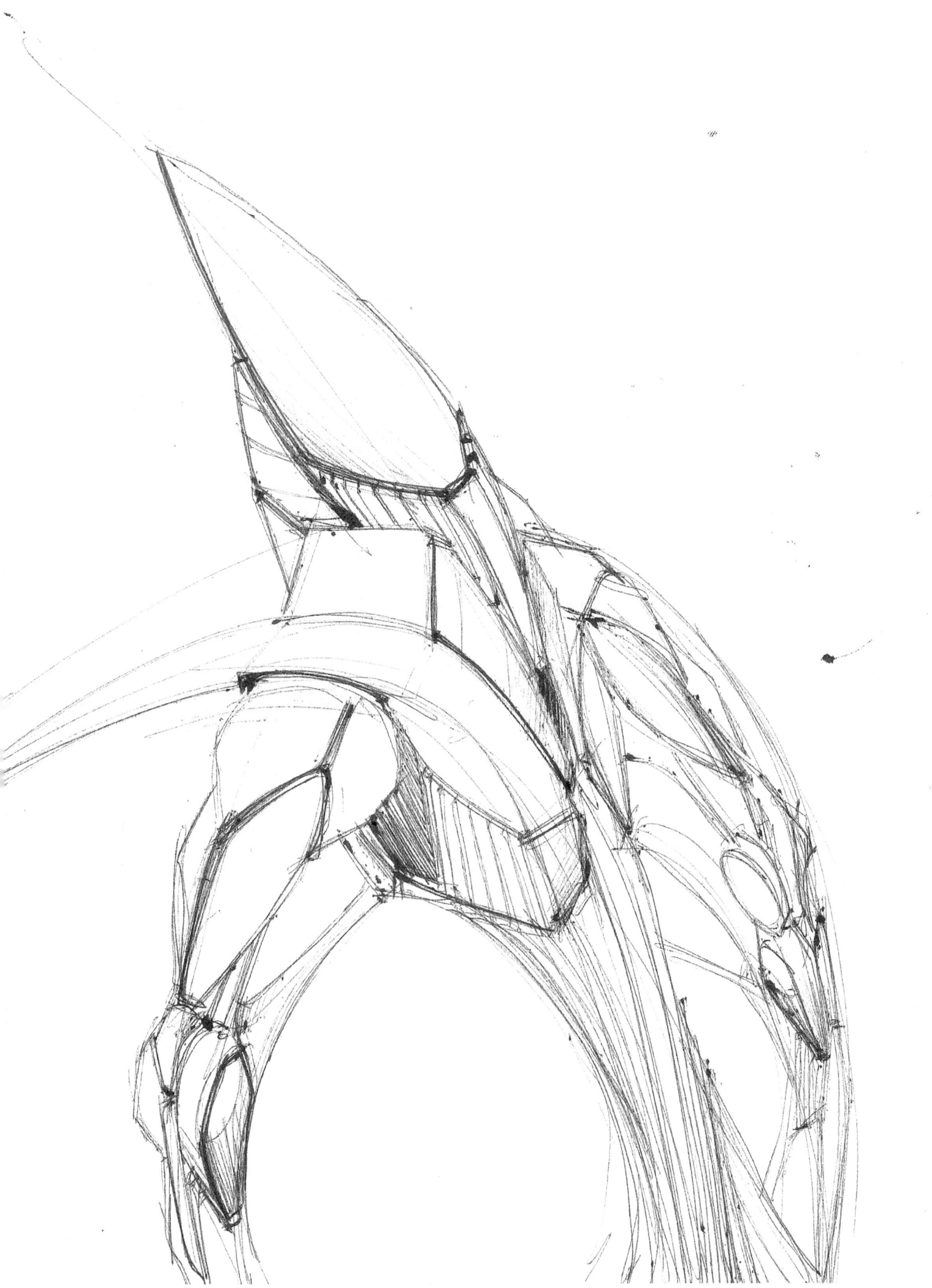

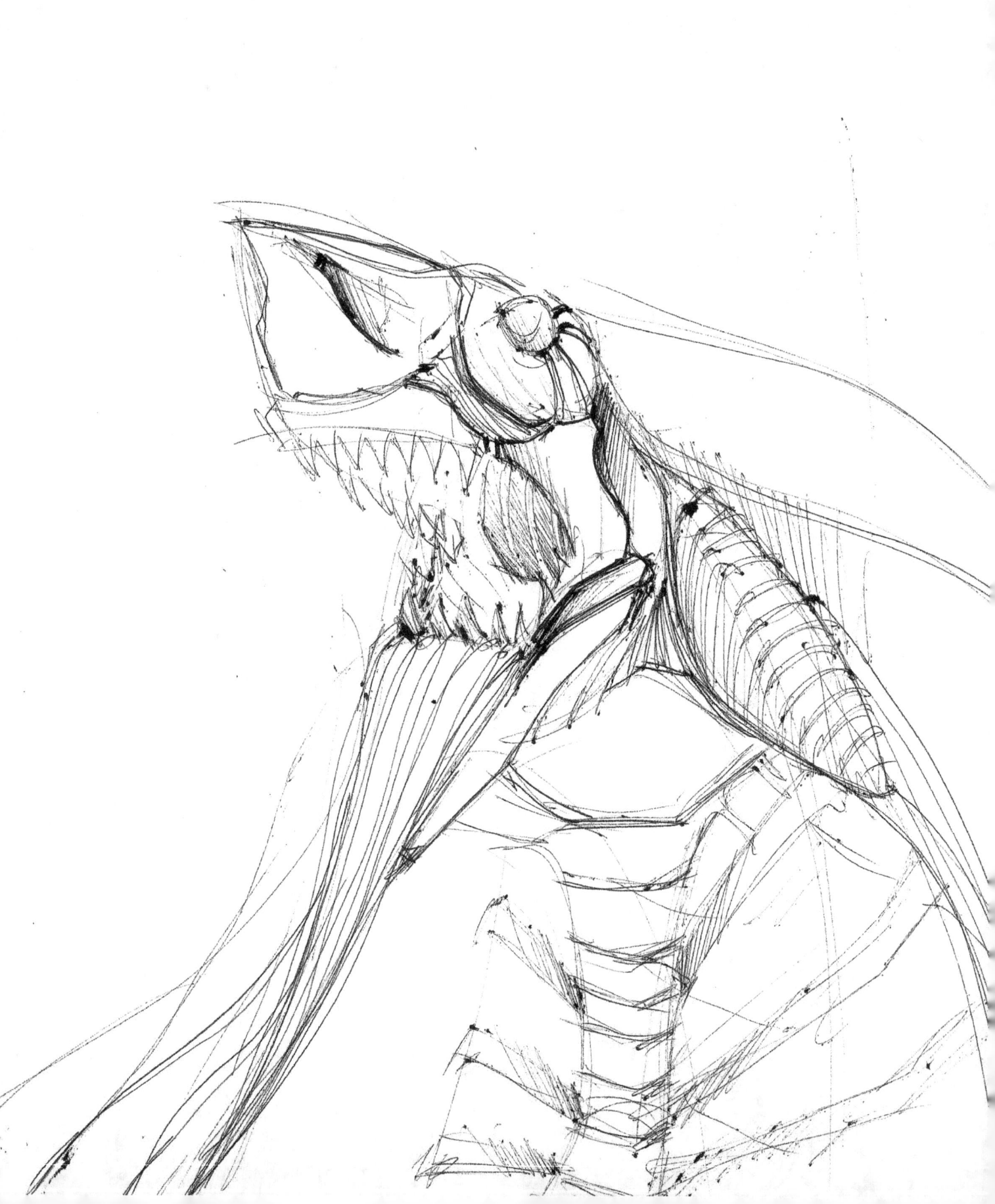

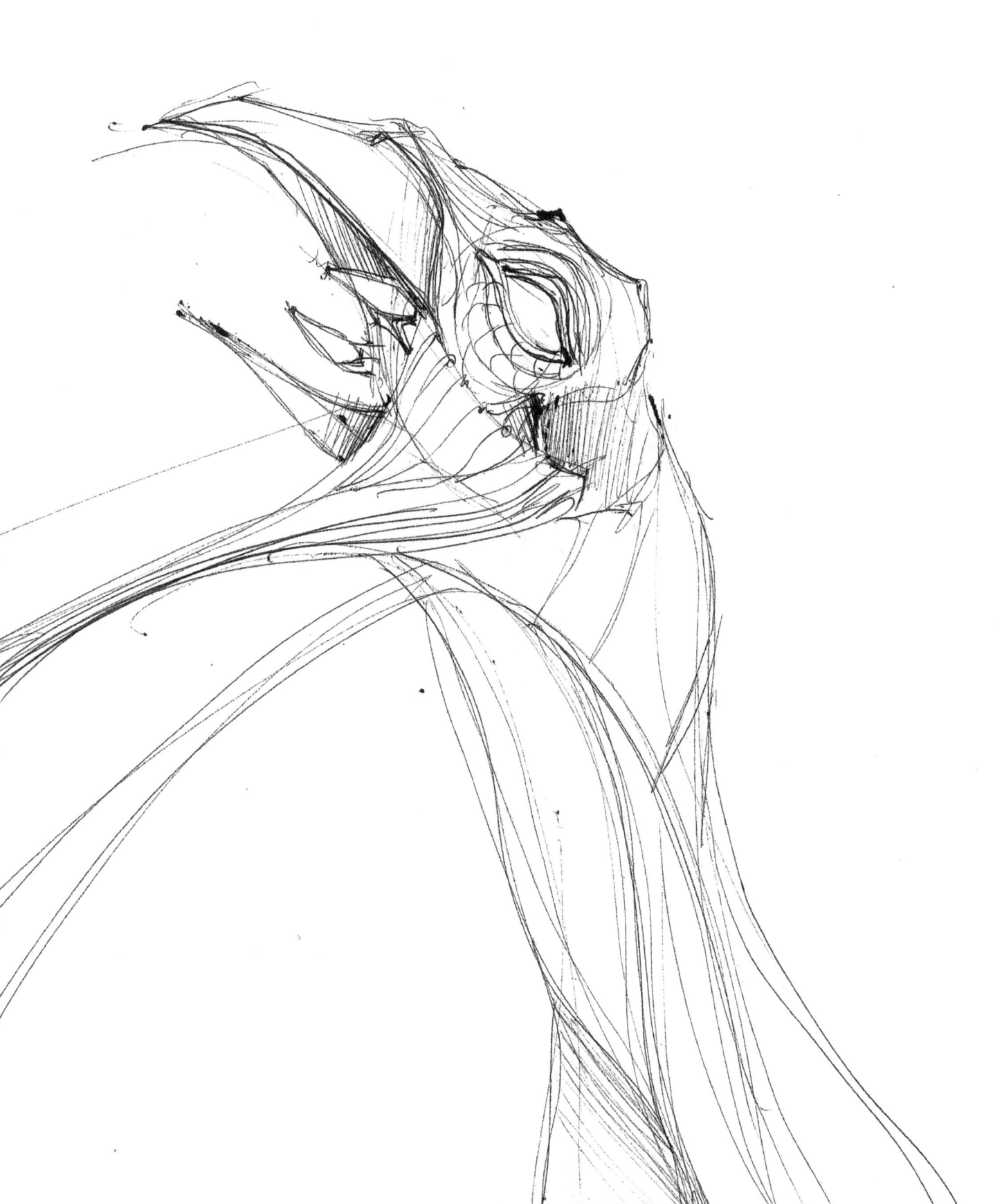

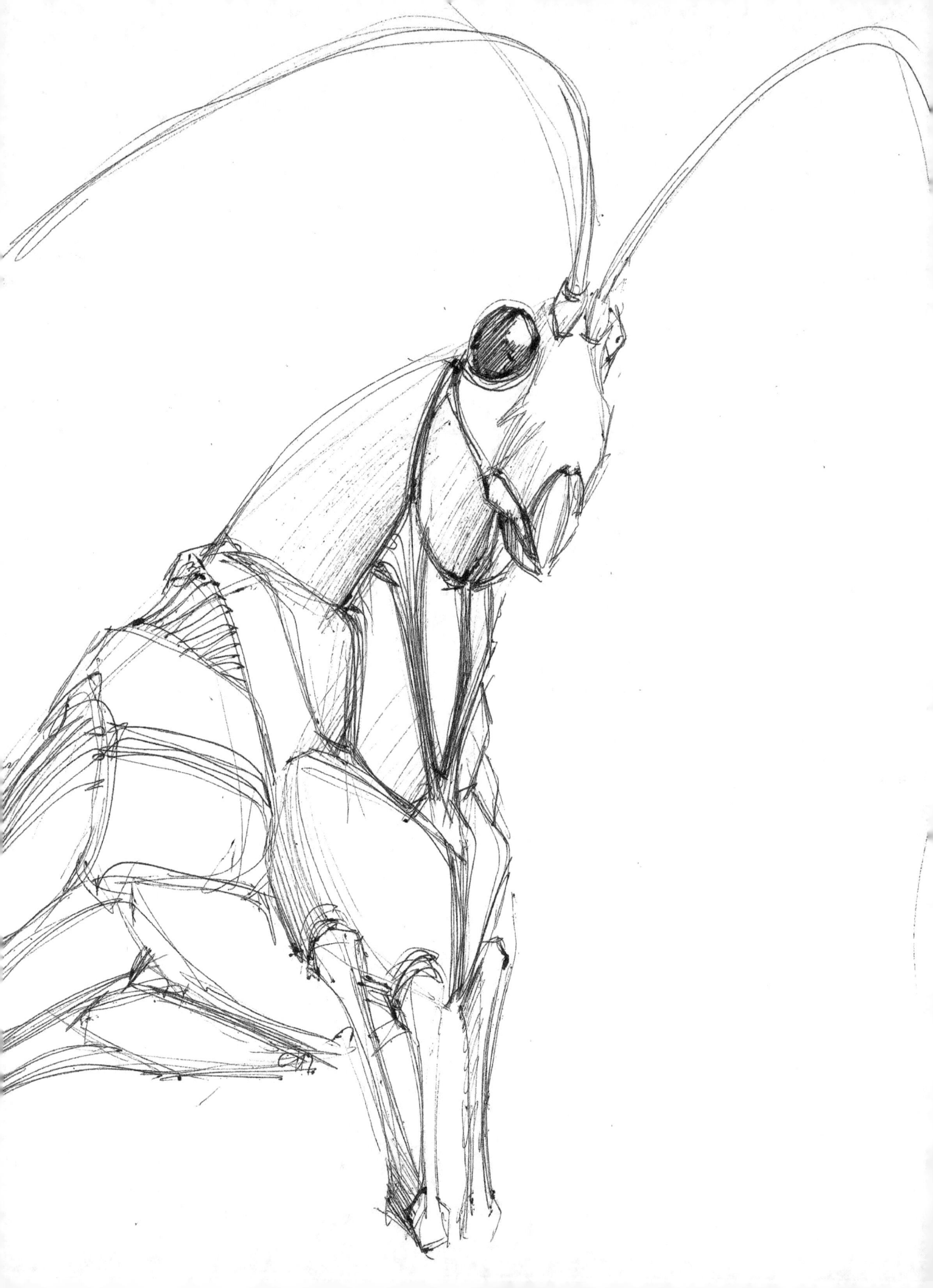

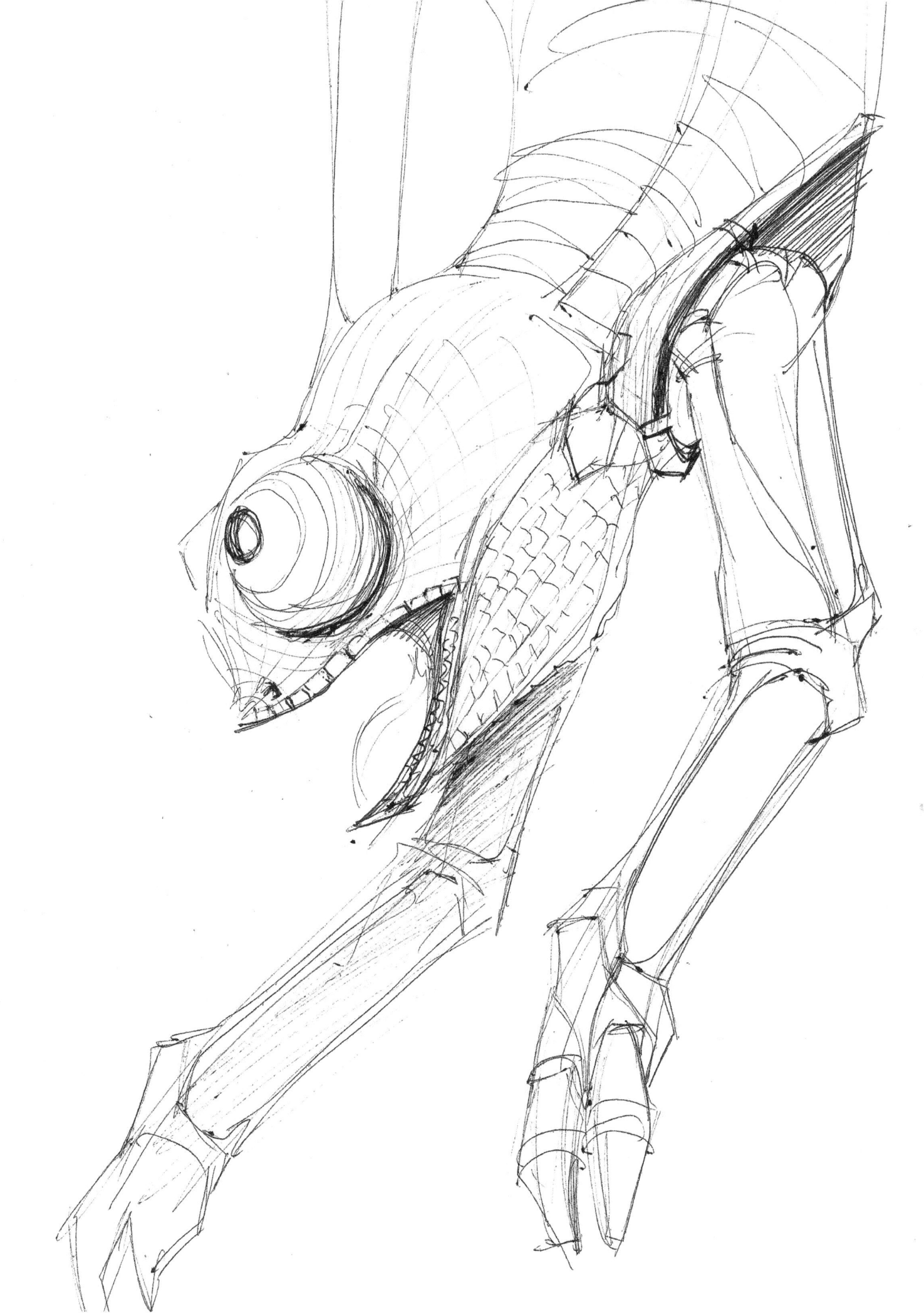

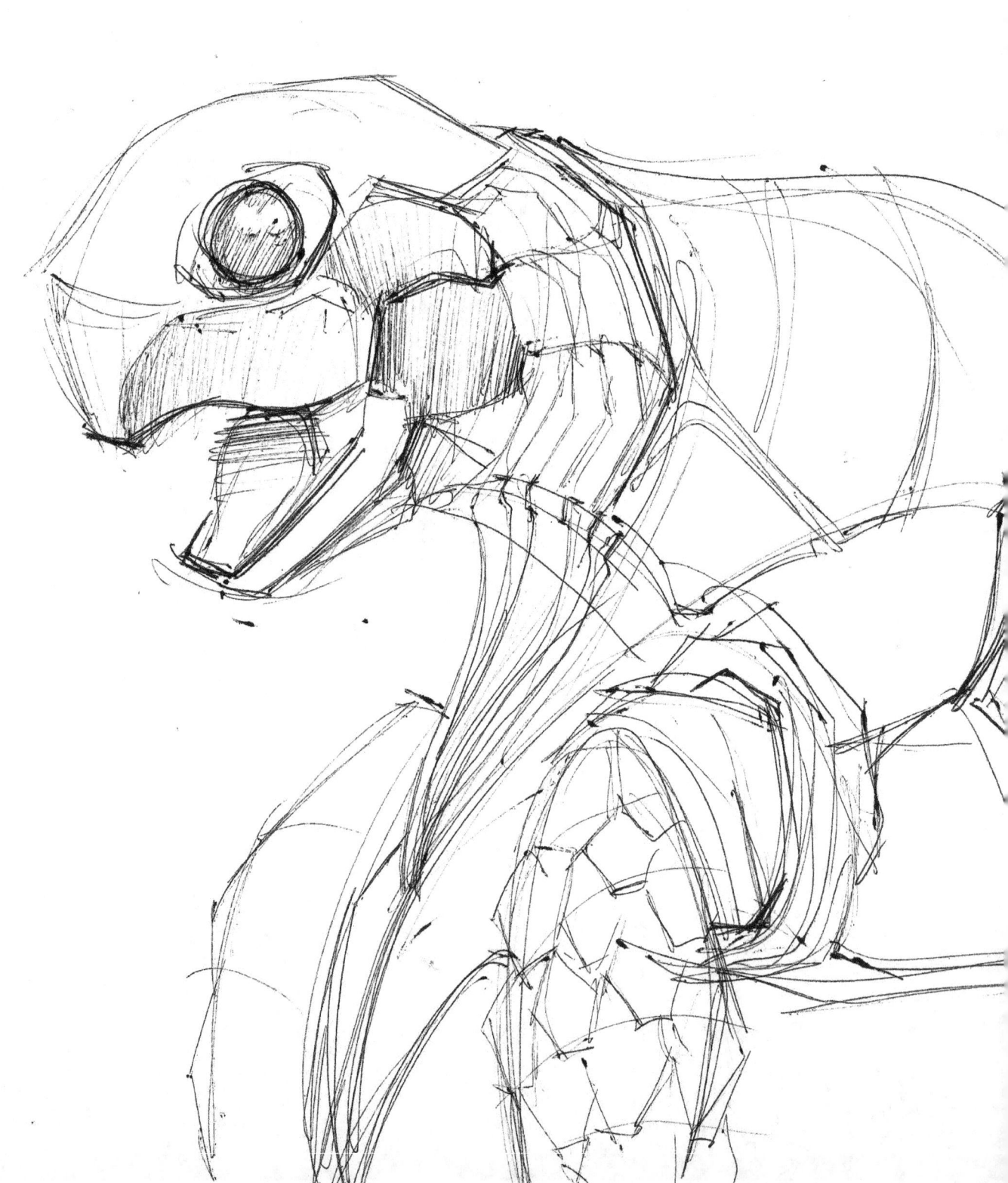

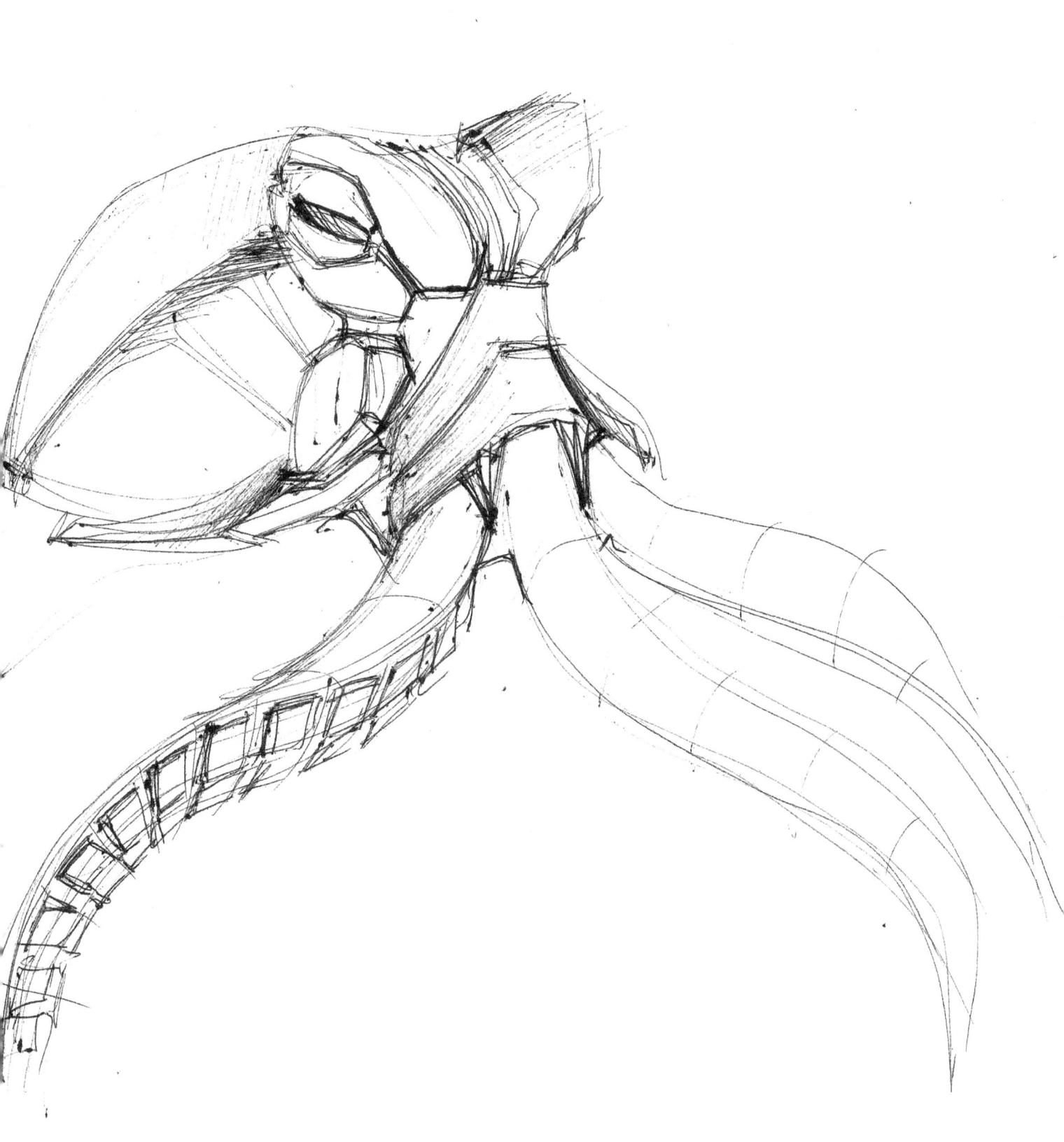

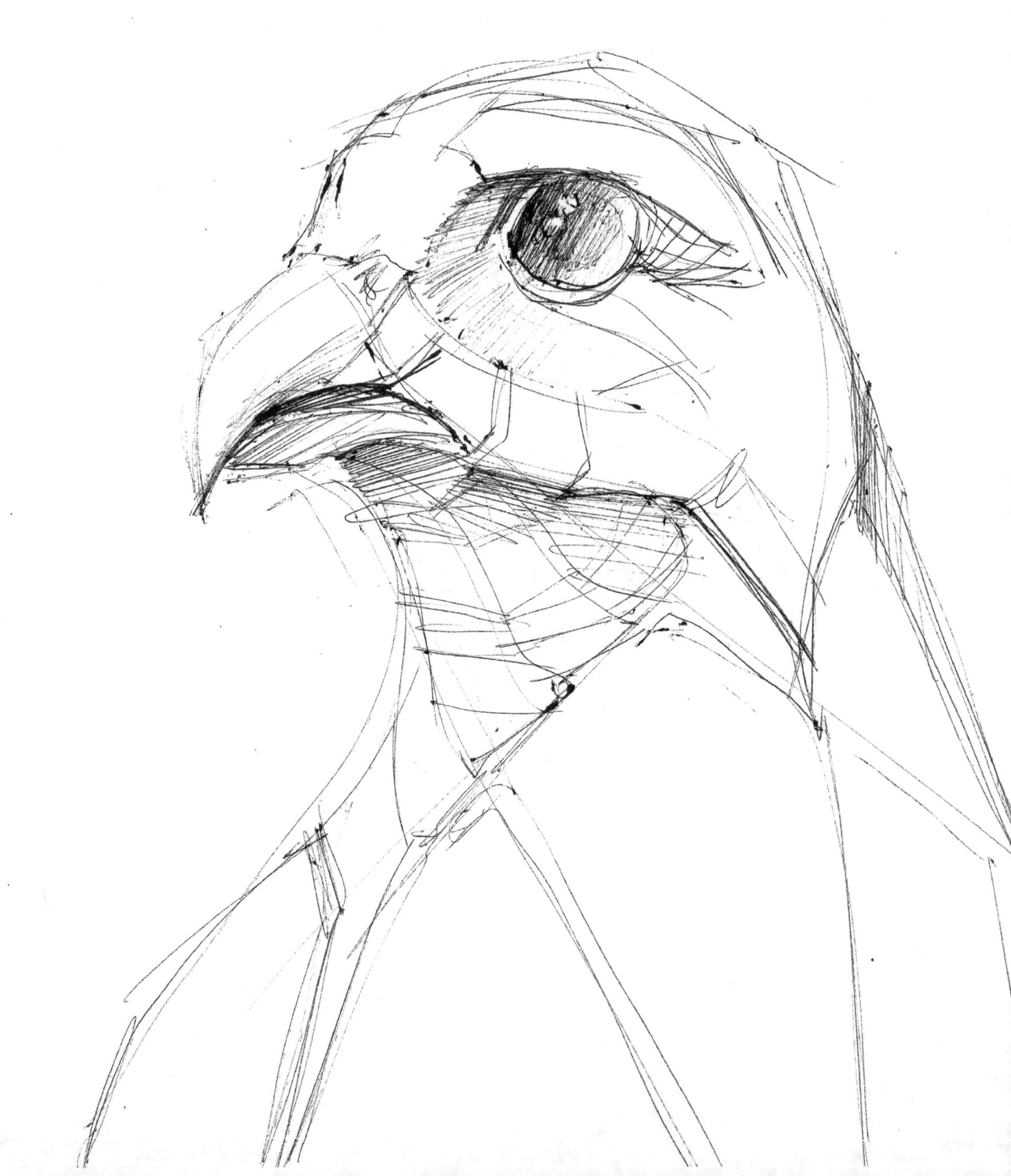

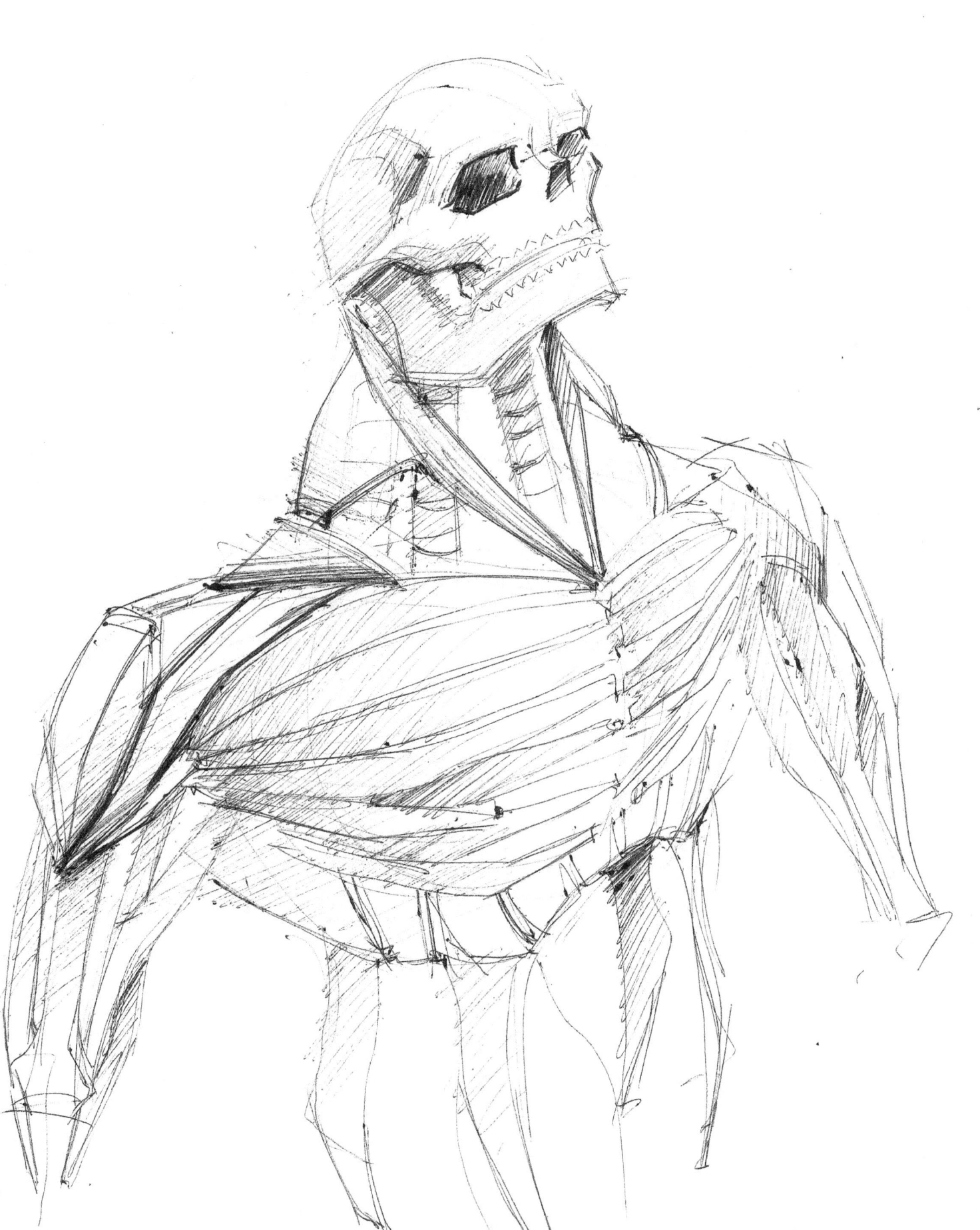

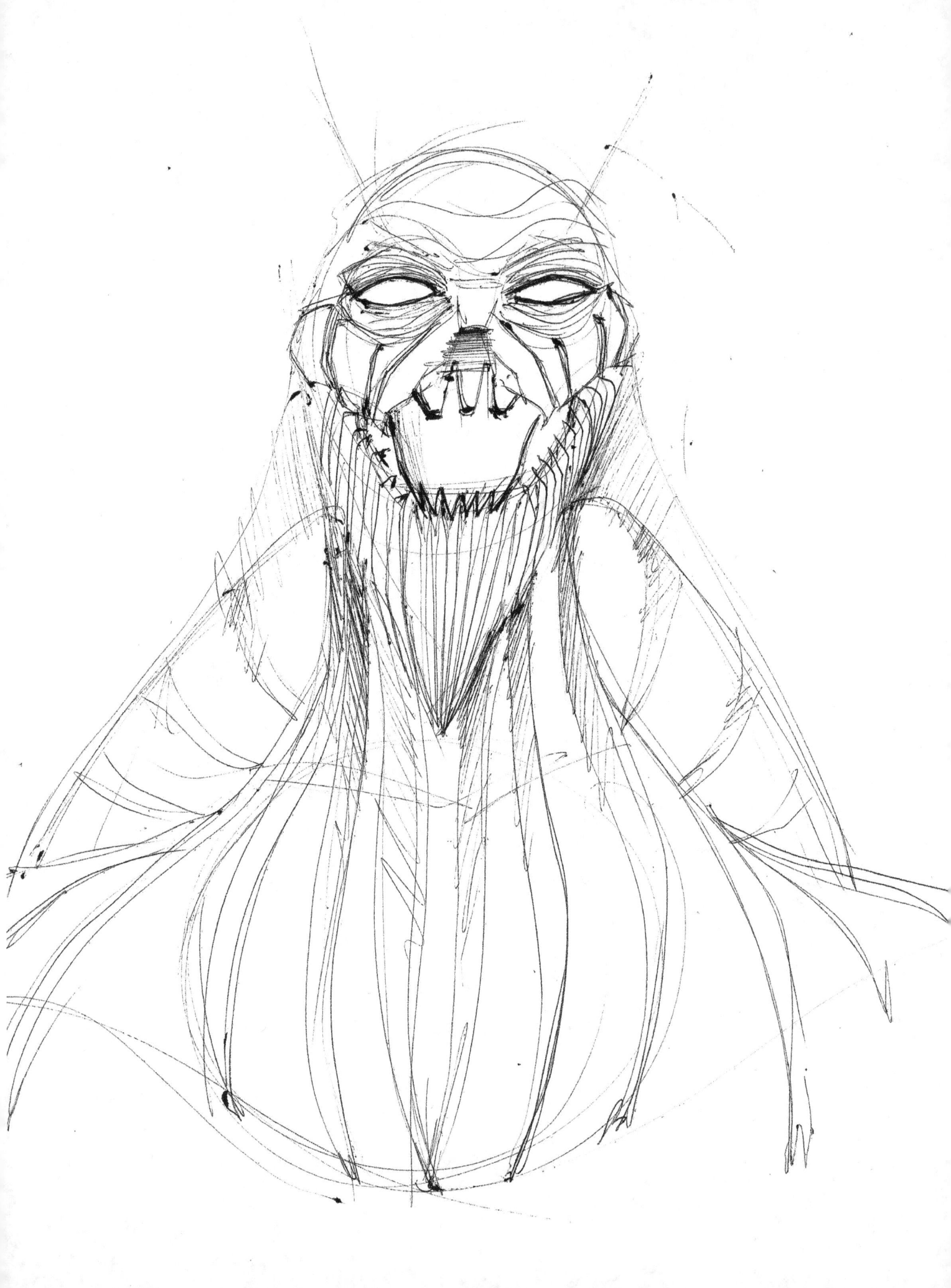

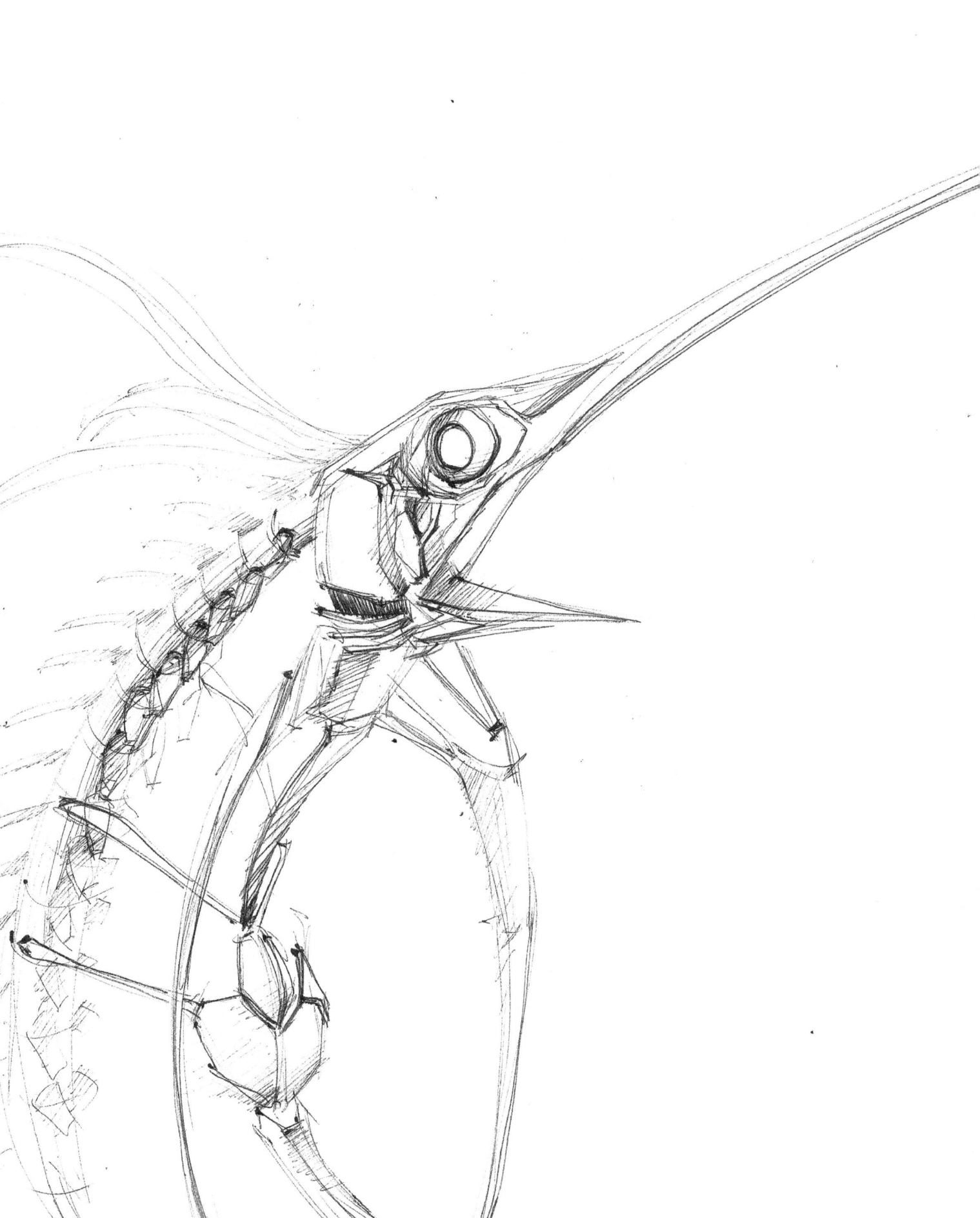

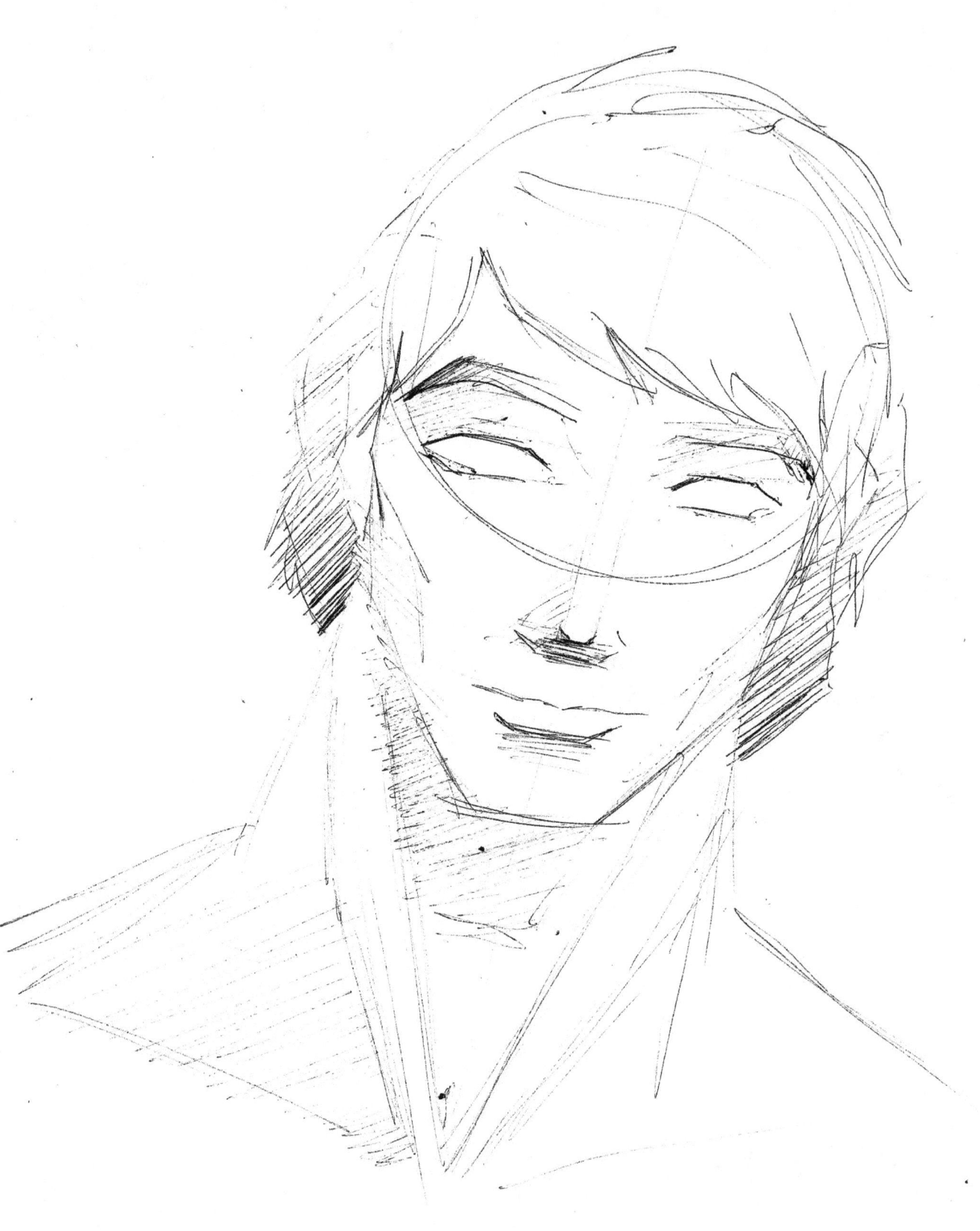

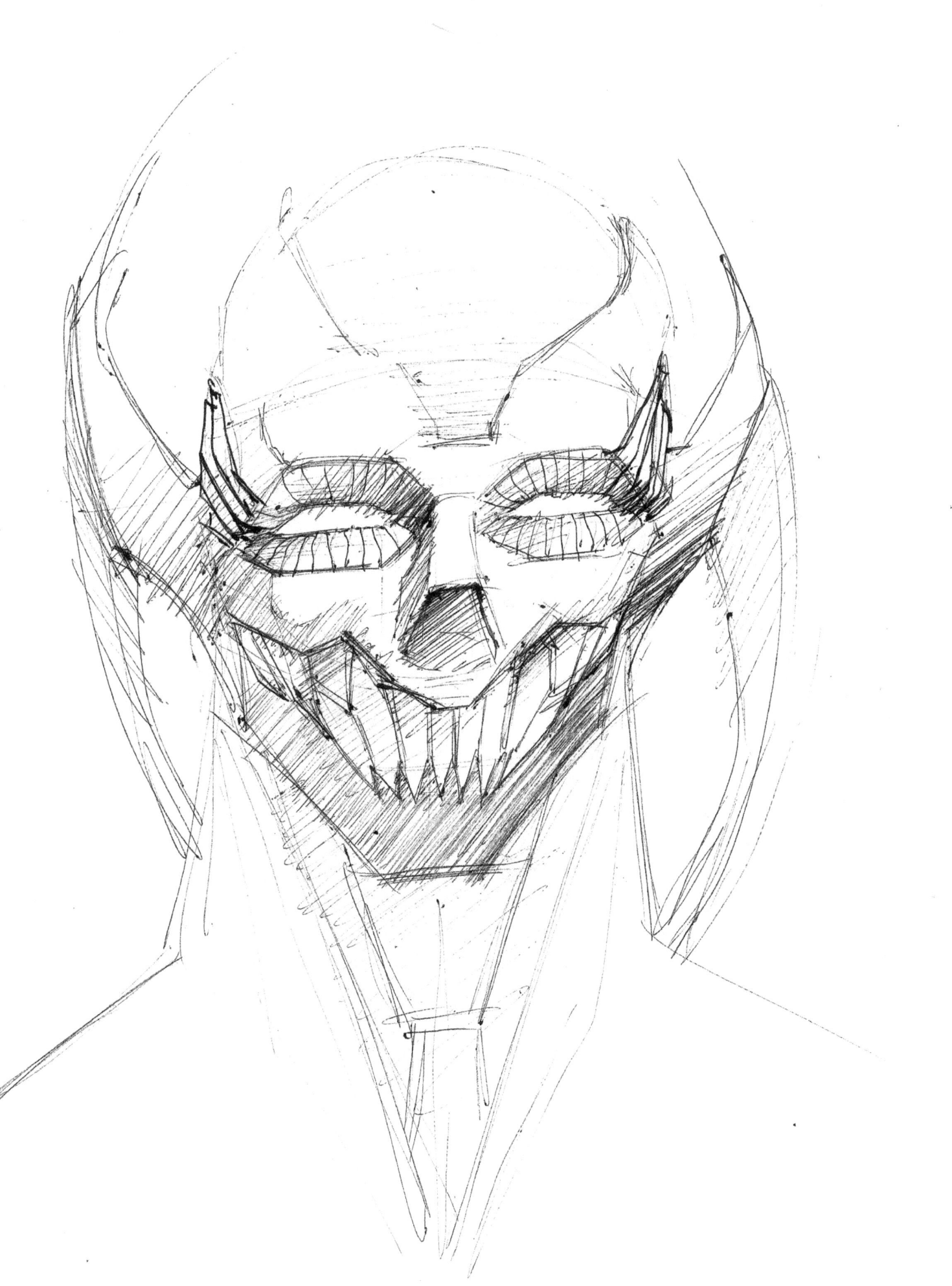

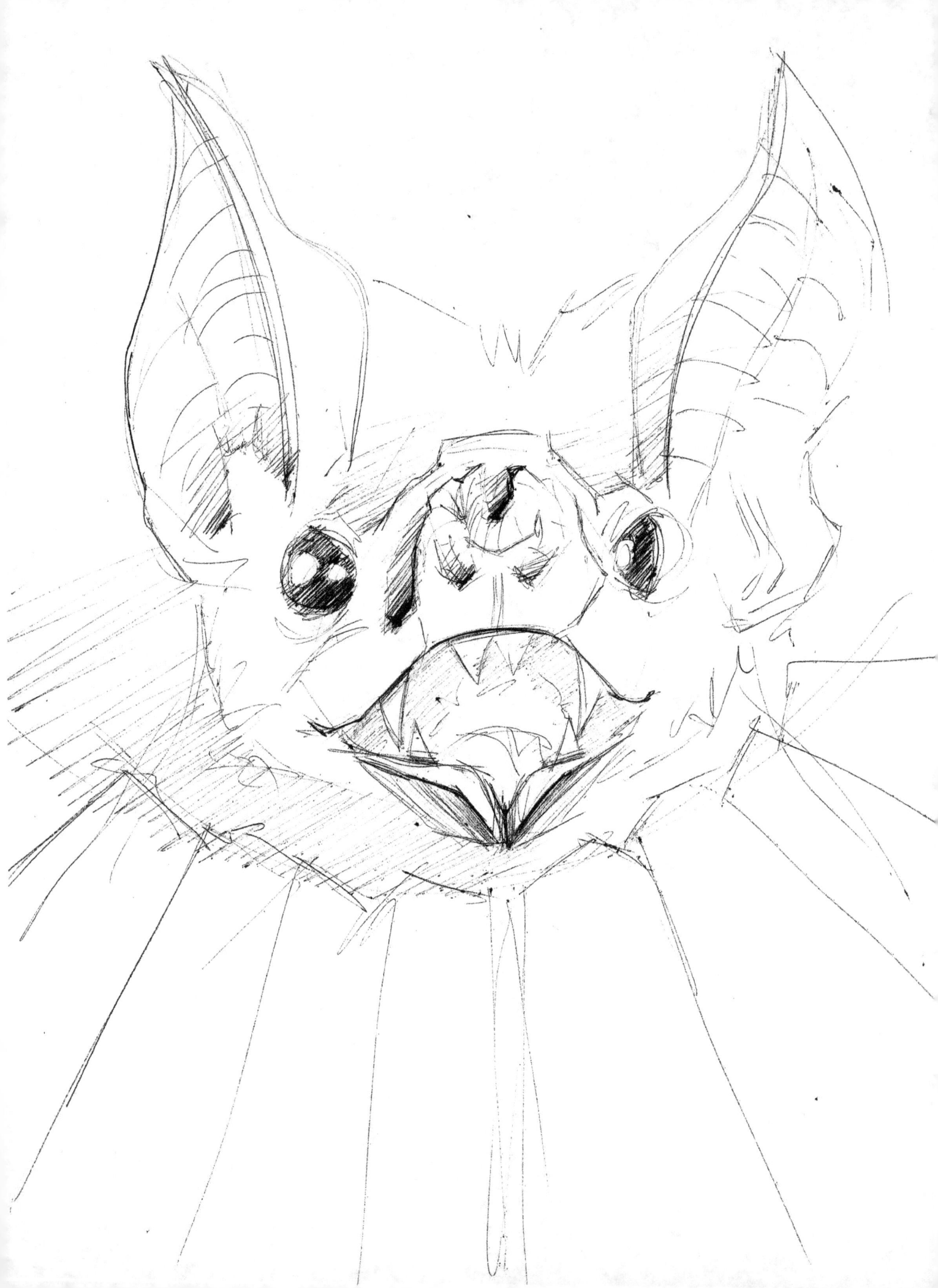

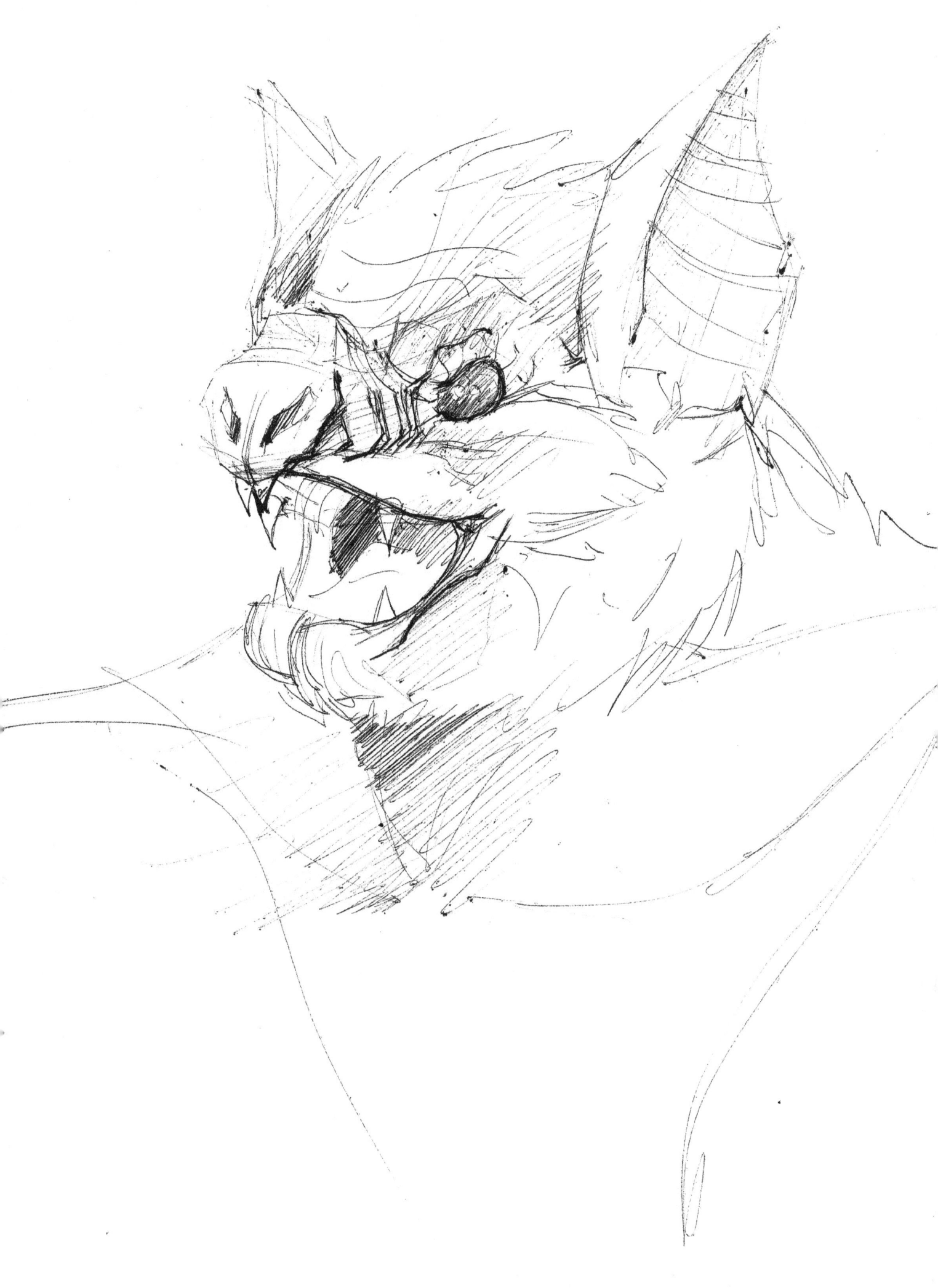

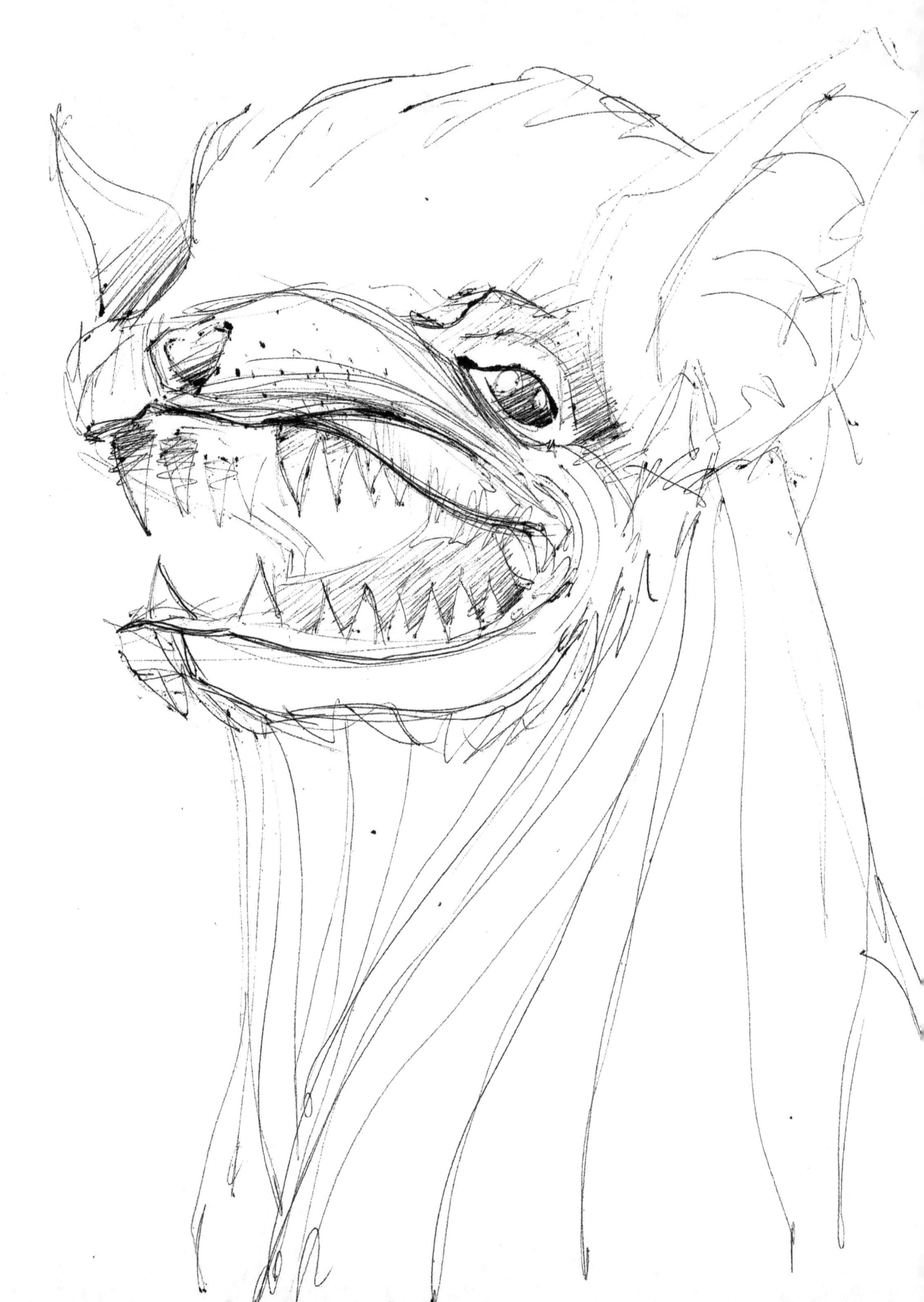

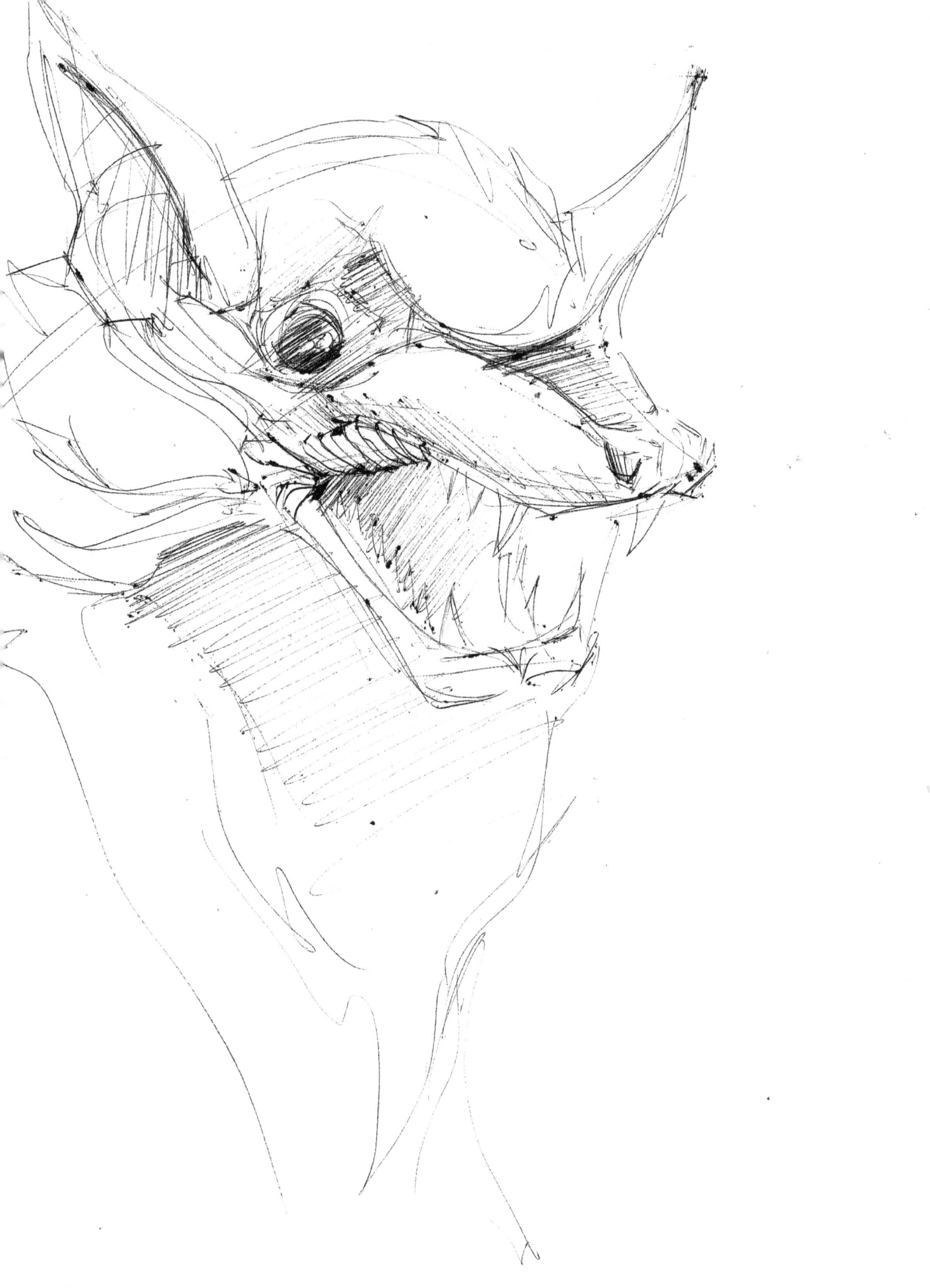

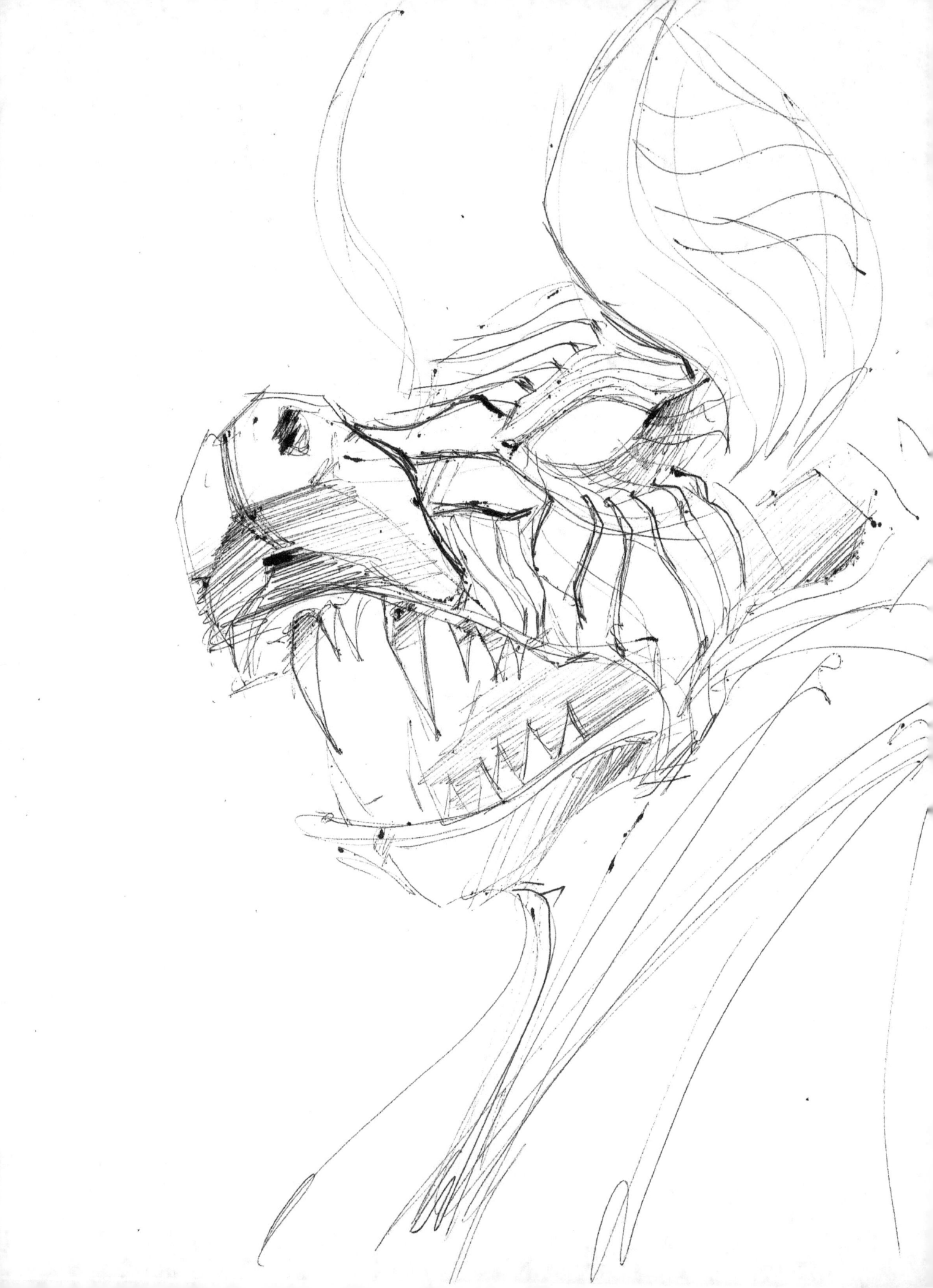

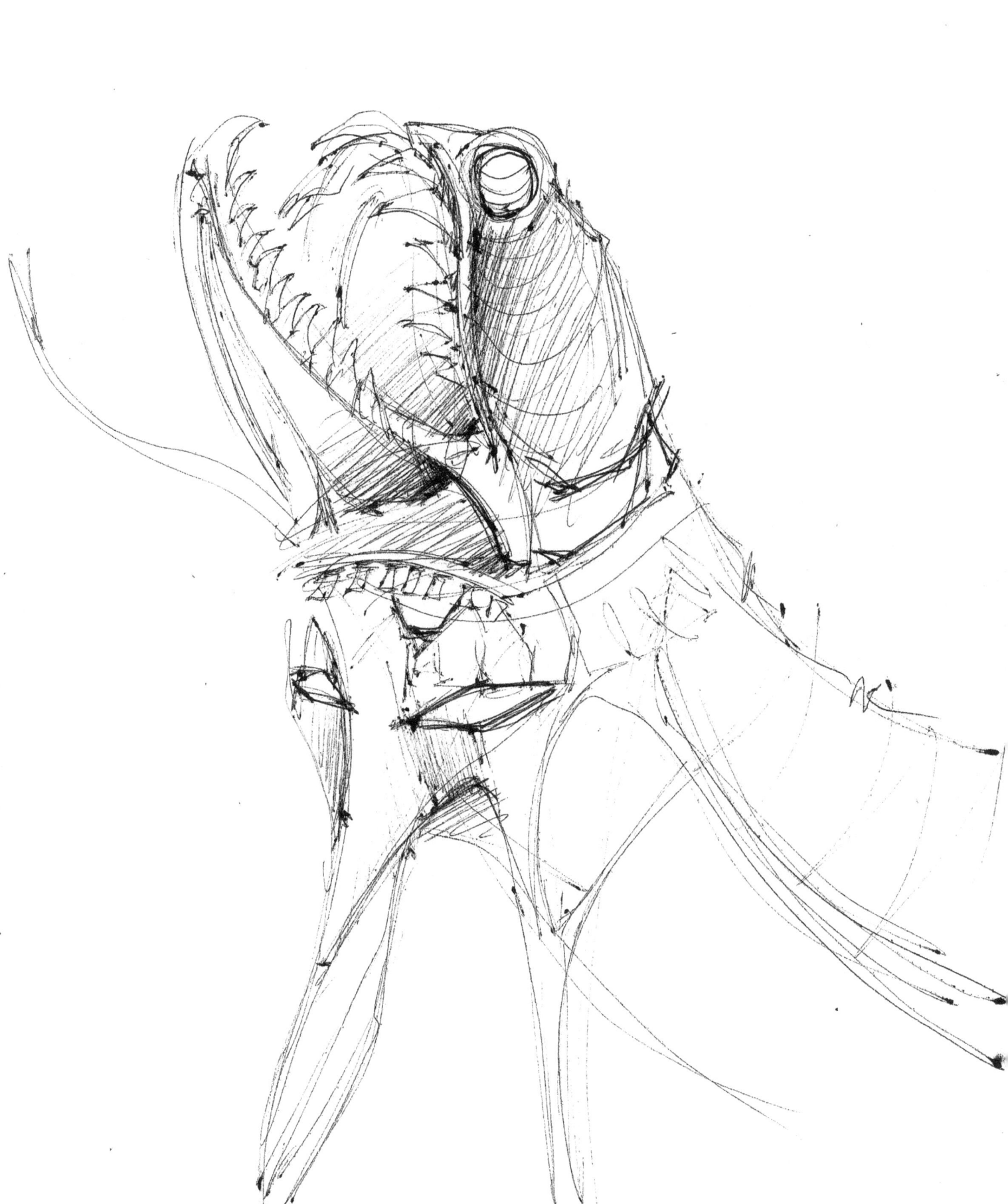

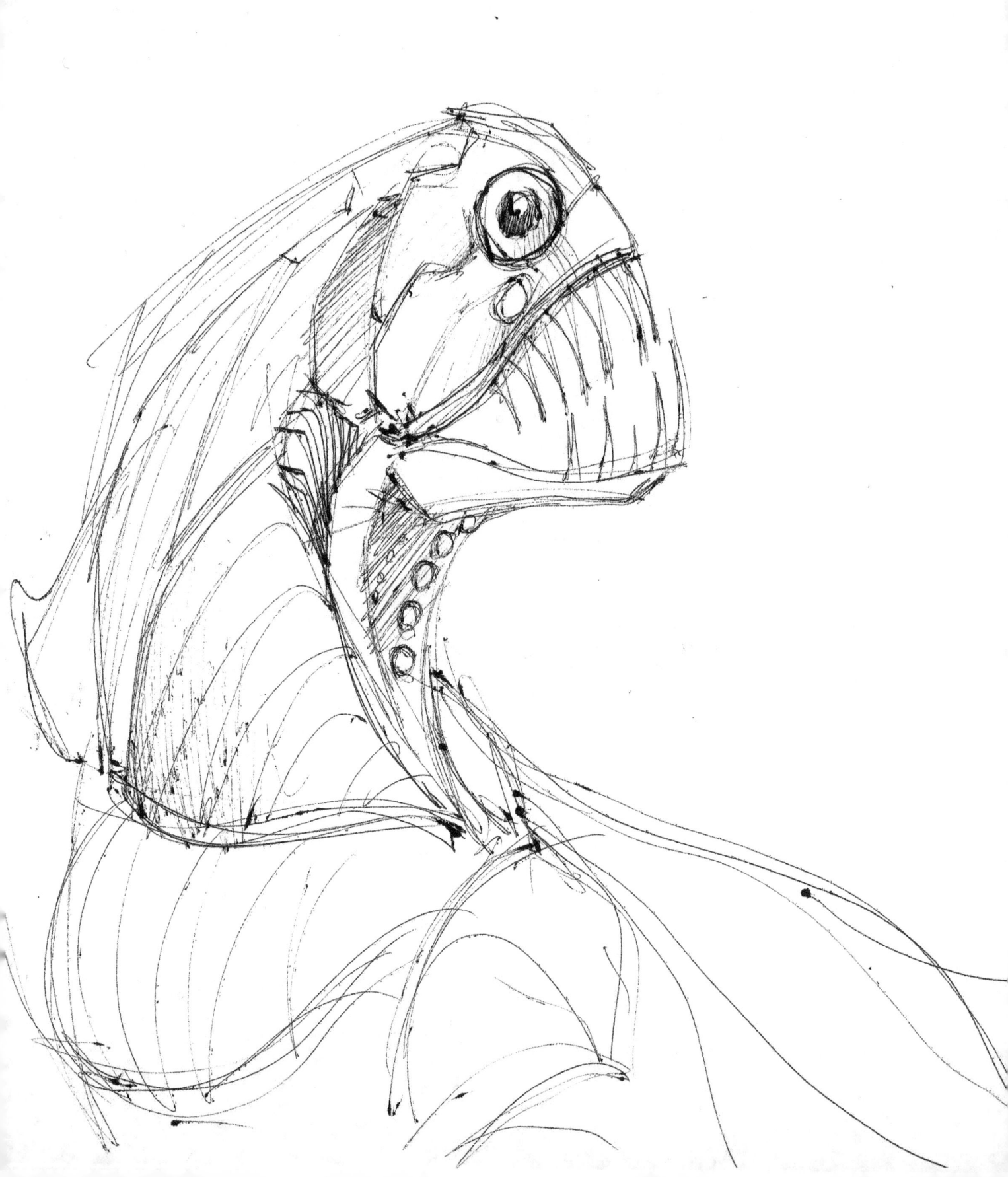

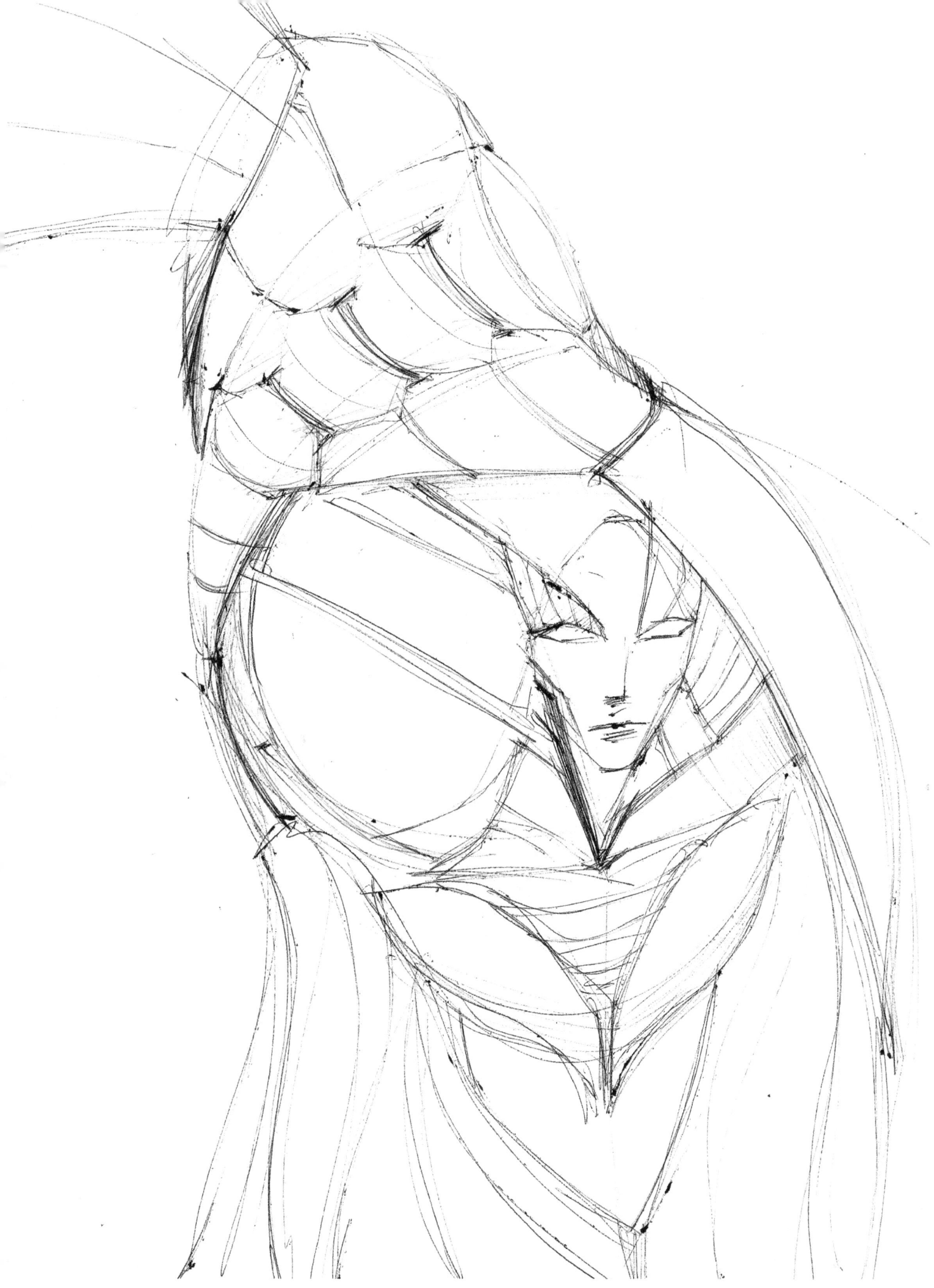

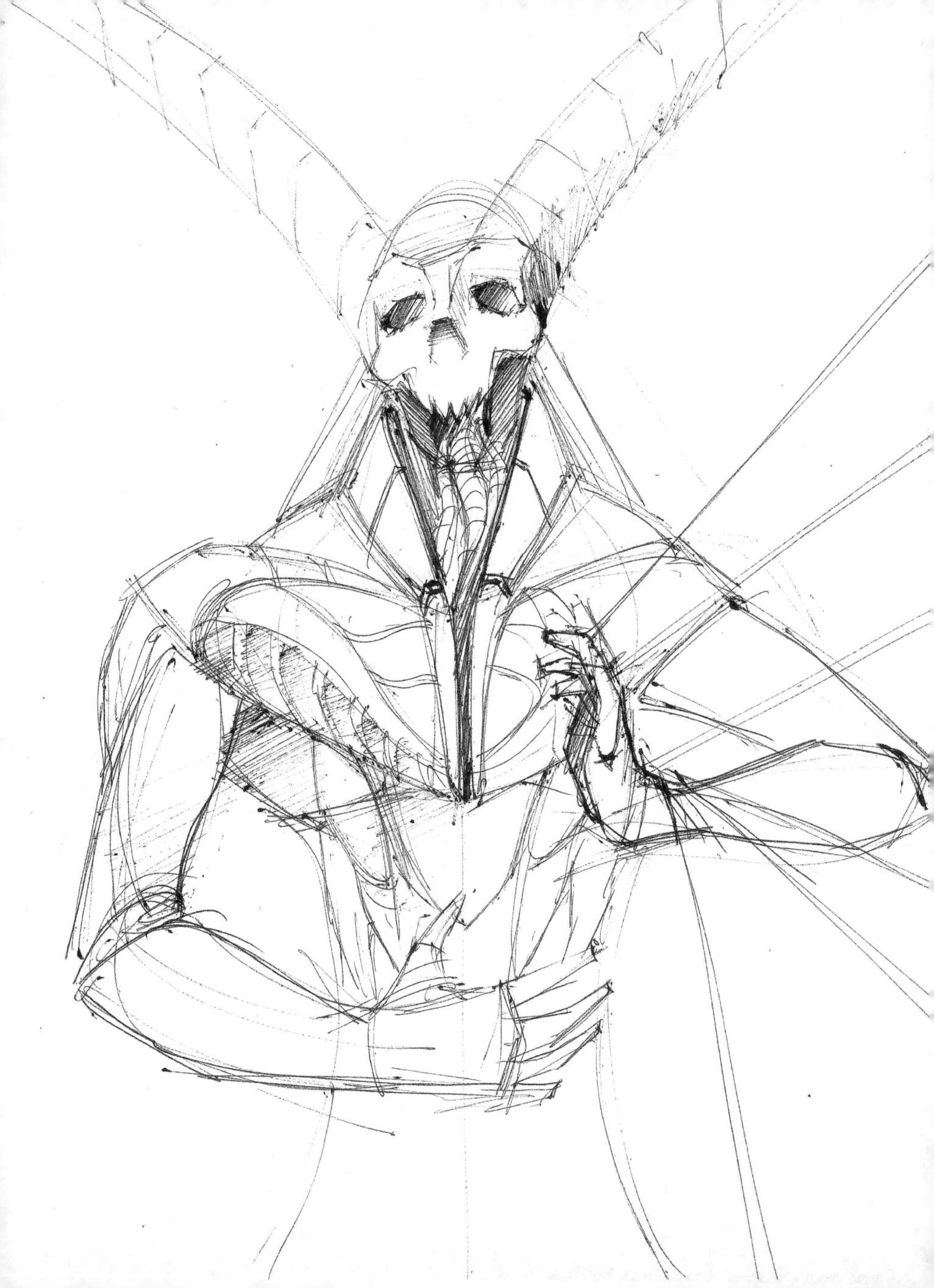

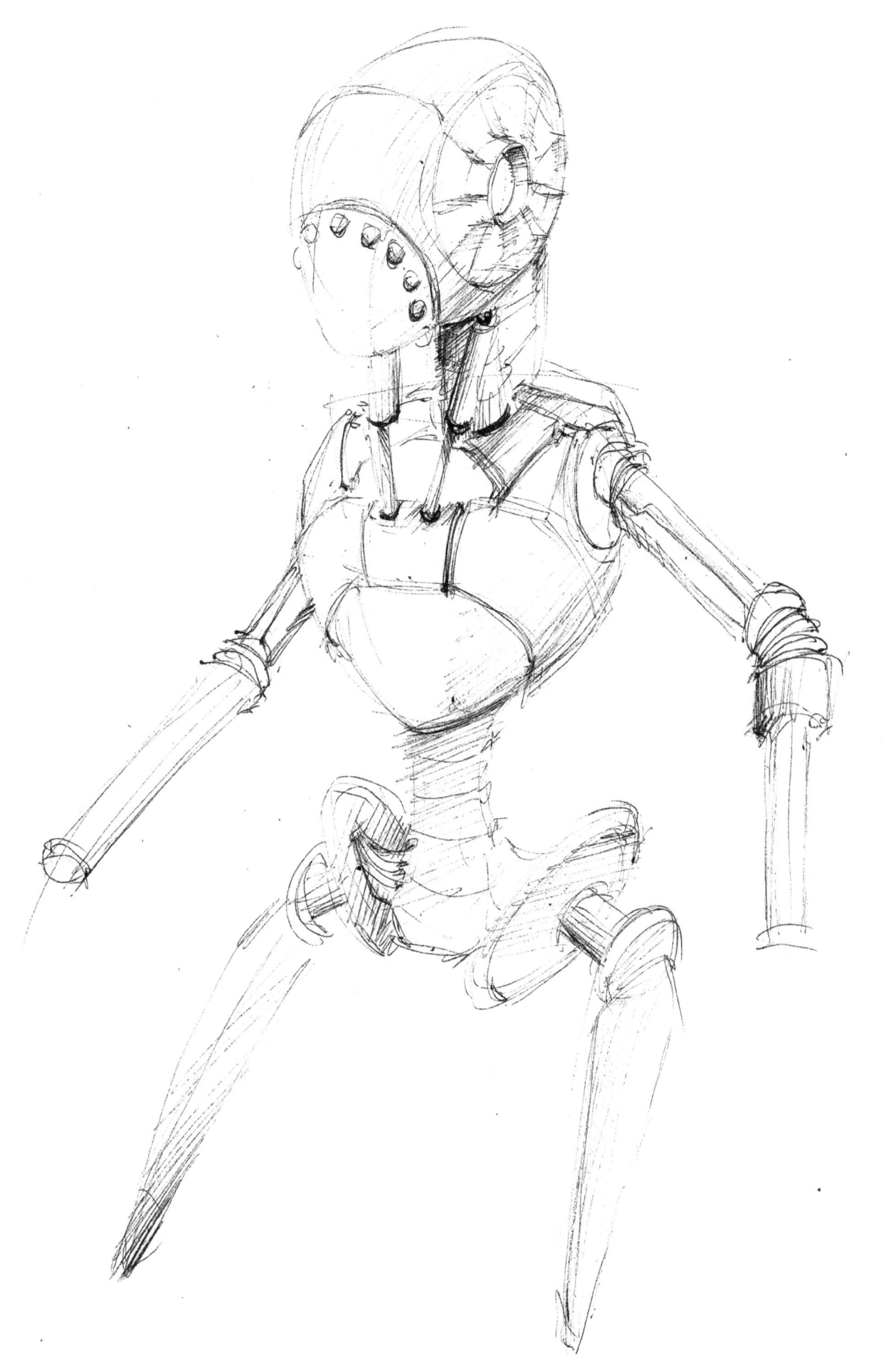

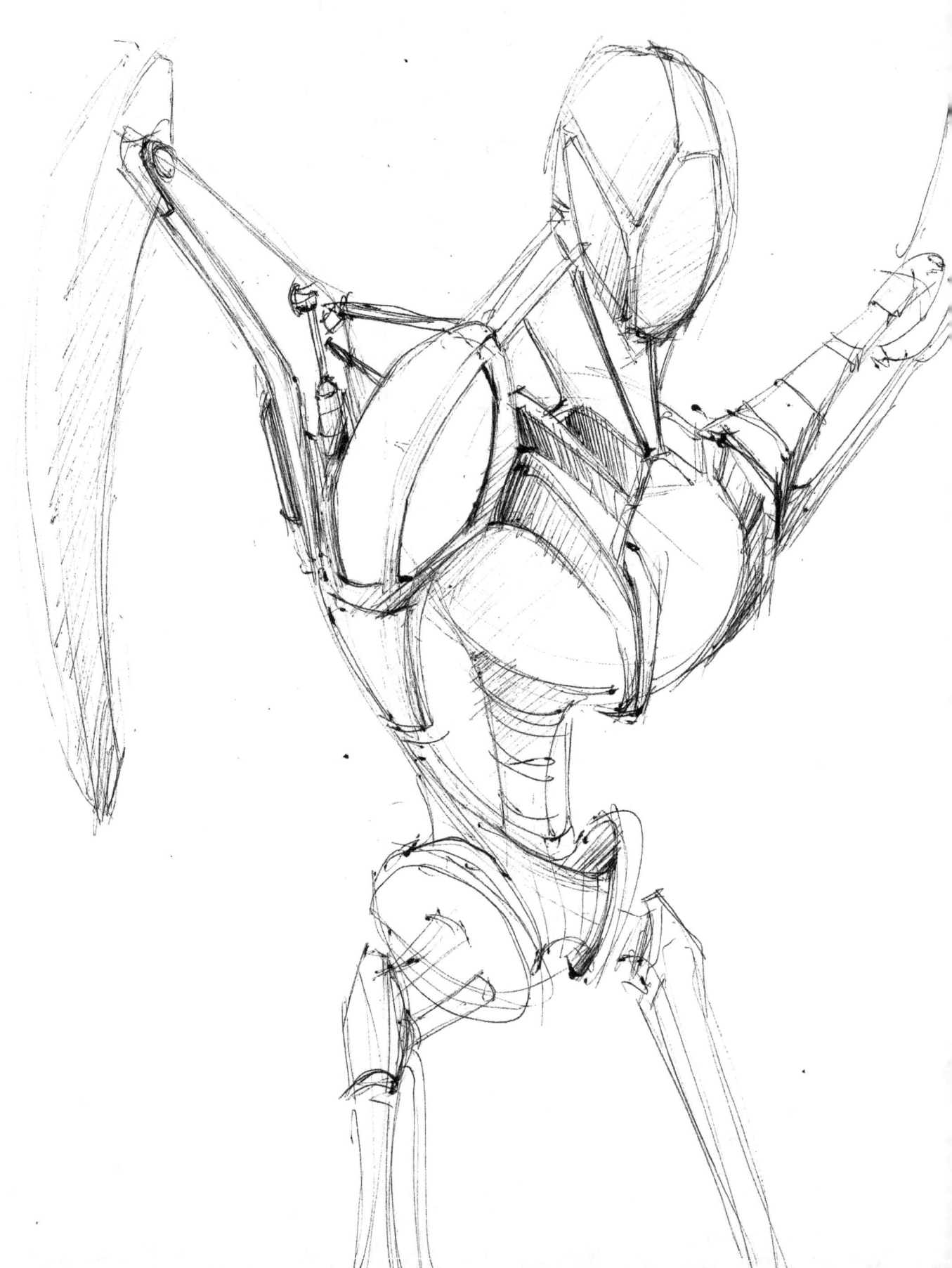

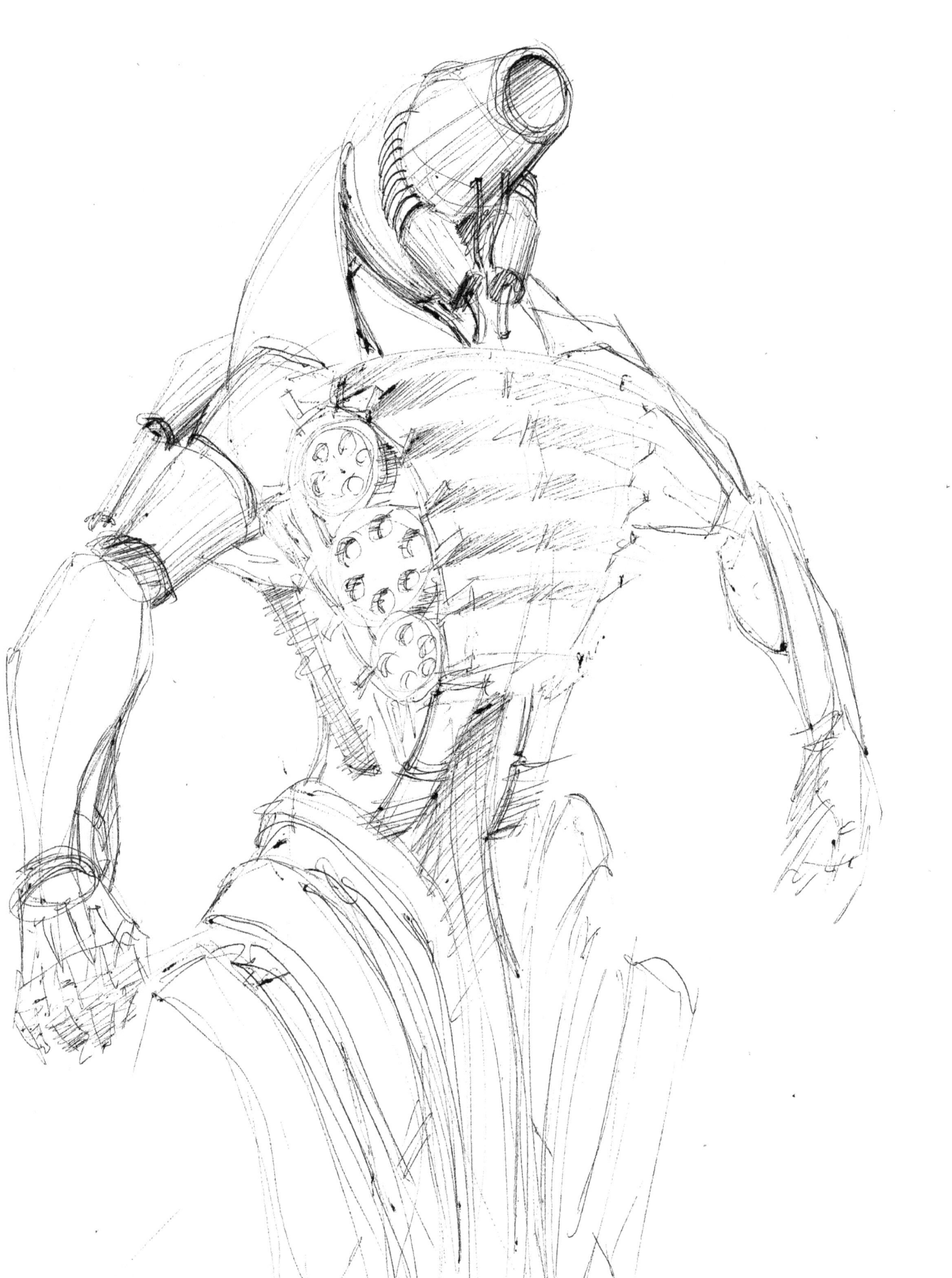

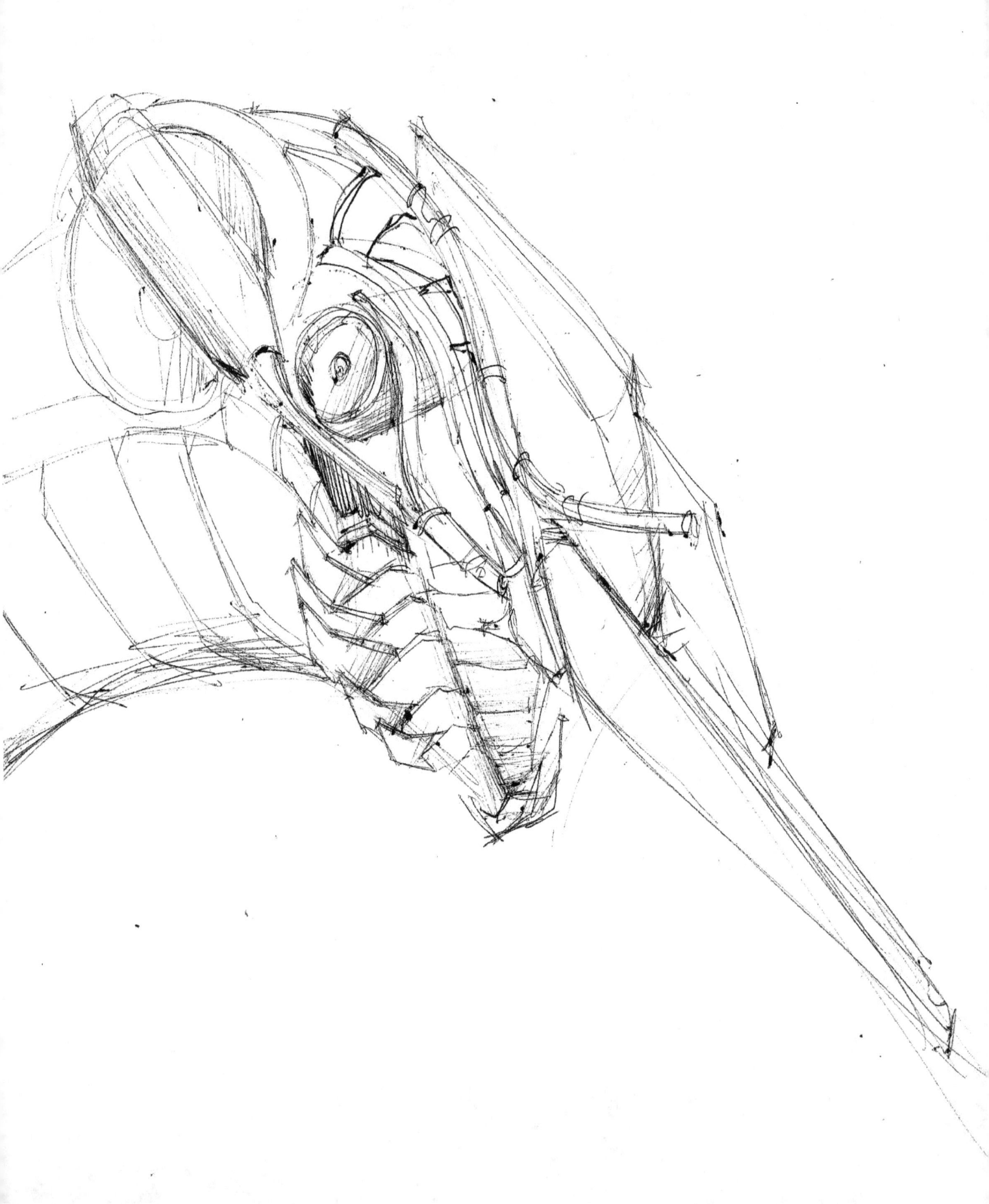

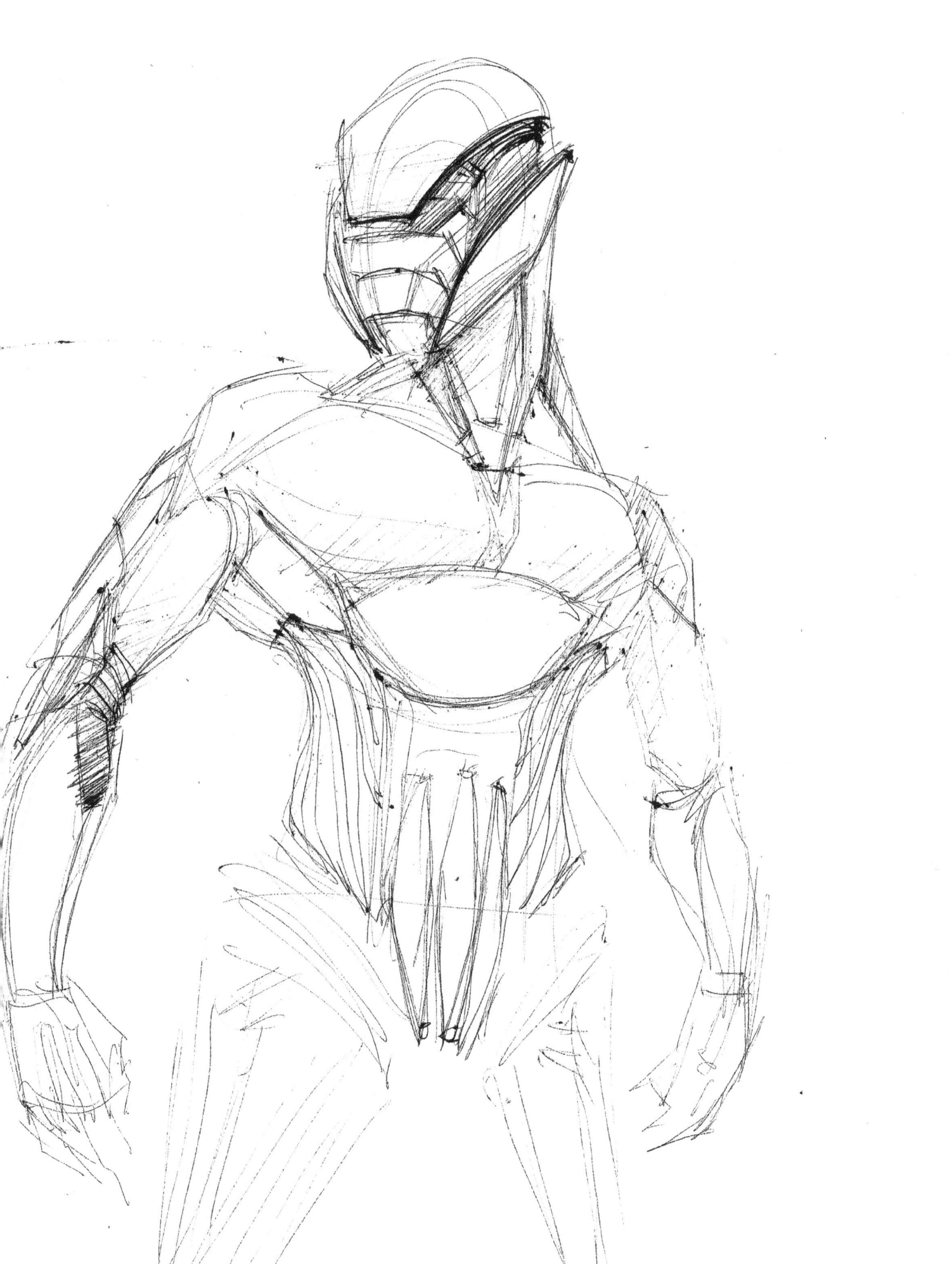

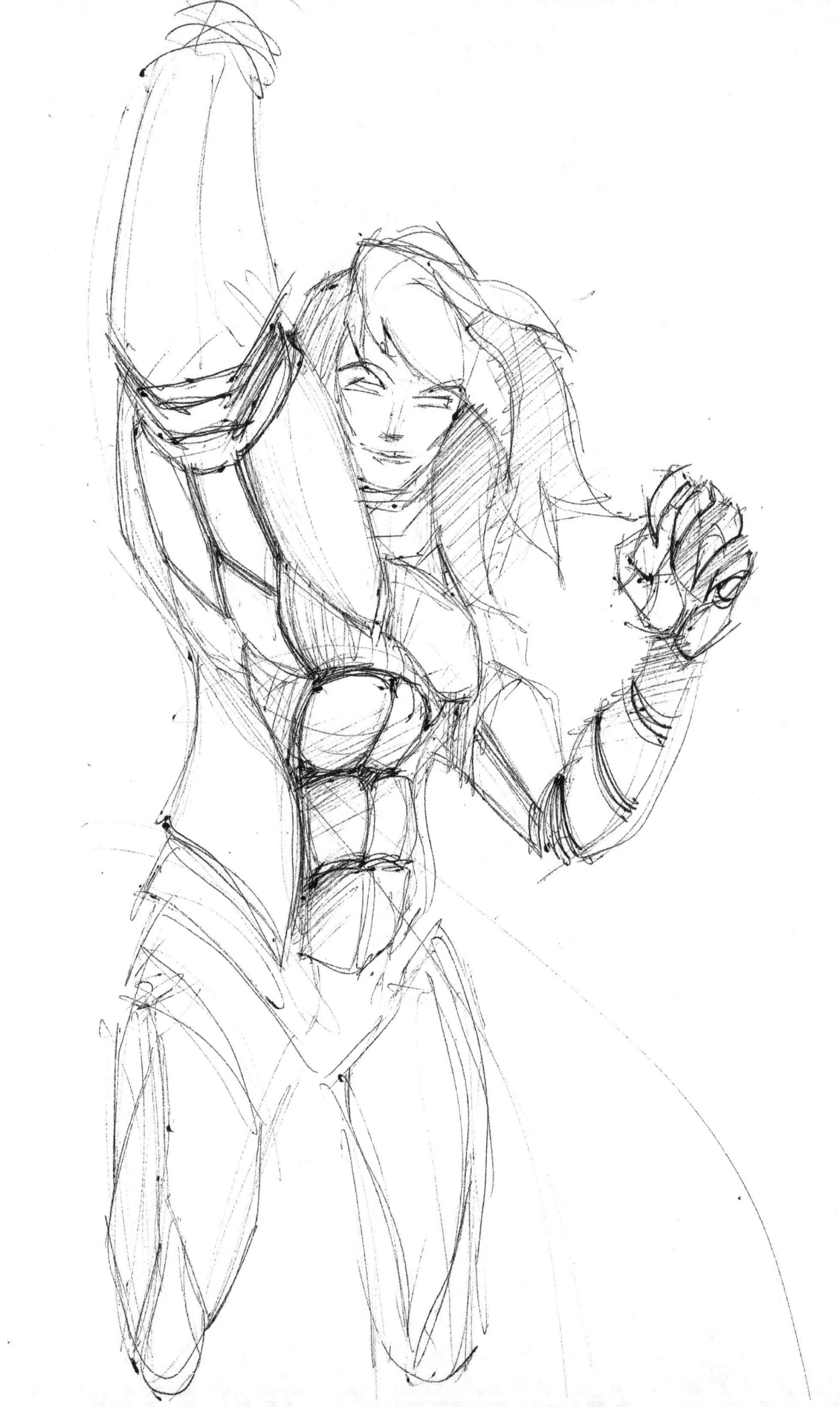

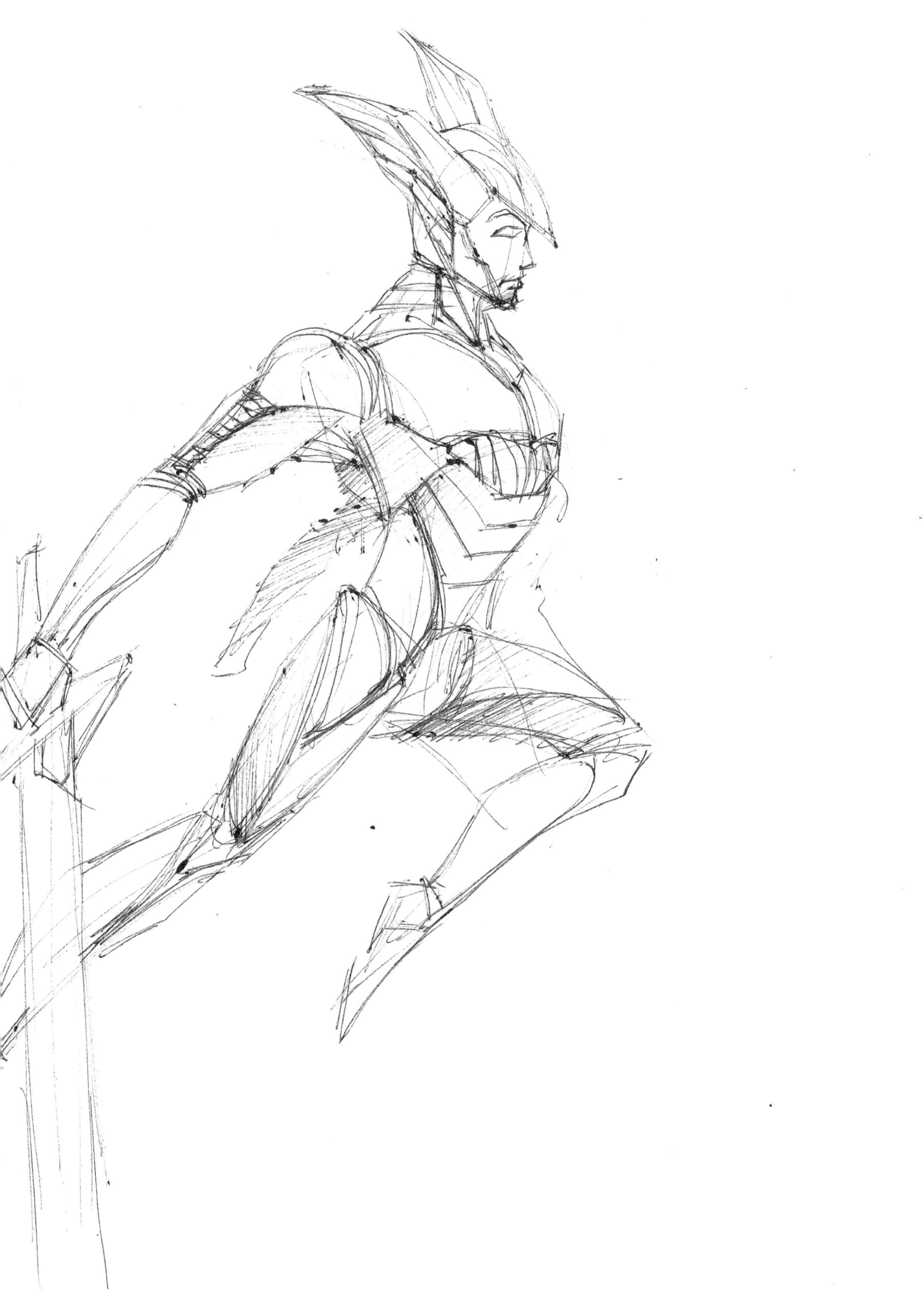

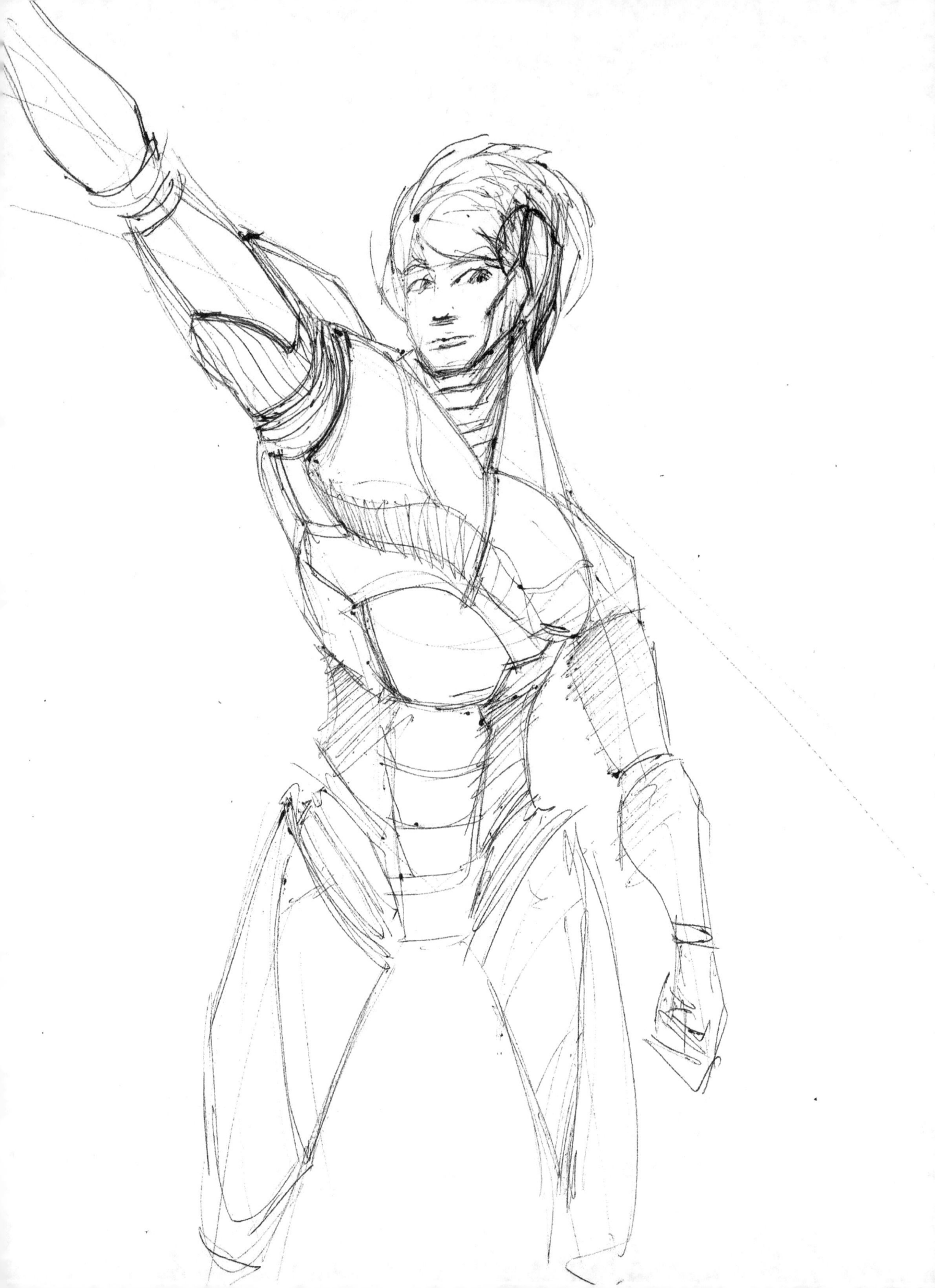

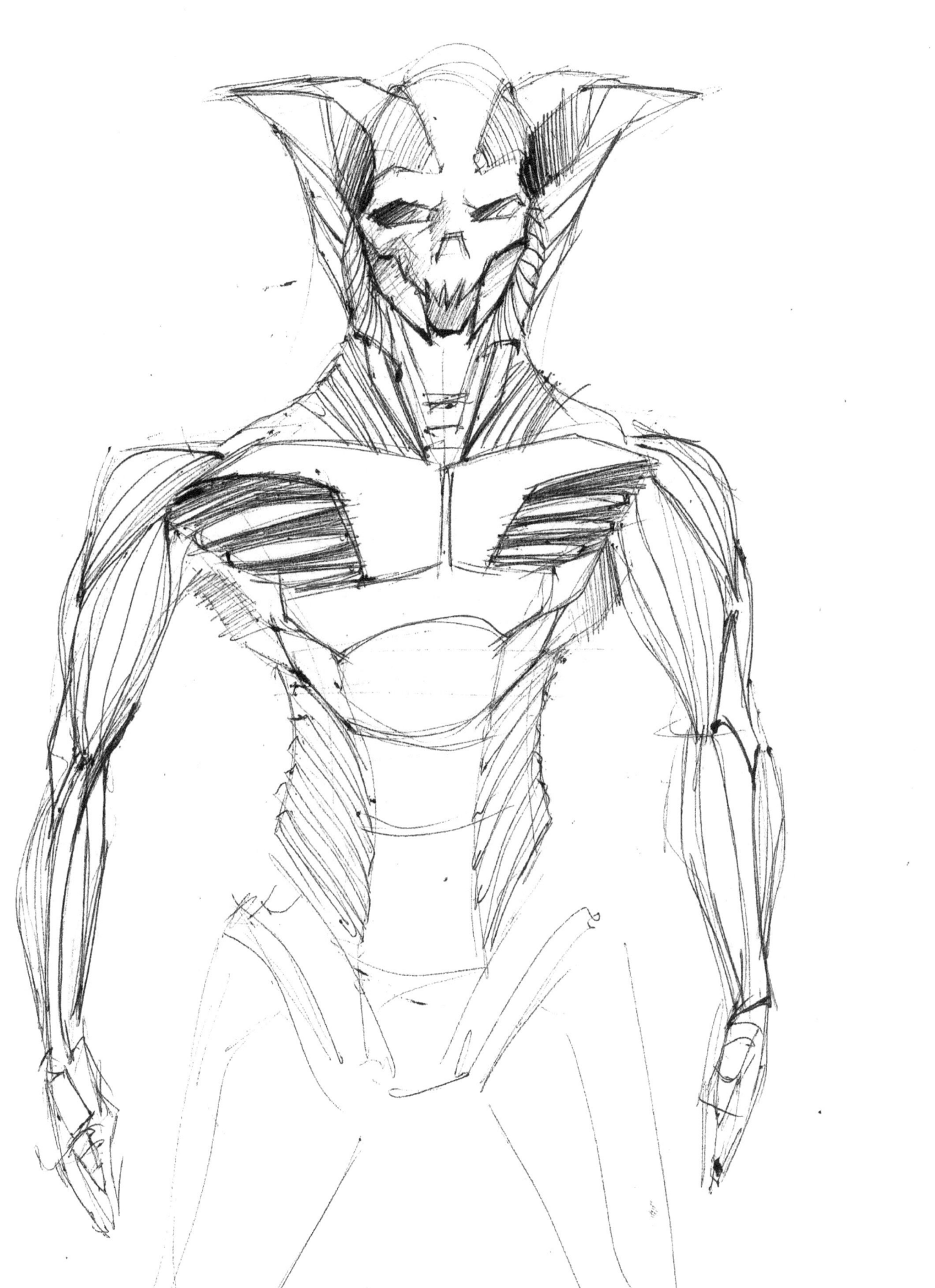

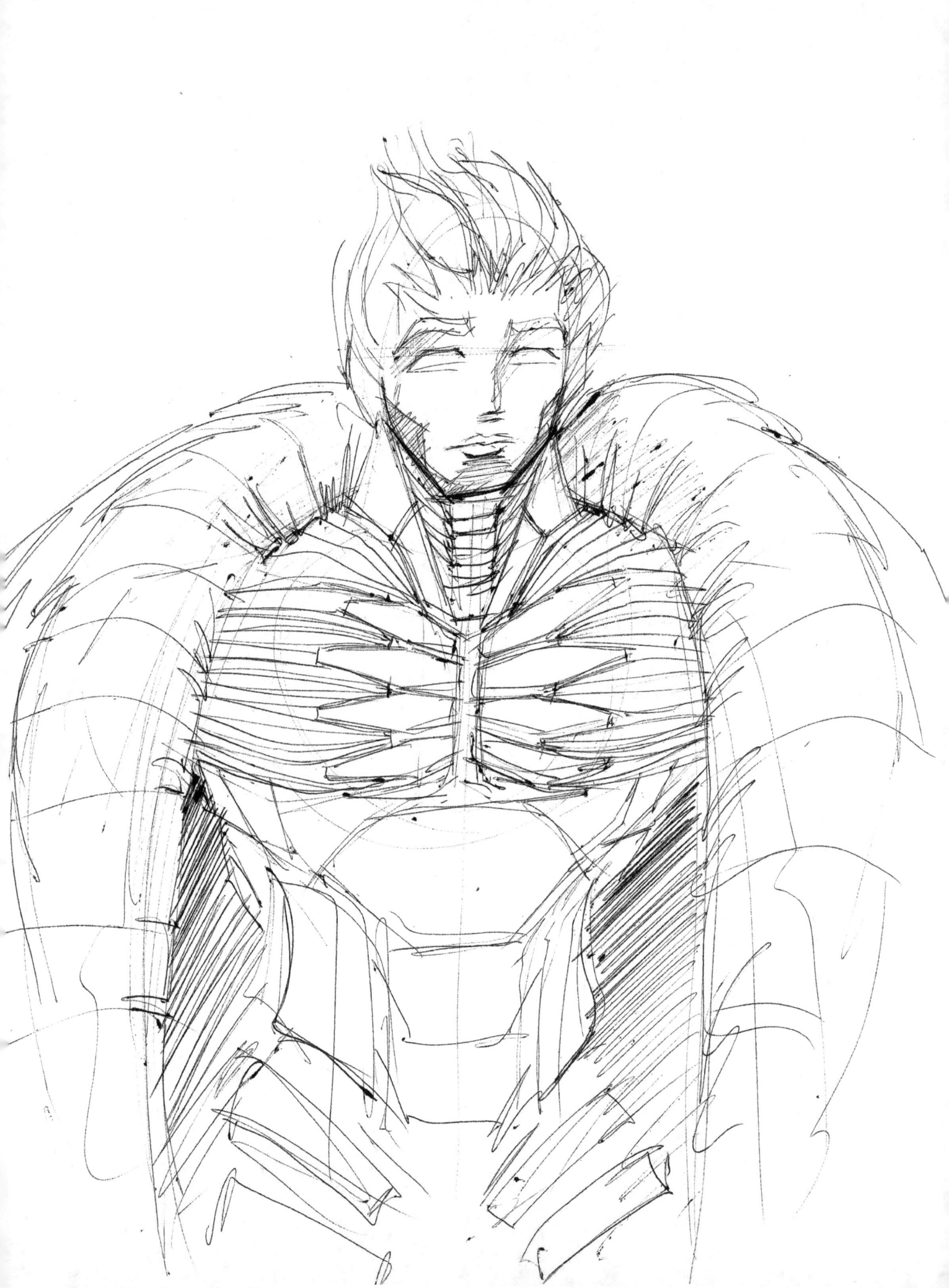

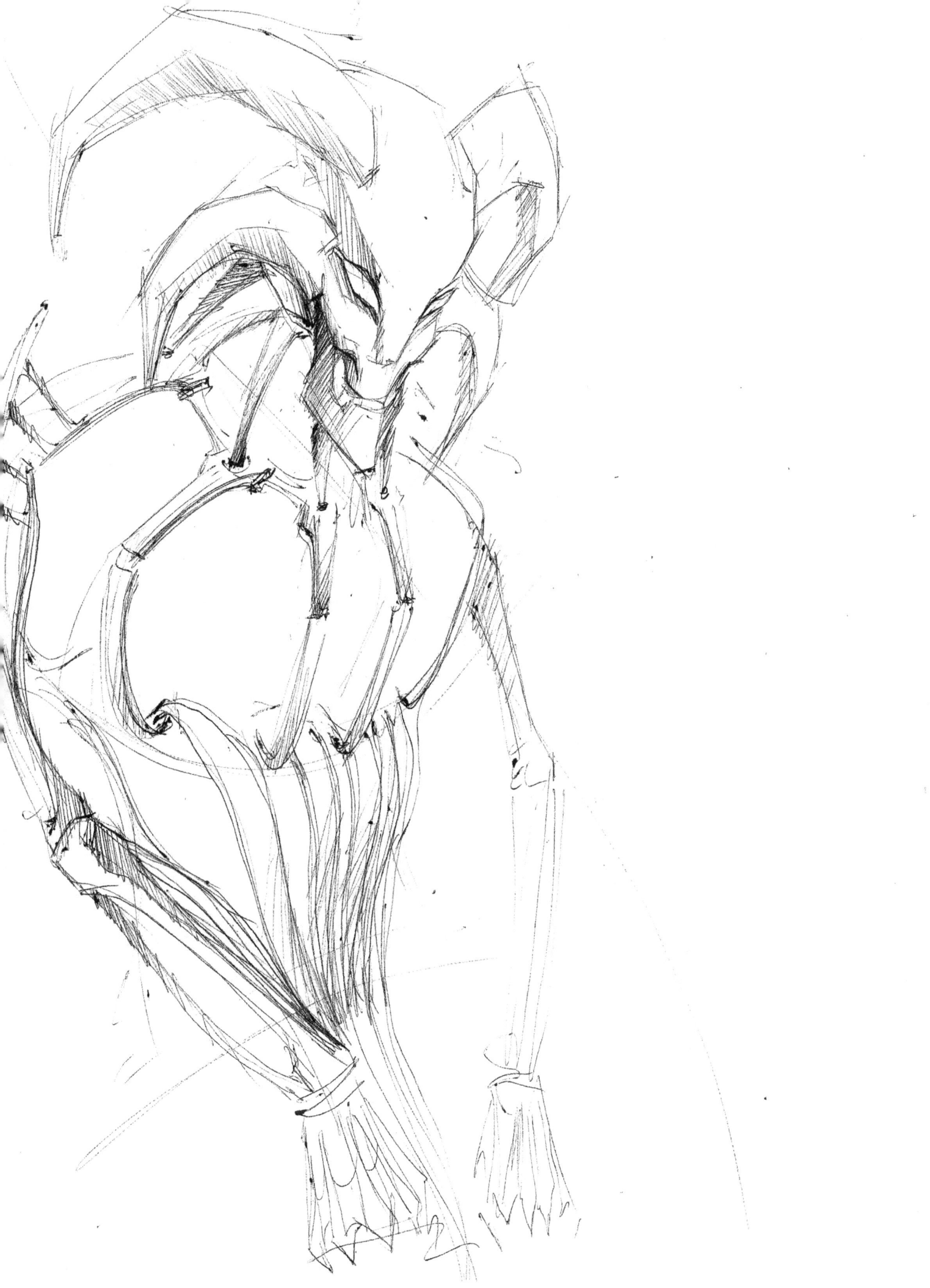

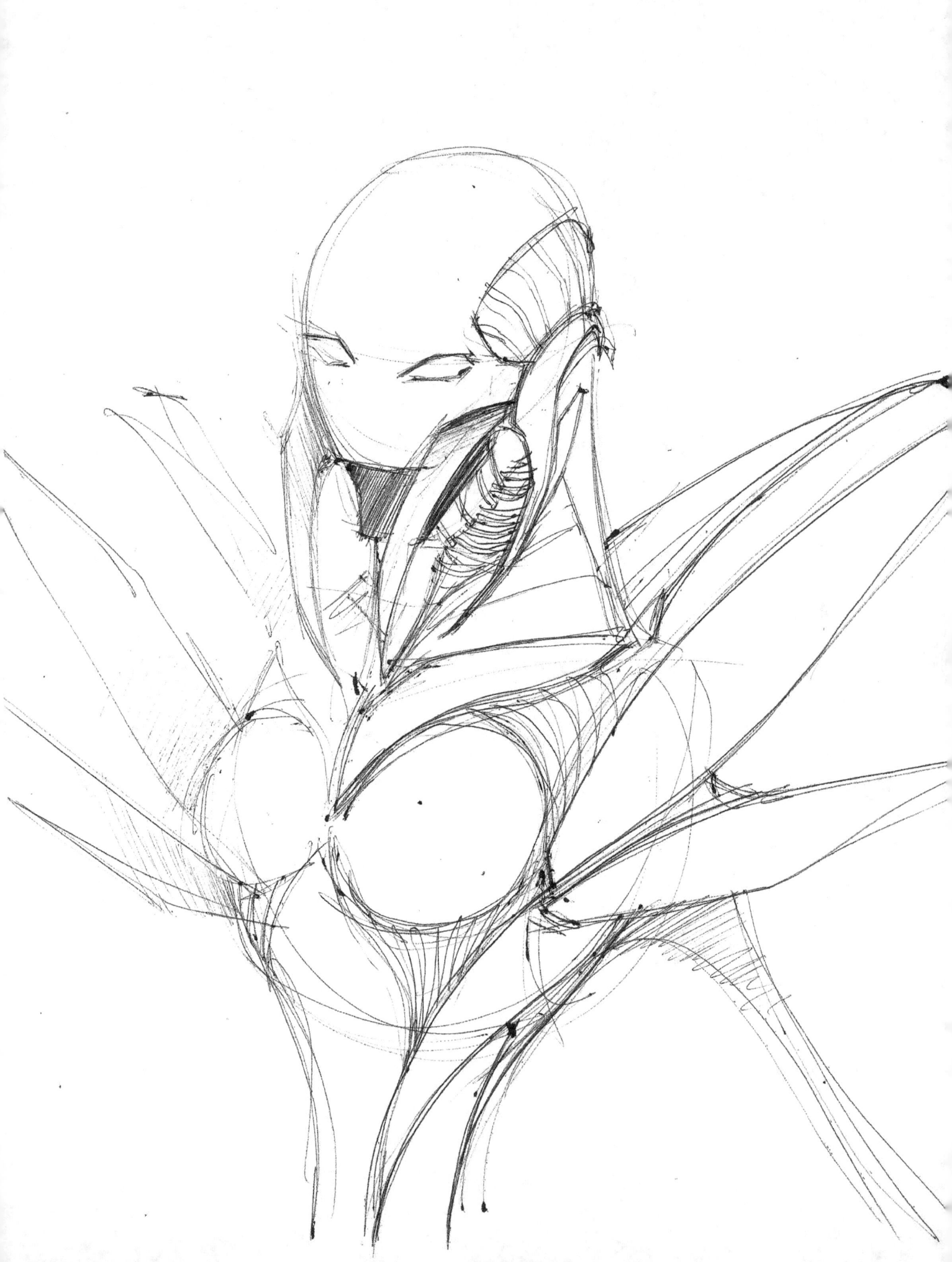

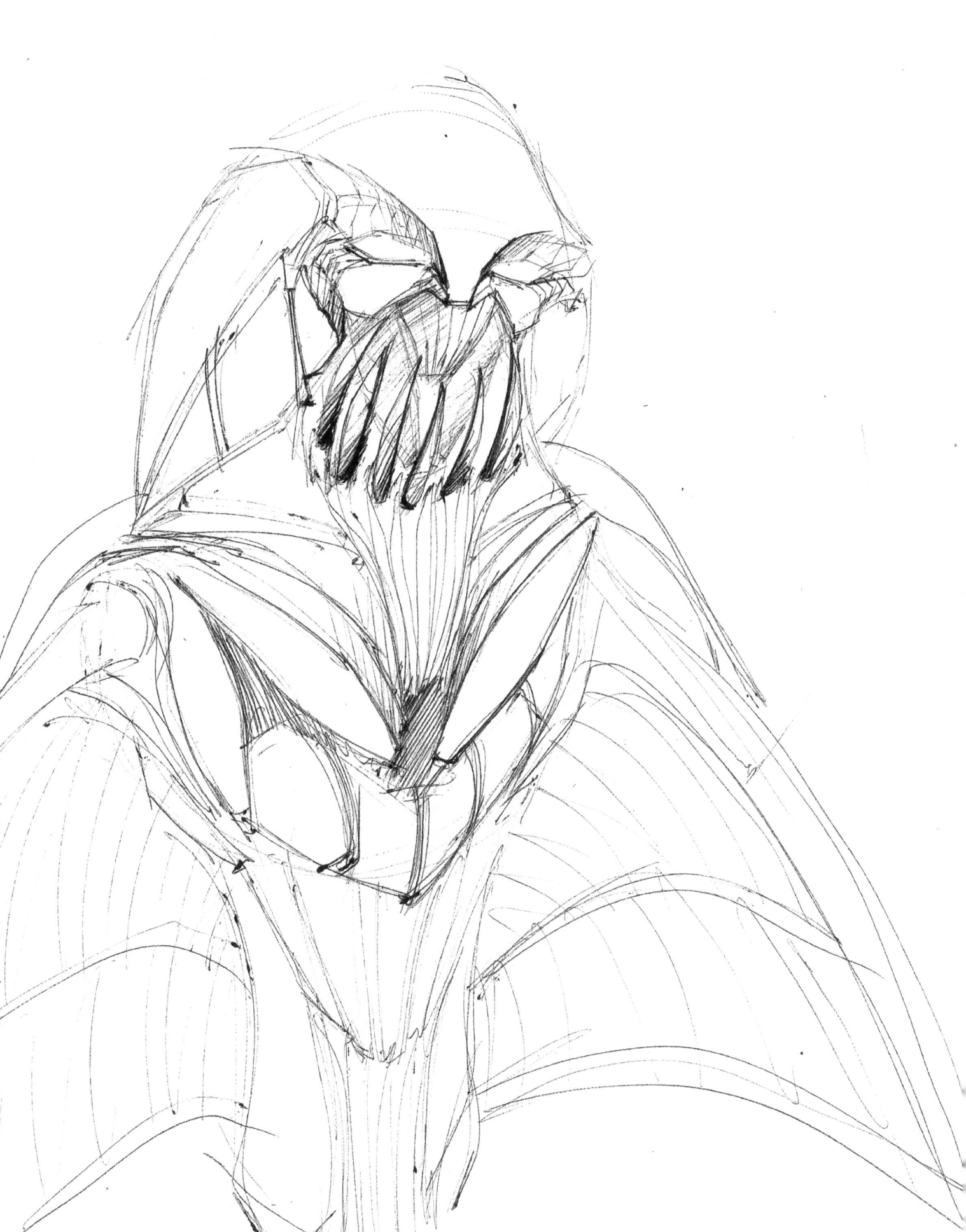

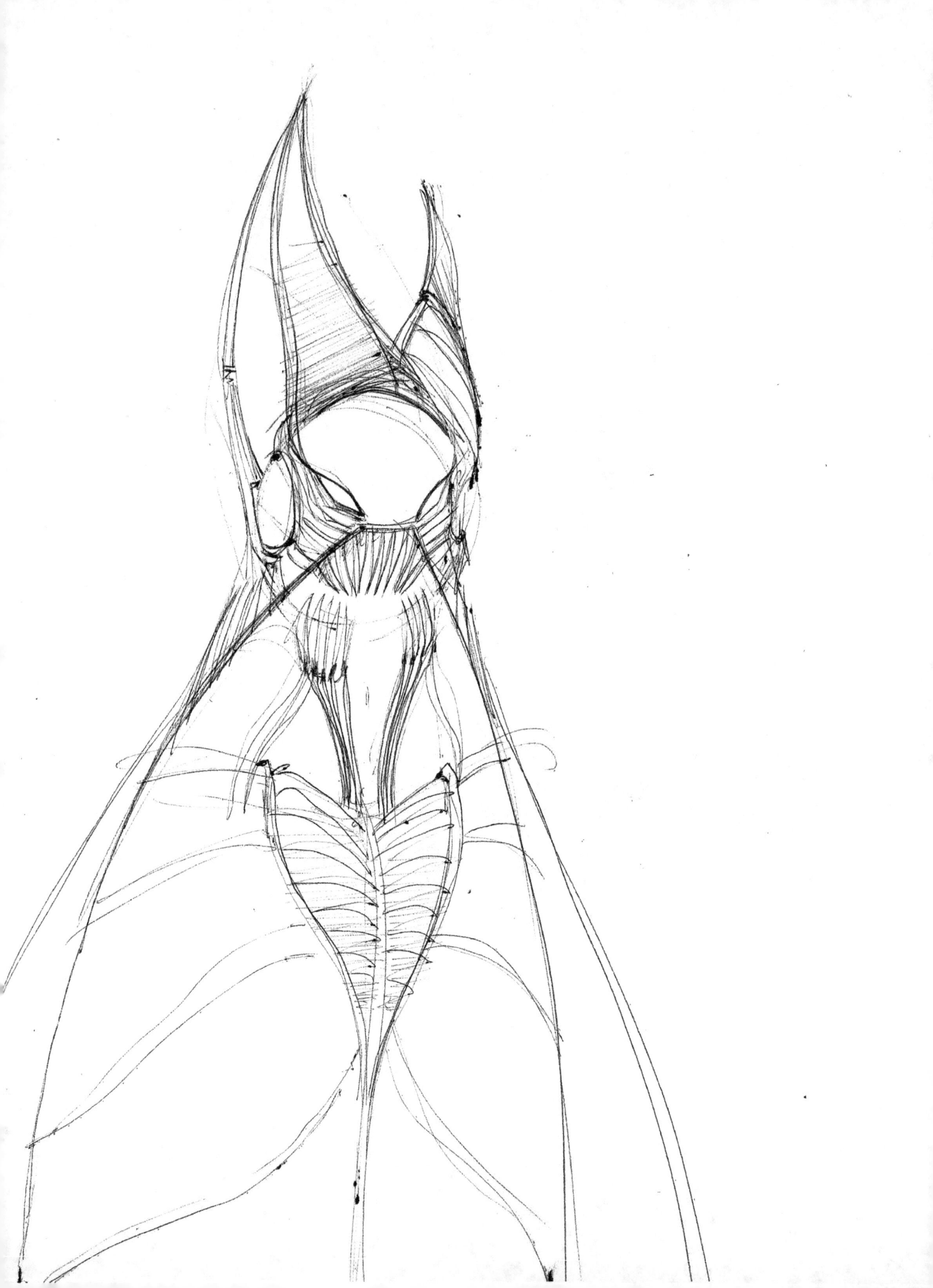

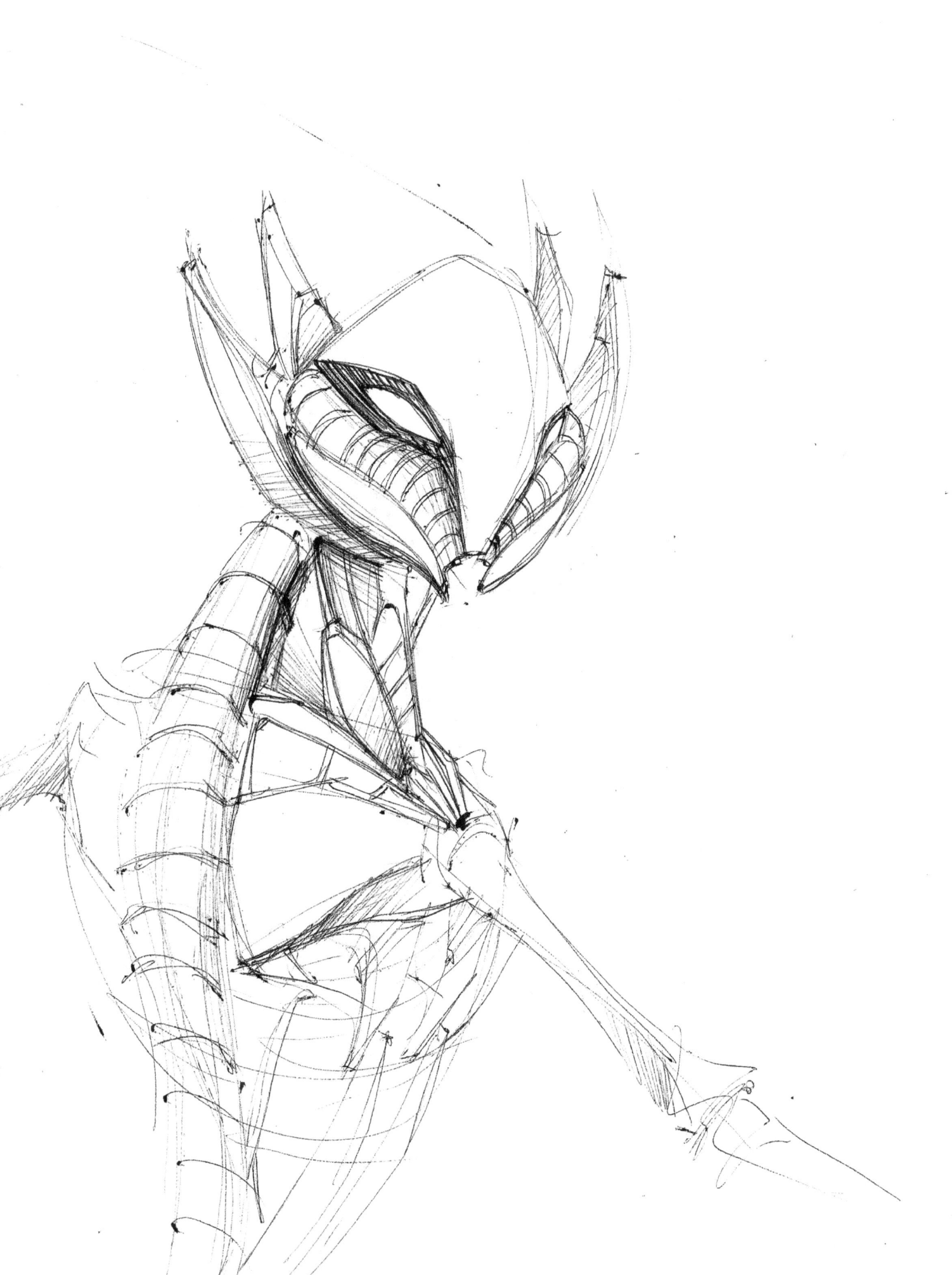

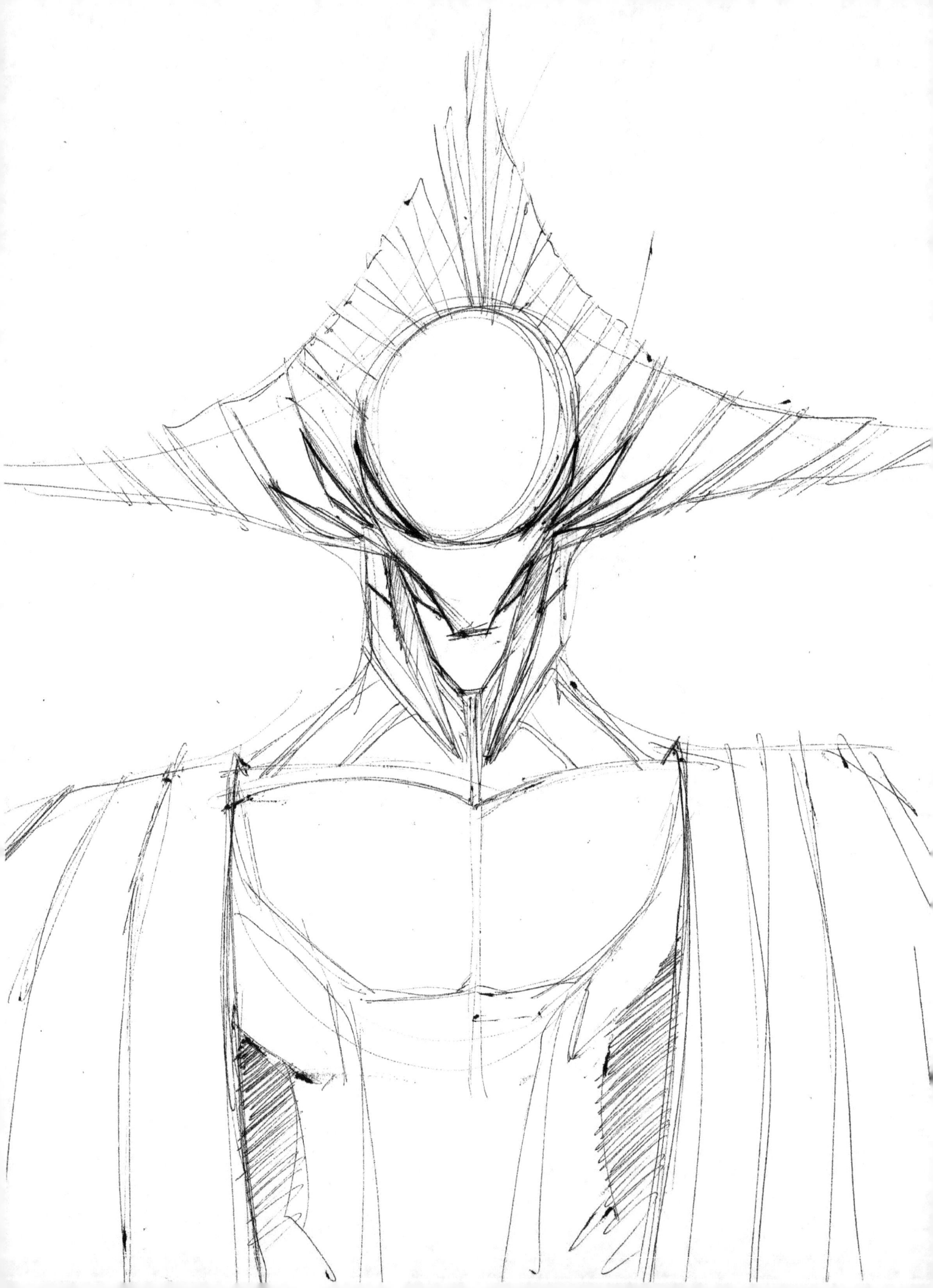

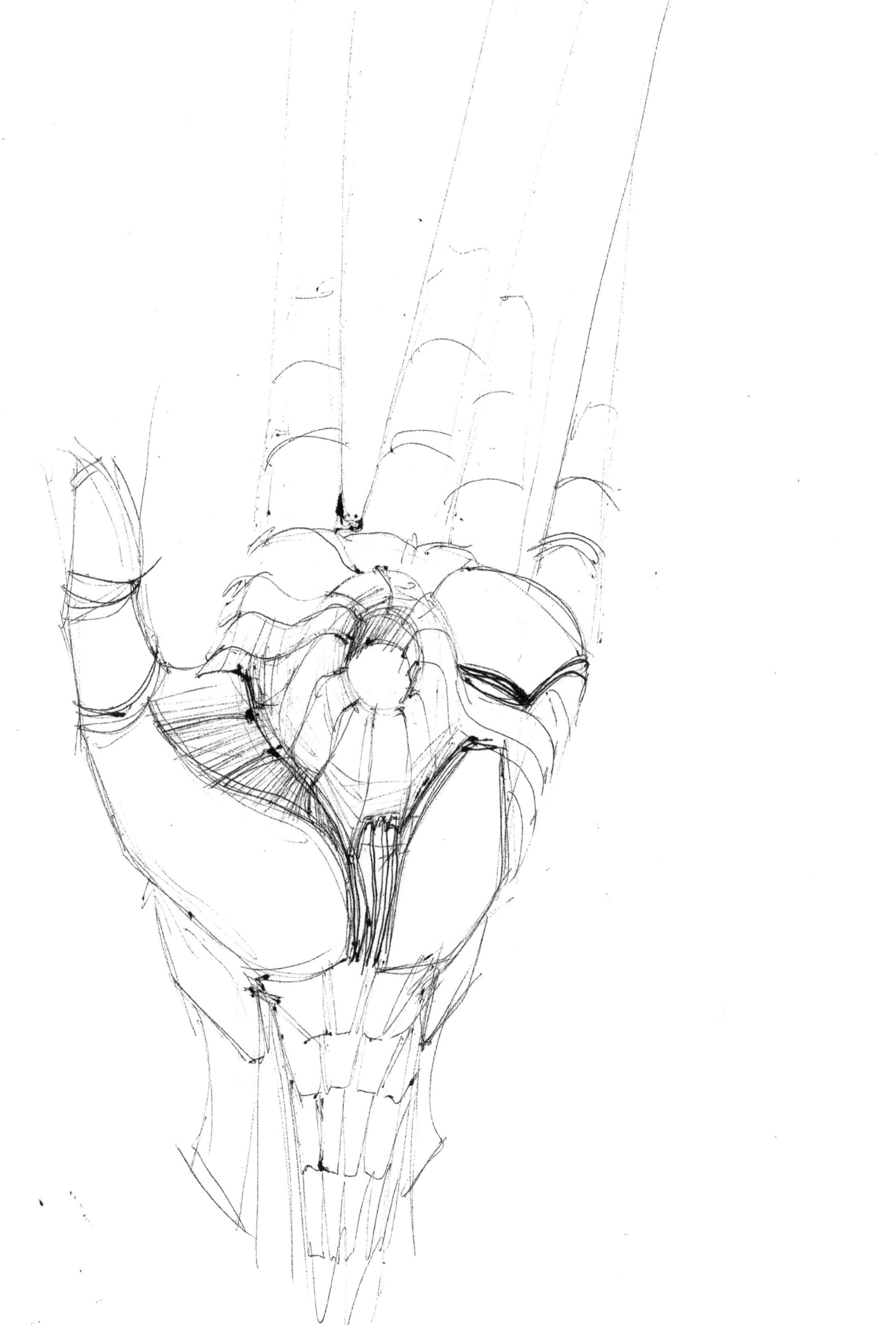

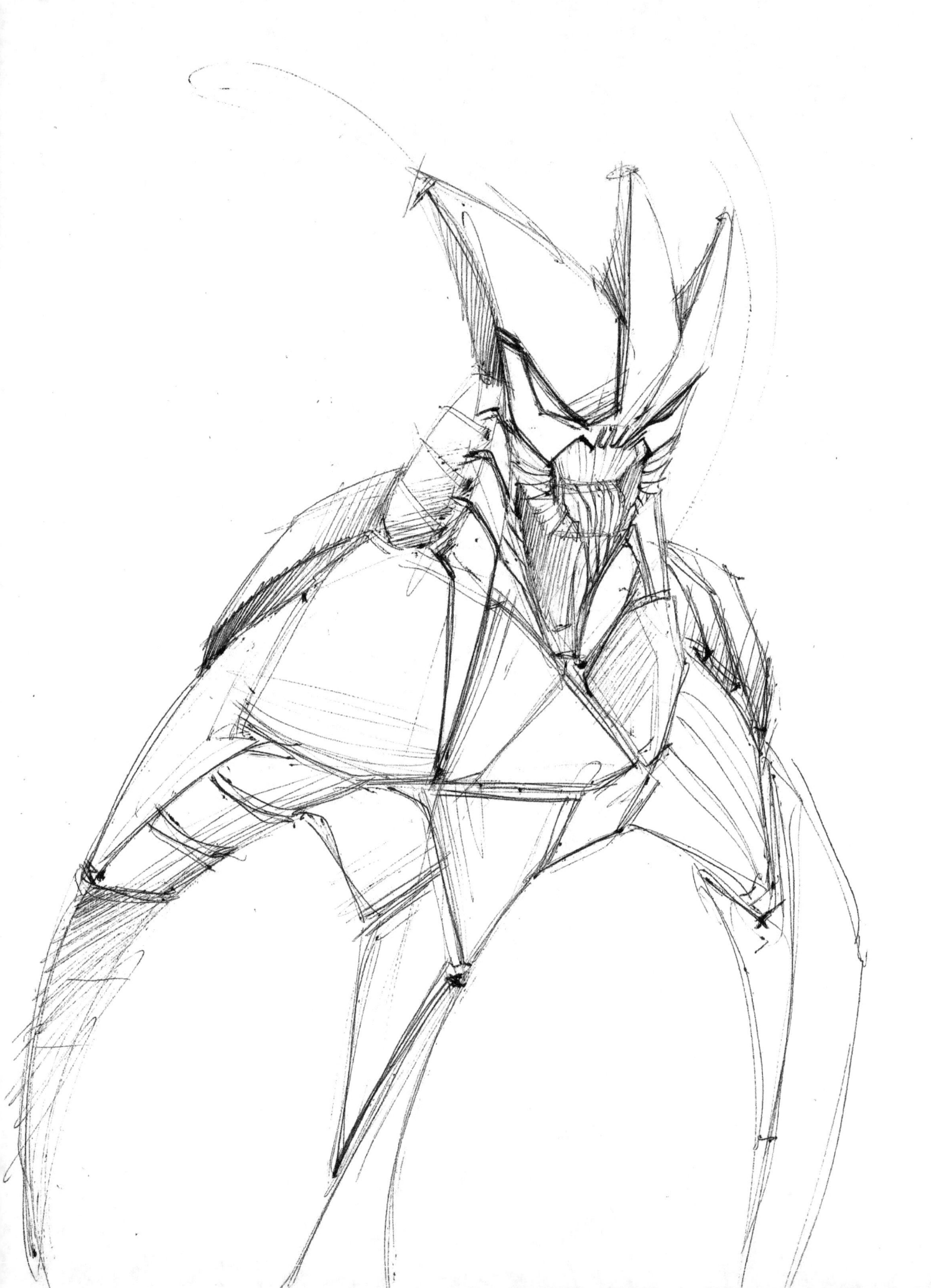

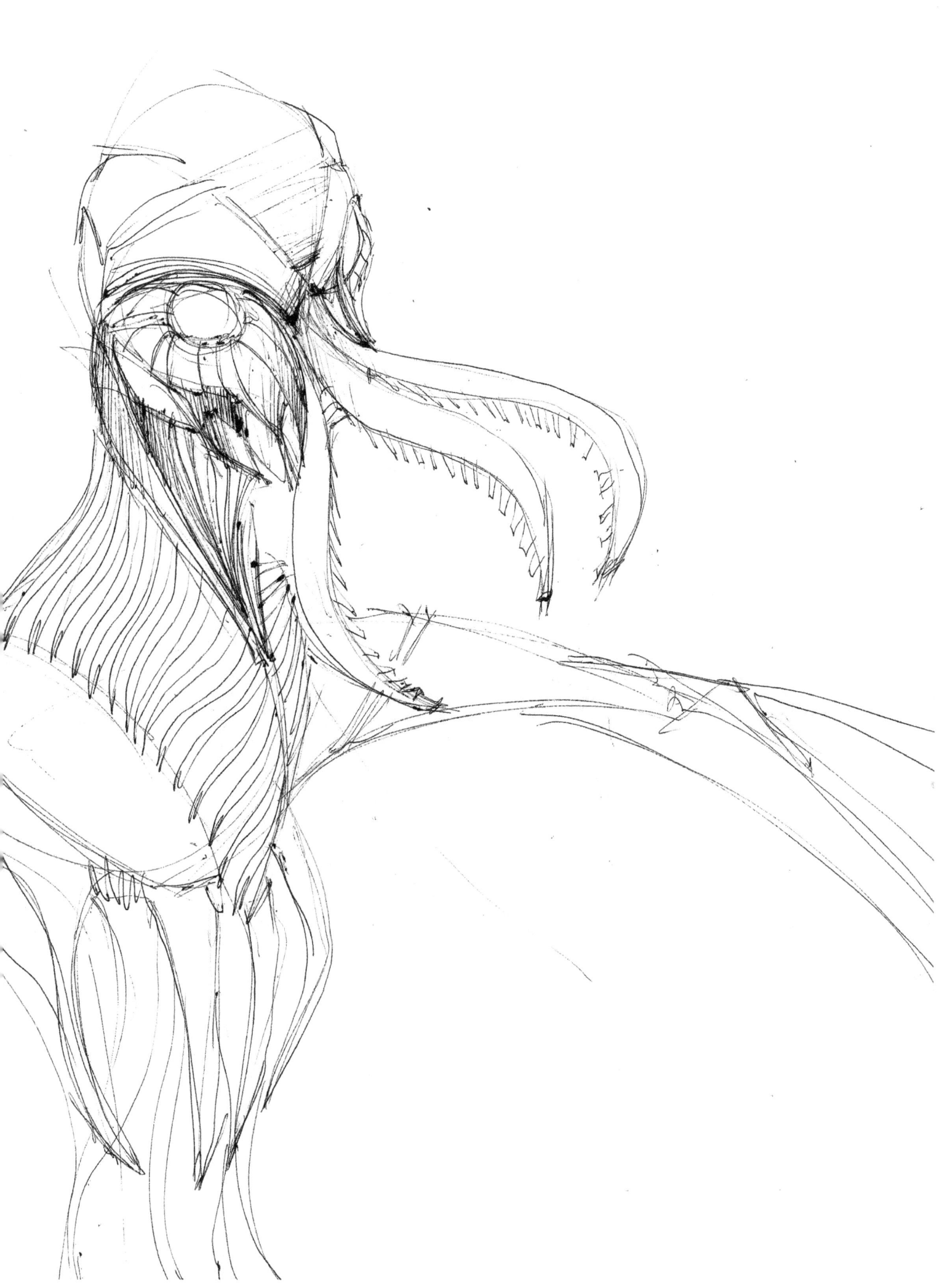

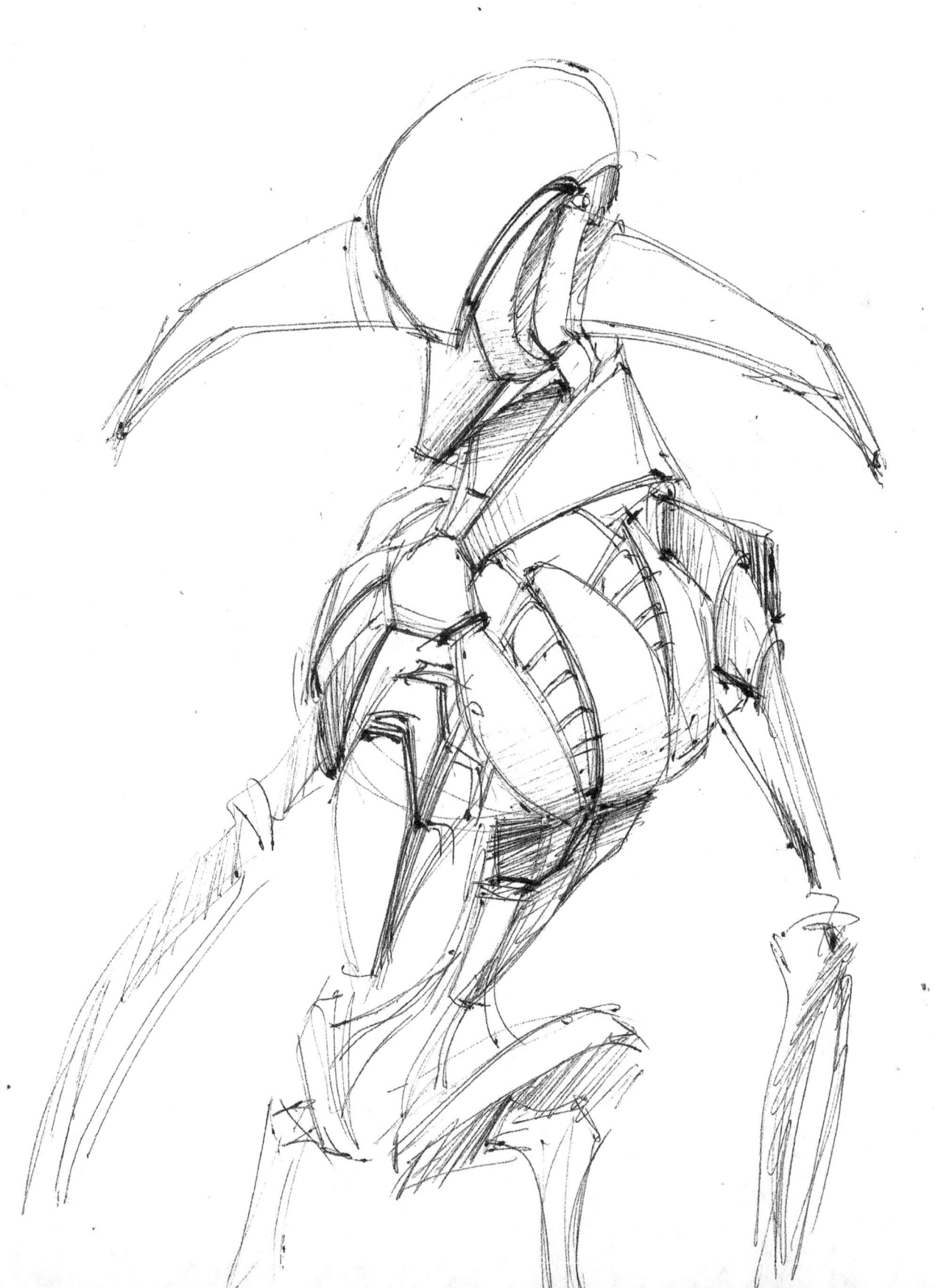

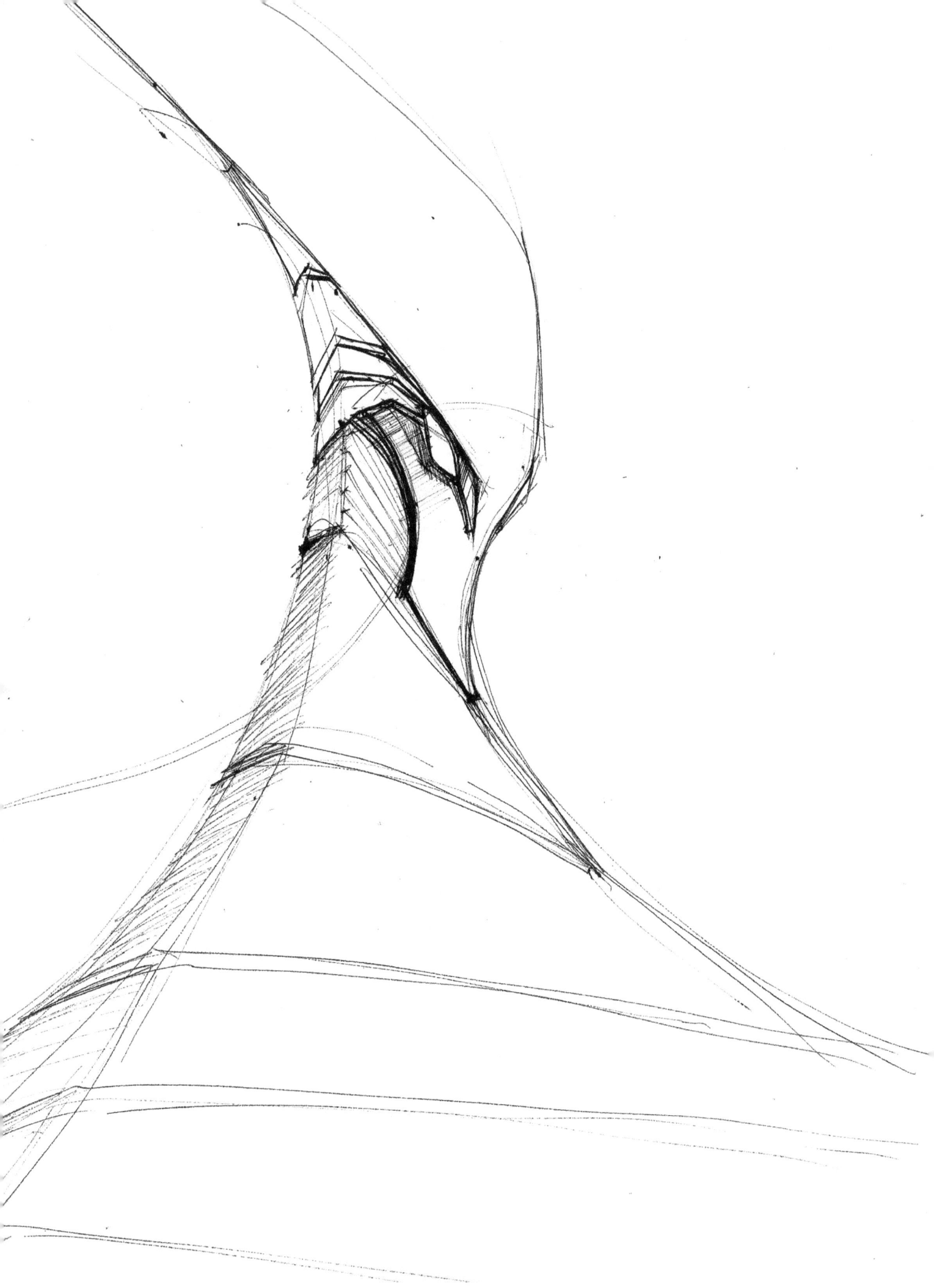

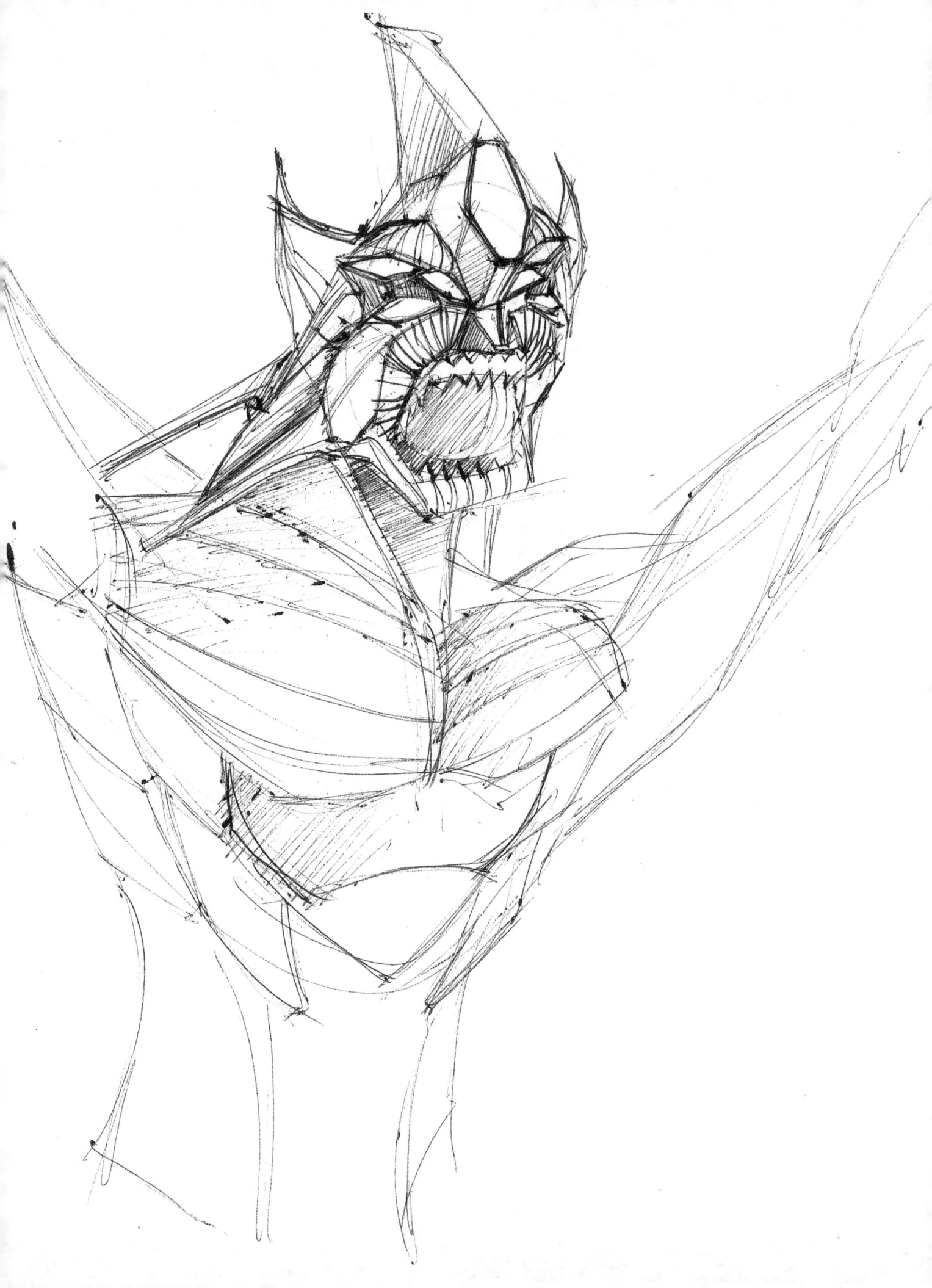

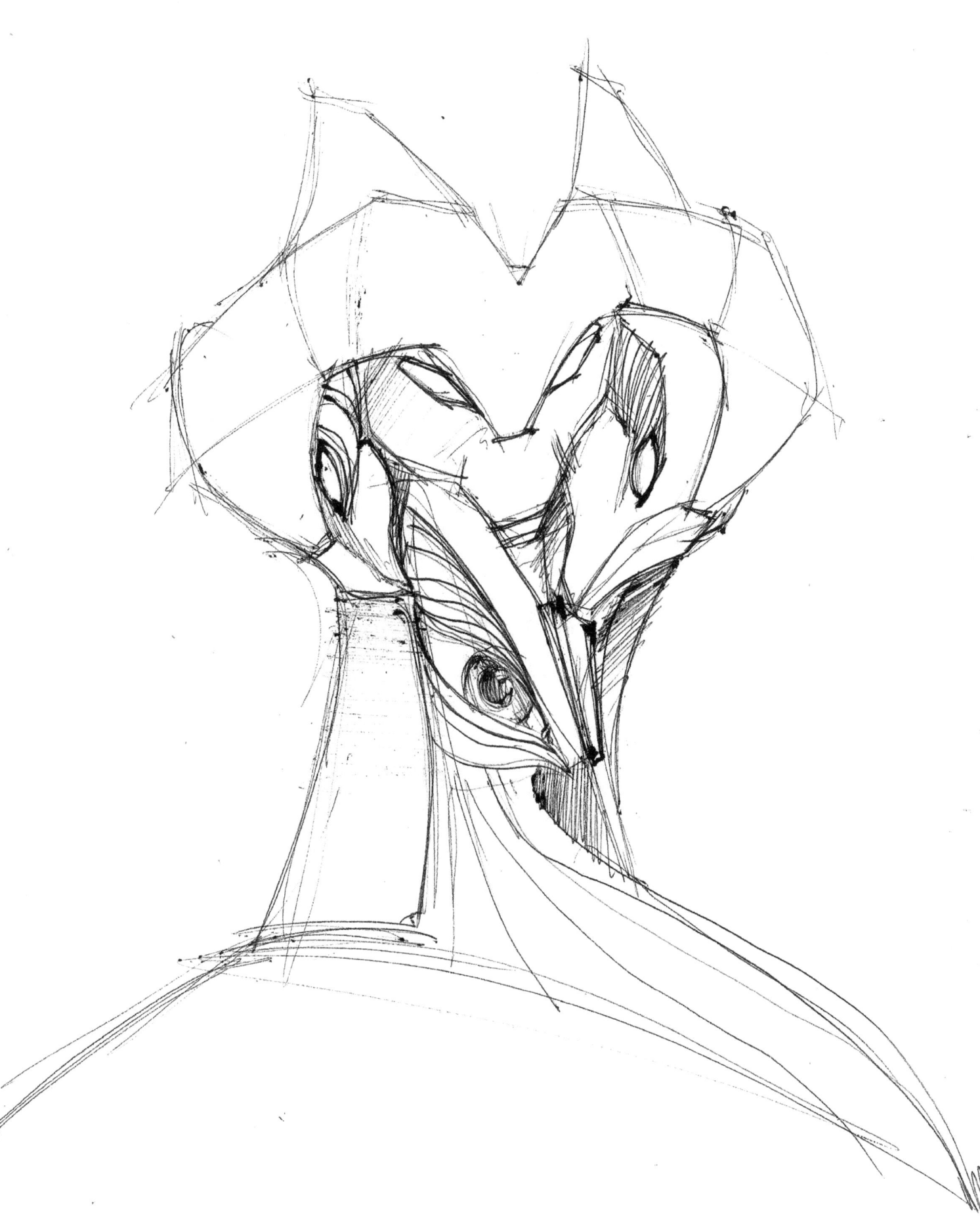

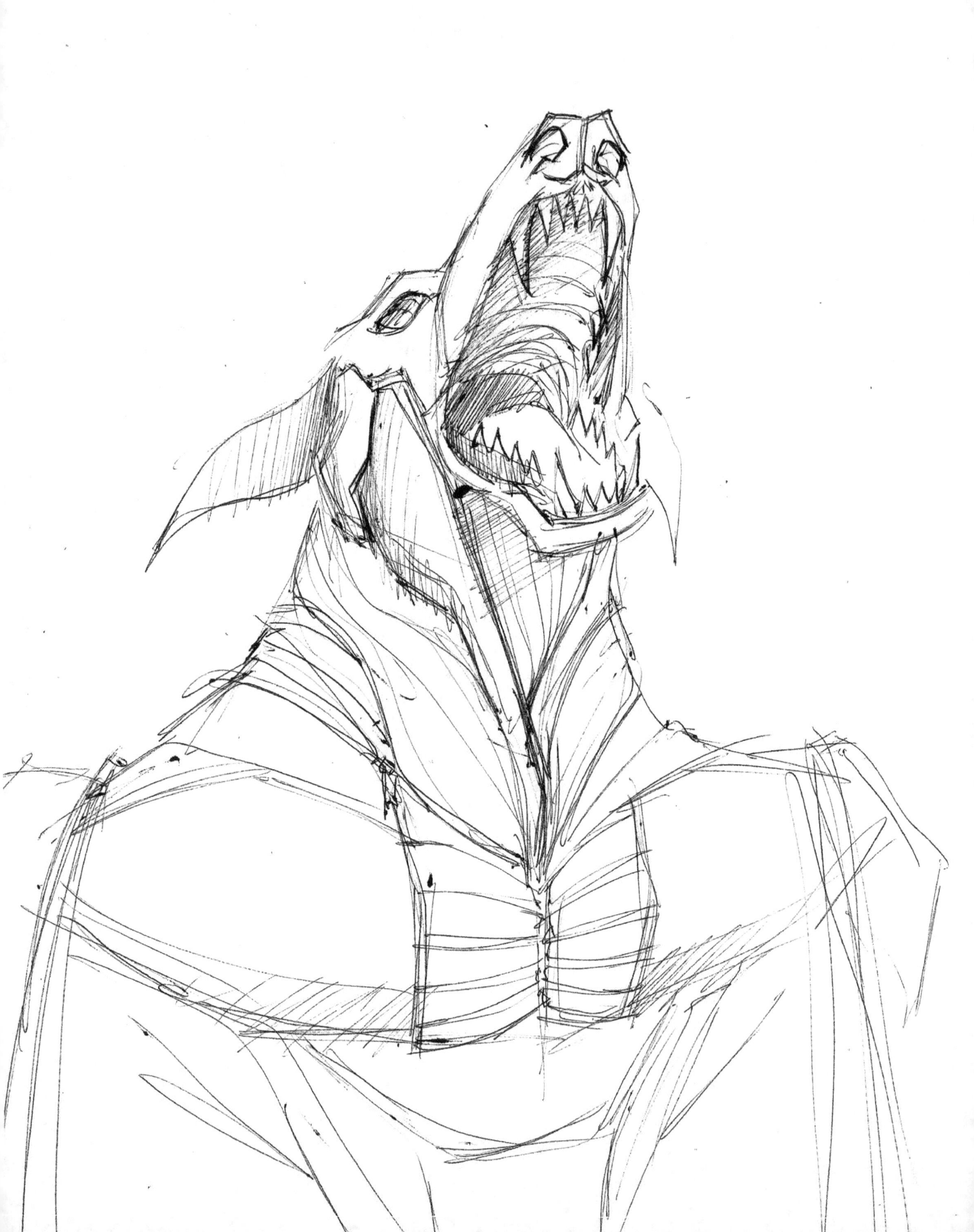

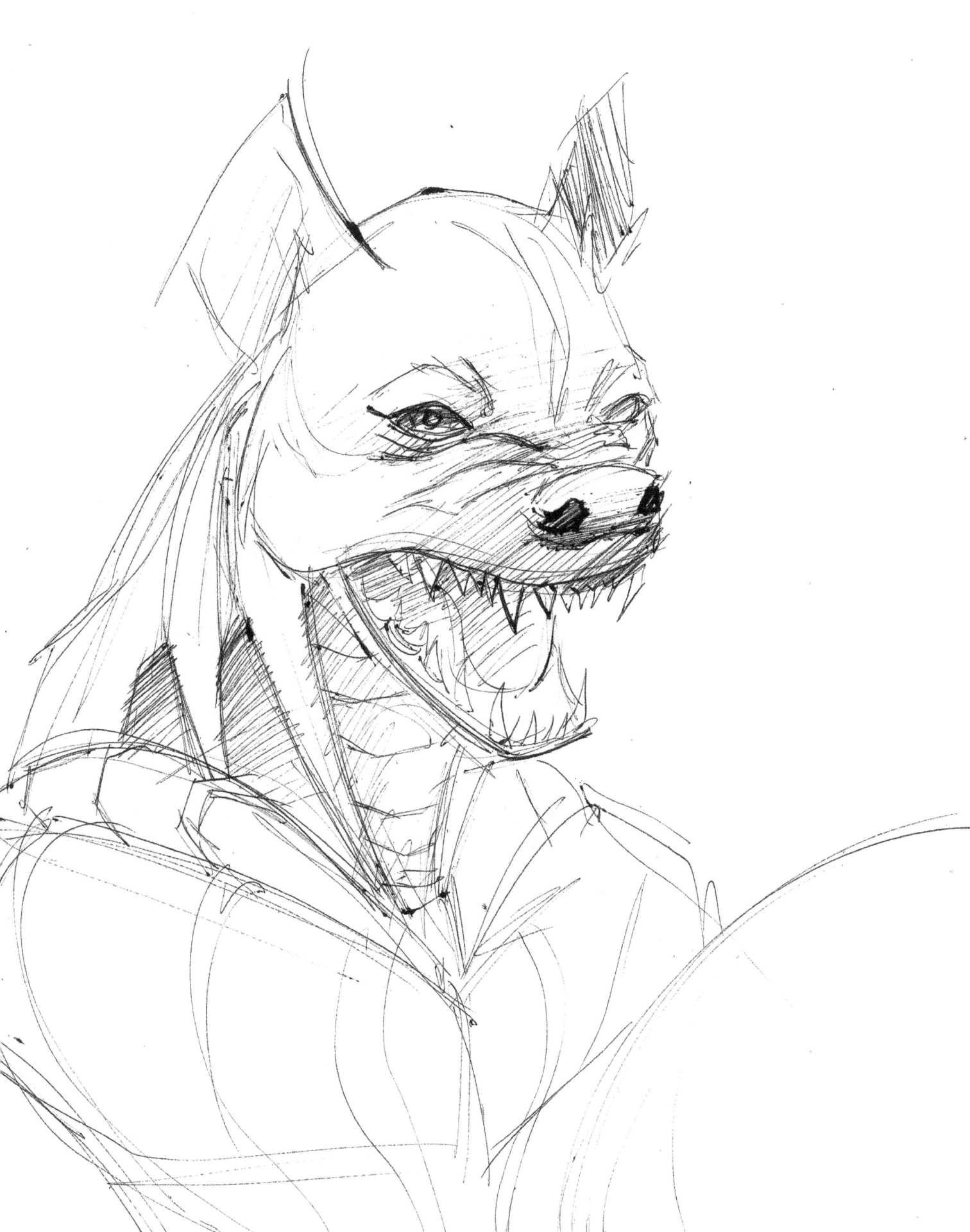

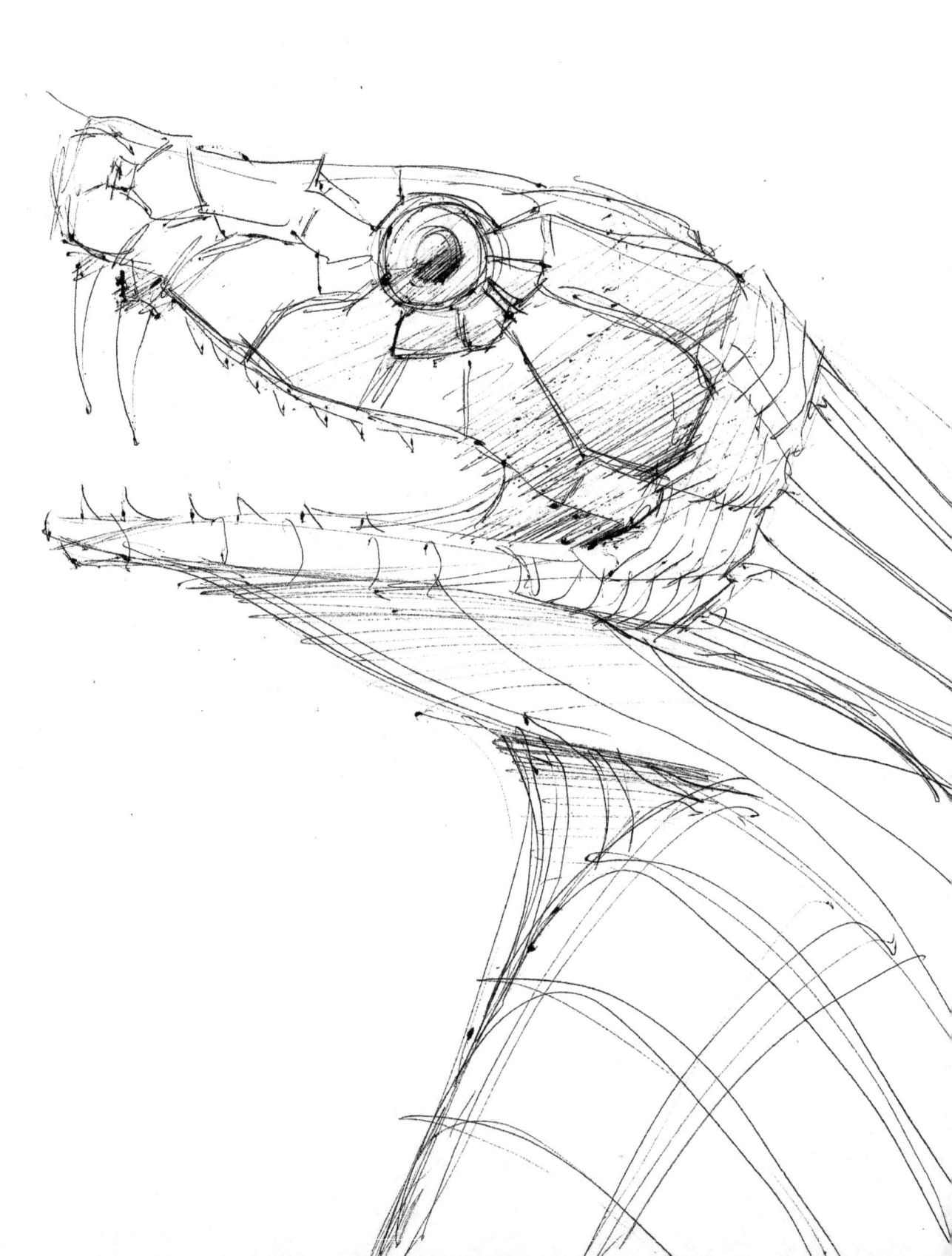

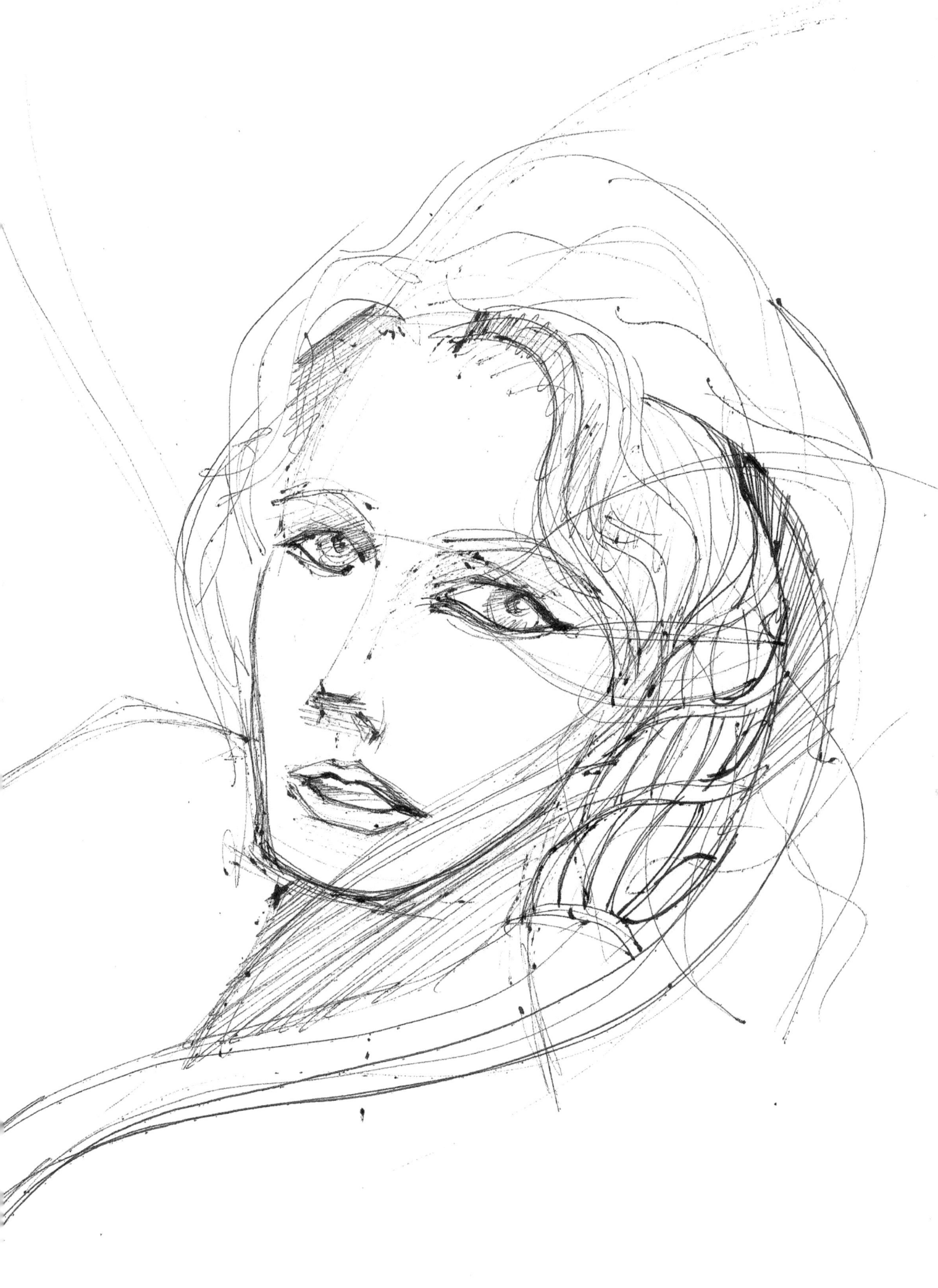

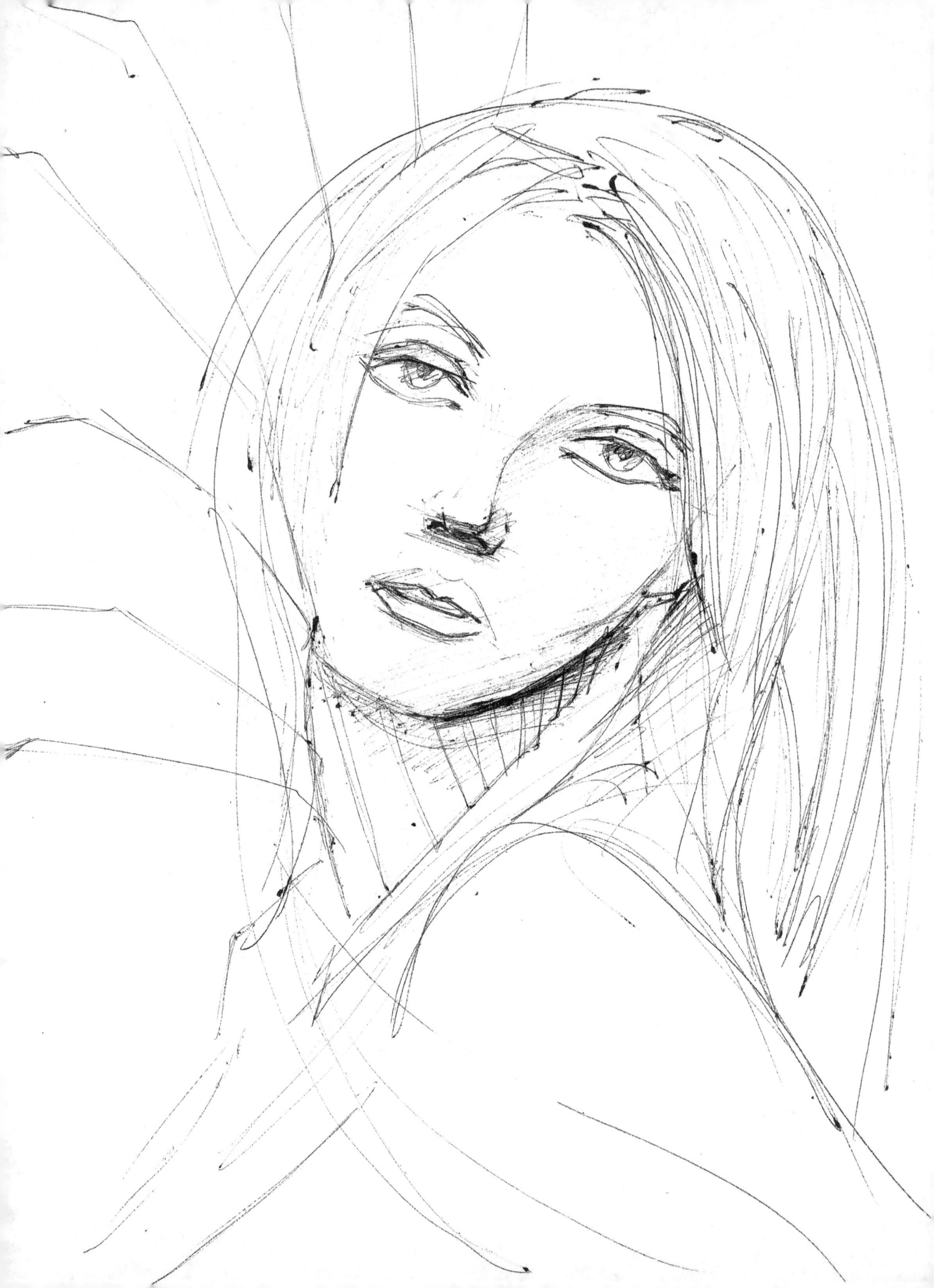

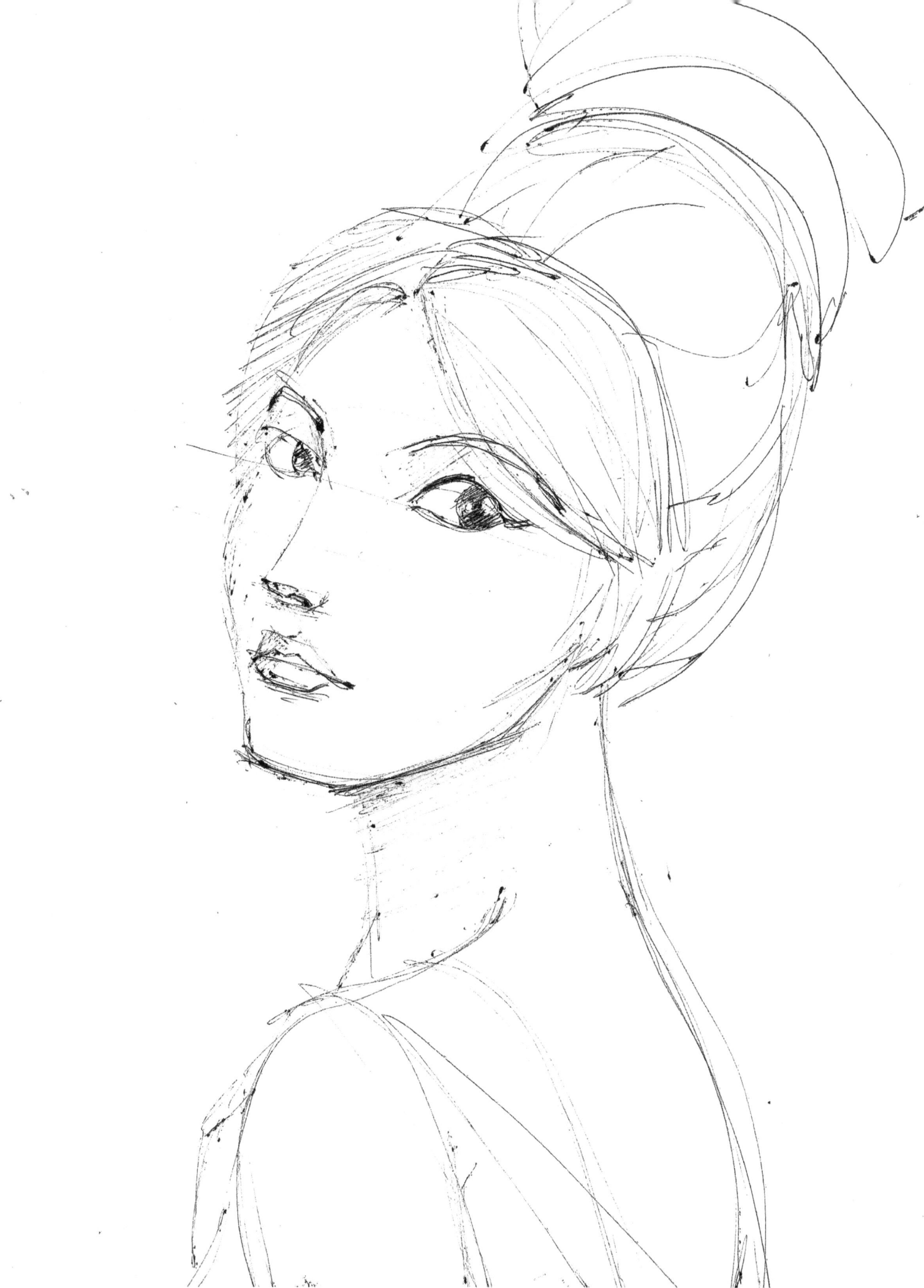

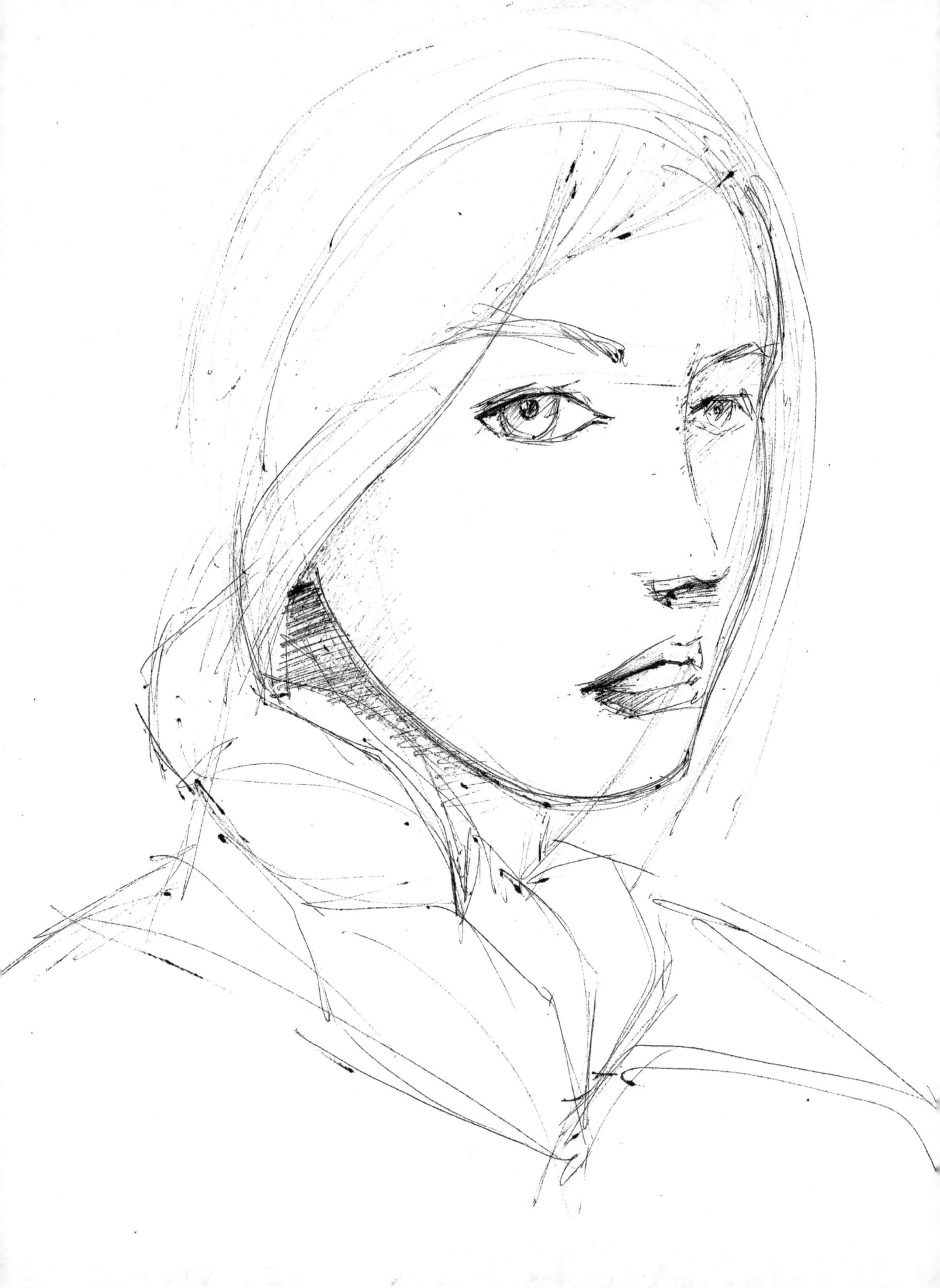

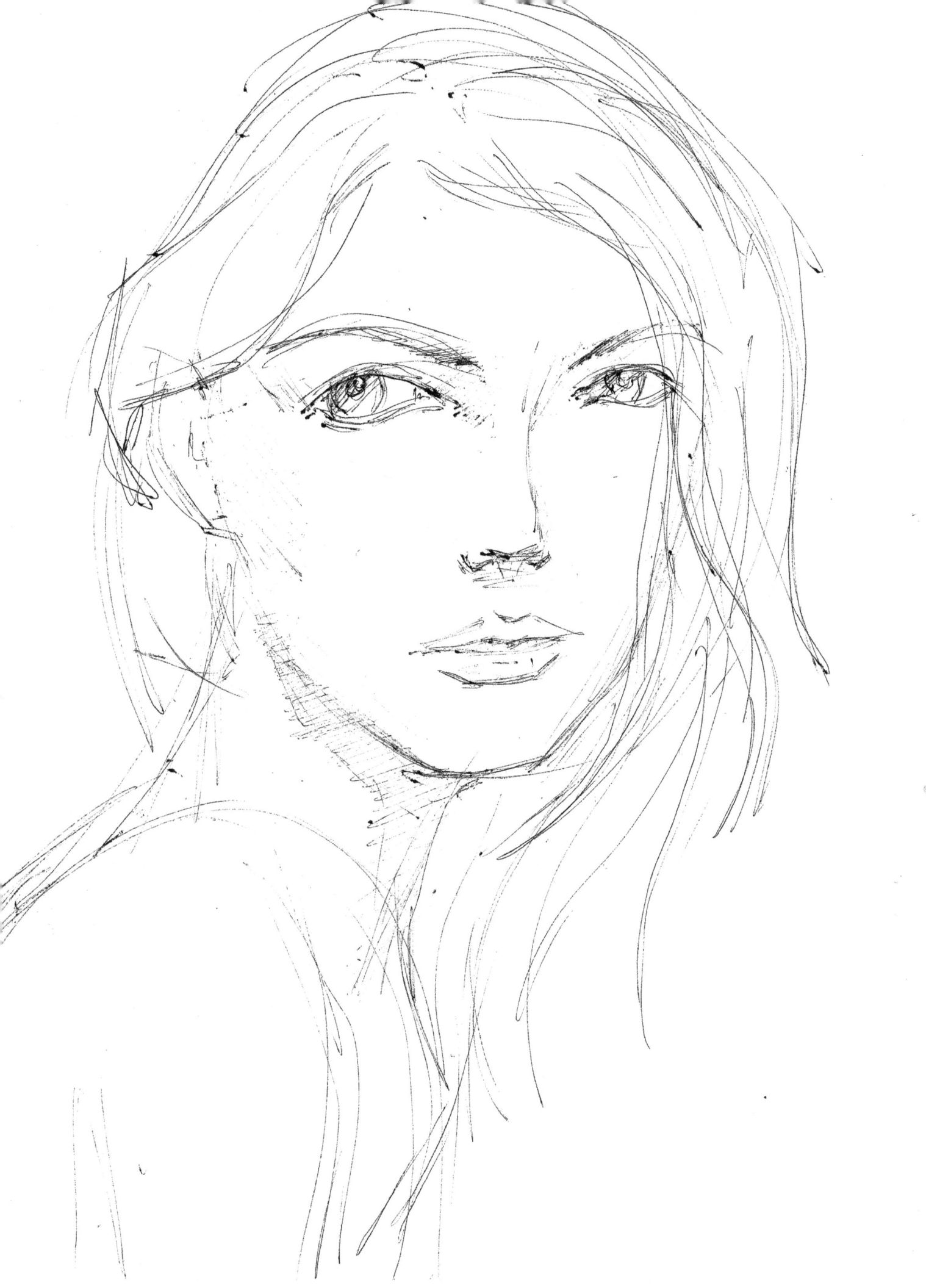

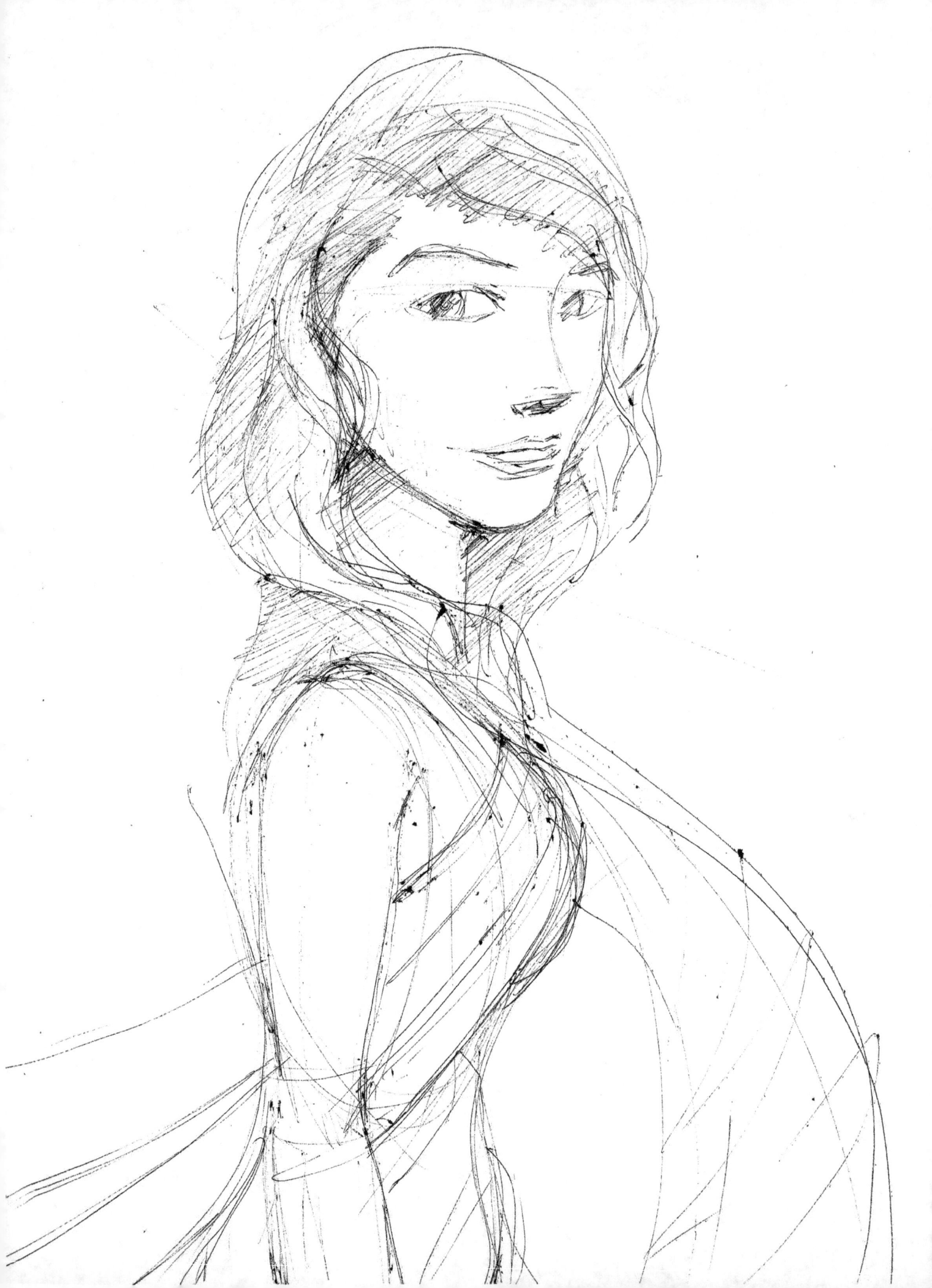

ABOUT THE AUTHOR

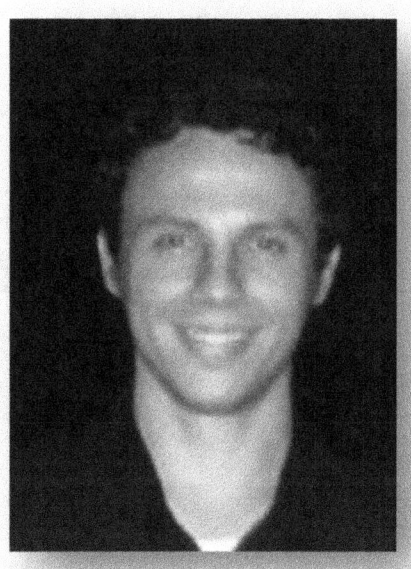

www.marcoaureliogalan.blogspot.com

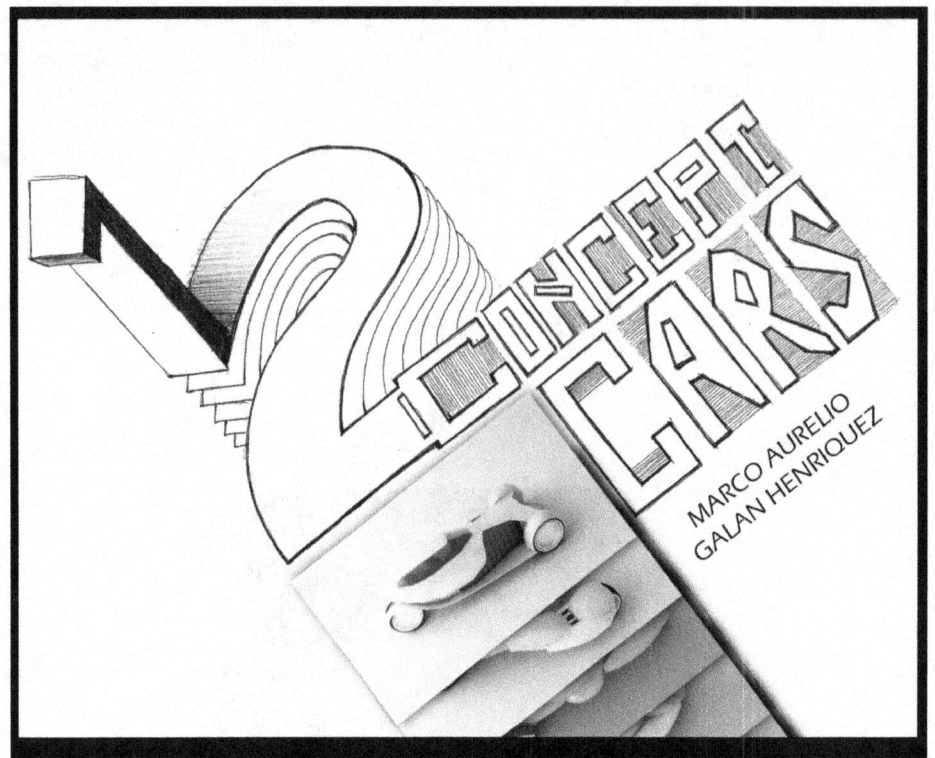

https://www.createspace.com/3671533

12 CONCEPT CARS

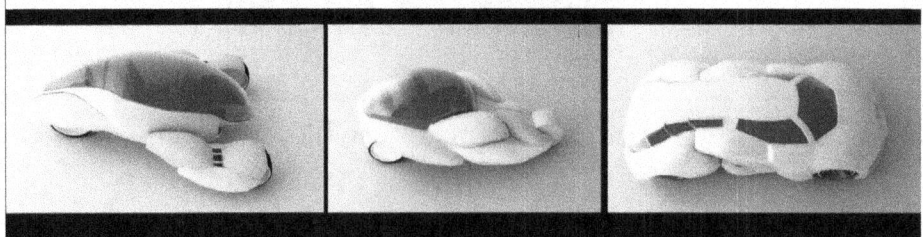

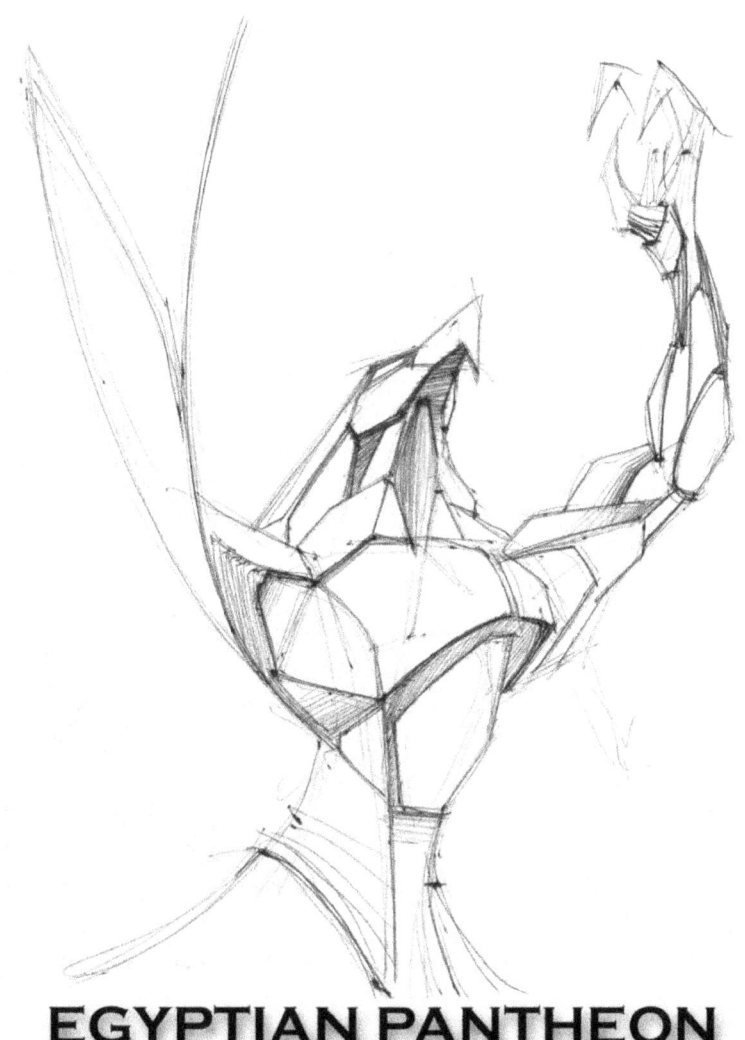

EGYPTIAN PANTHEON
A GRAPHIC JOURNEY THROUGH
ANCIENT GODS

https://www.createspace.com/3711902

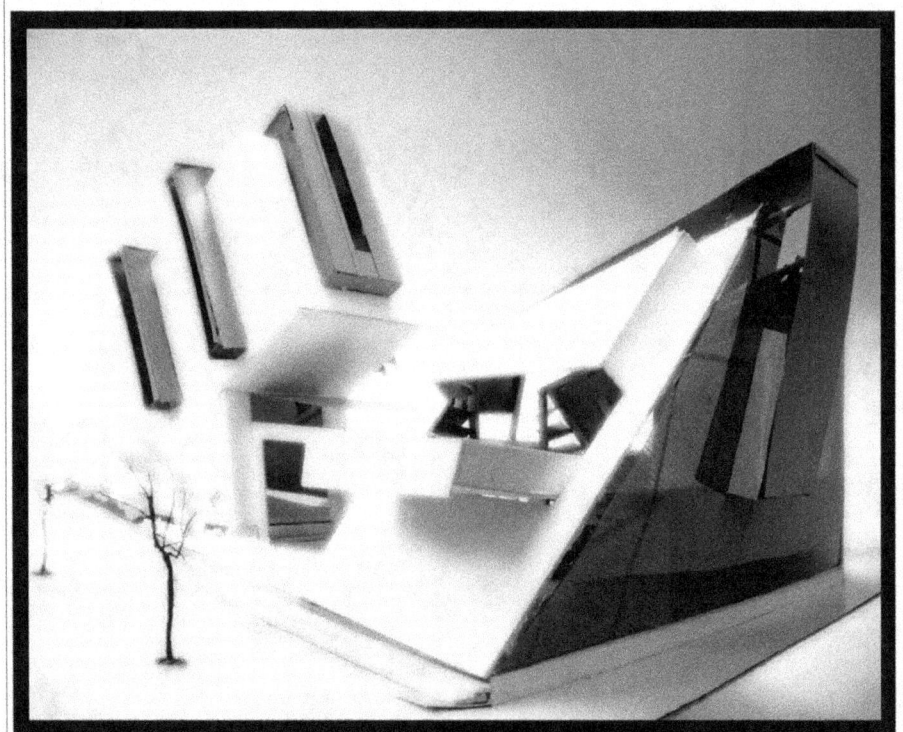

DESIGN STAGE 1

MARCO AURELIO GALAN HENRIQUEZ

https://www.createspace.com/3777840

Art gallery by Eliana Paola Gomez (Cover)

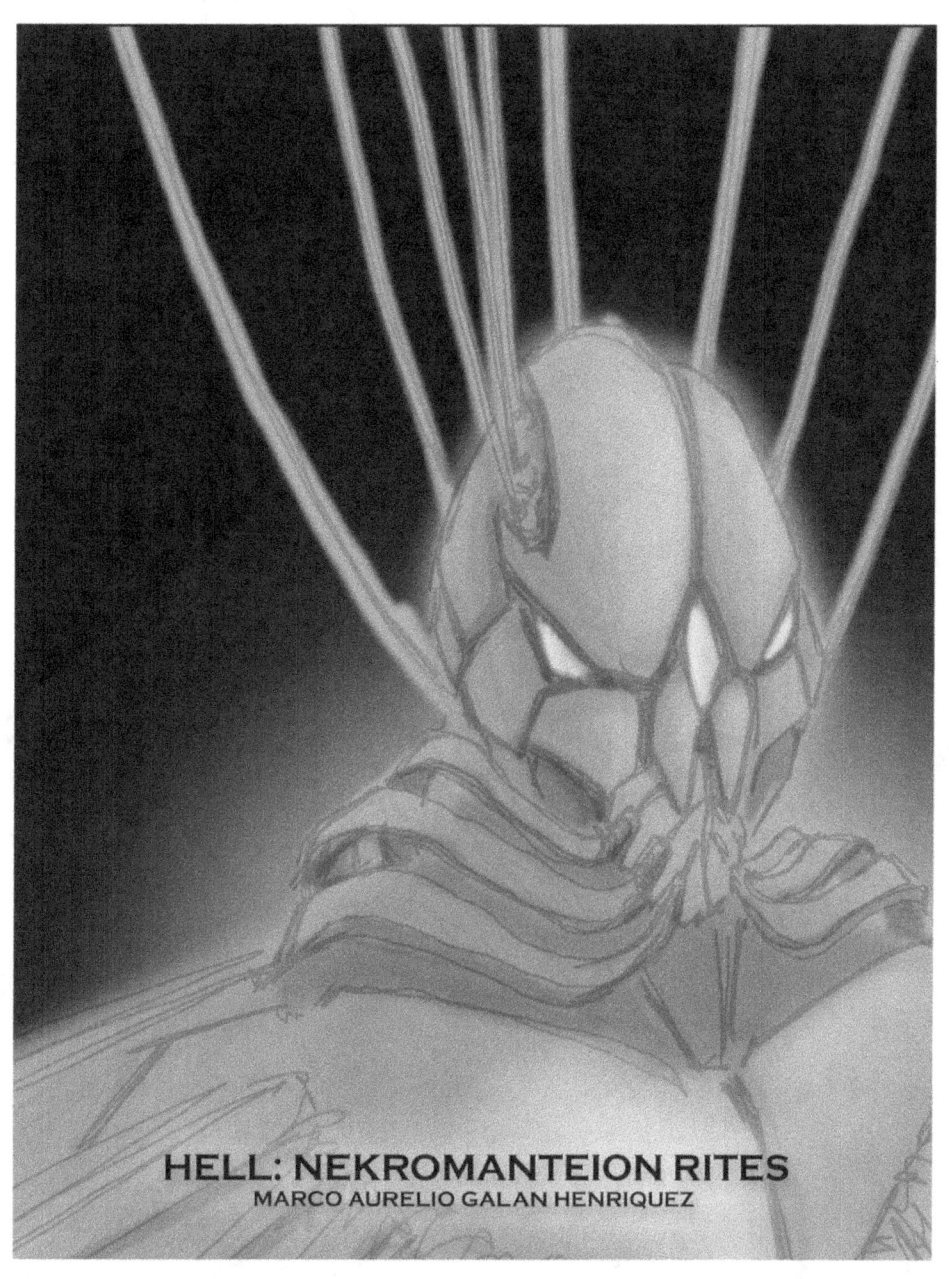

HELL: NEKROMANTEION RITES
MARCO AURELIO GALAN HENRIQUEZ

https://www.createspace.com/3833646

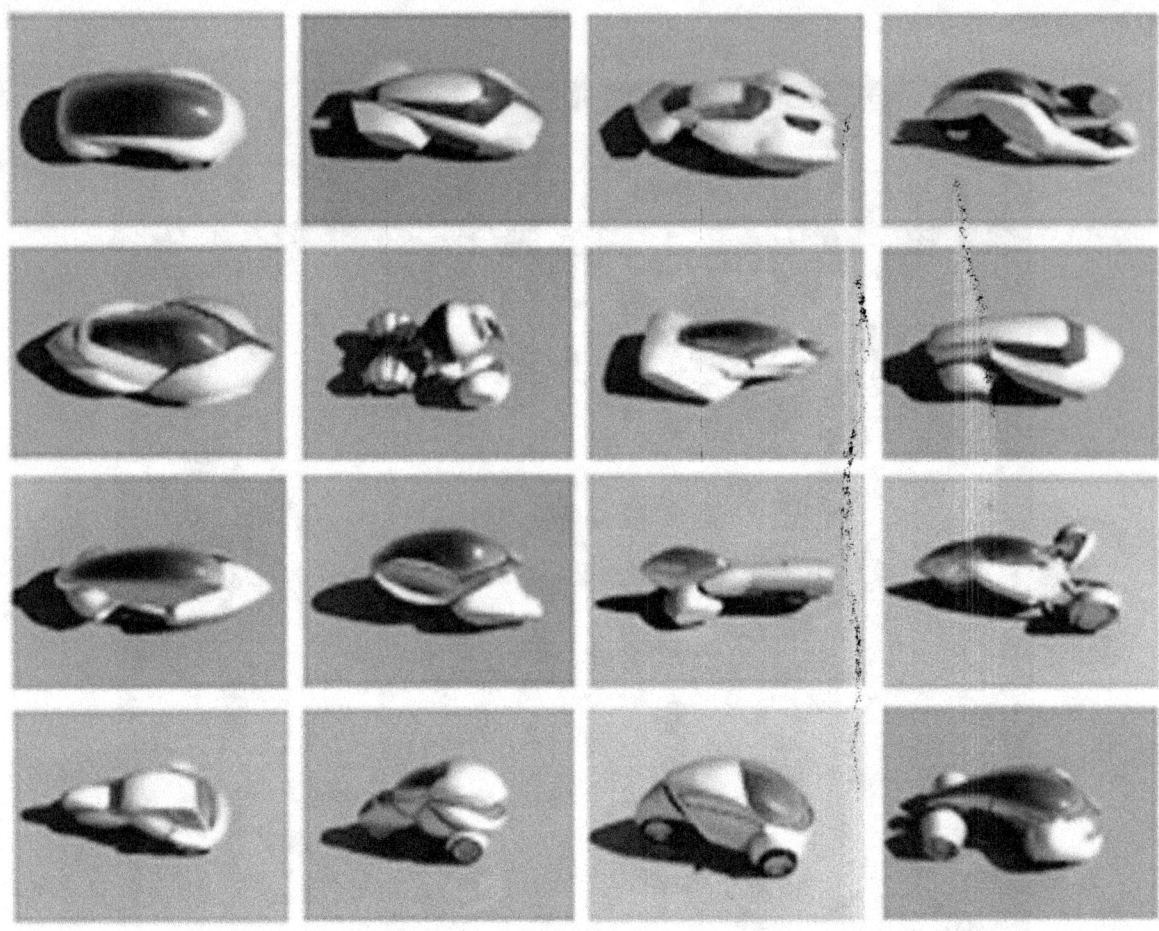

24 BIONIC CARS
MARCO AURELIO GALAN HENRIQUEZ

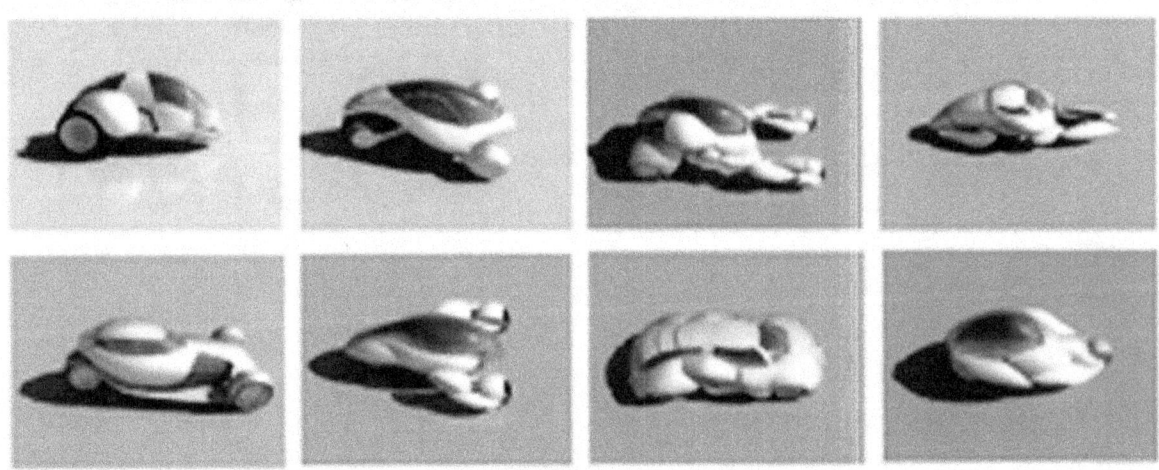

https://www.createspace.com/3942876

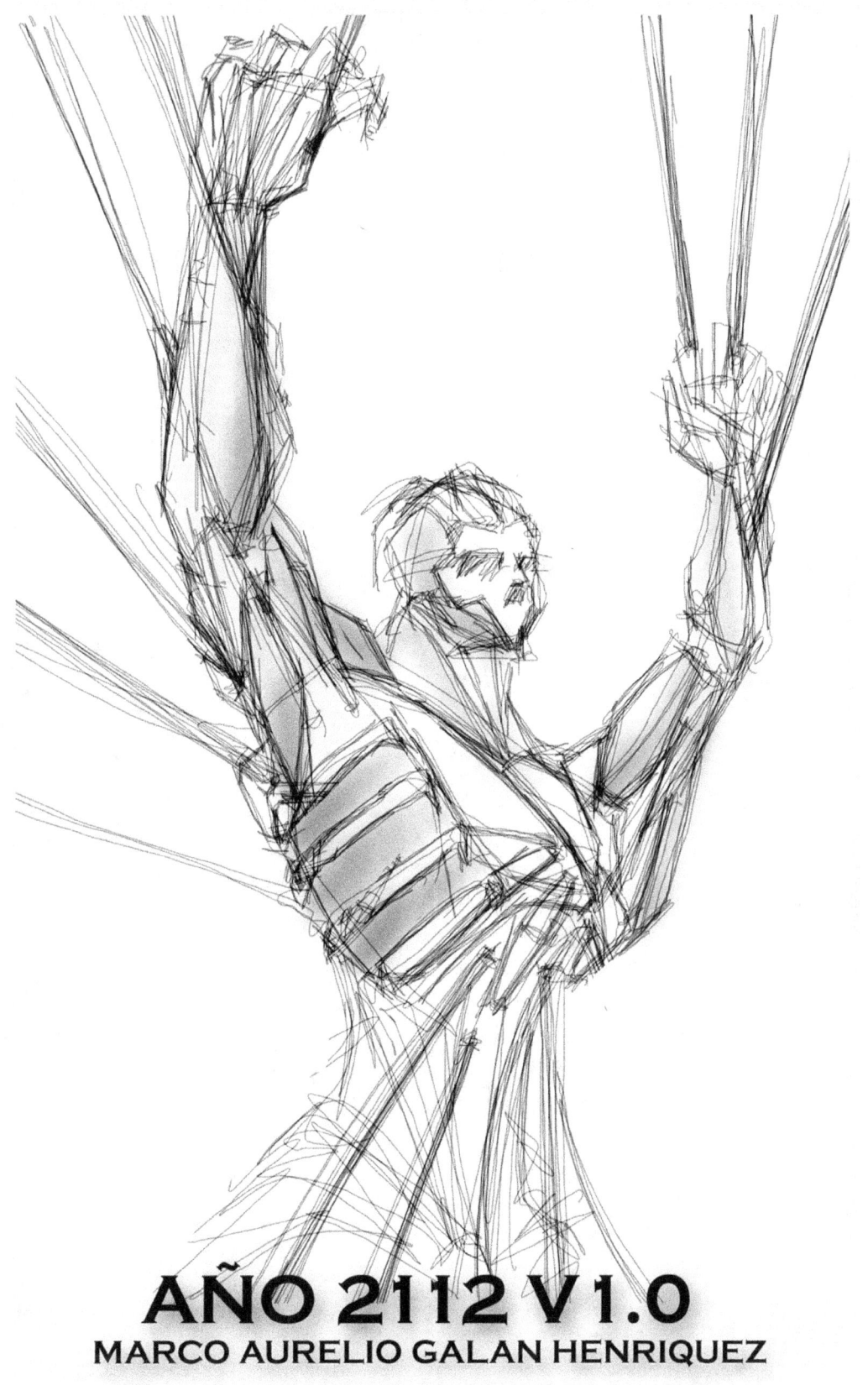

AÑO 2112 V1.0
MARCO AURELIO GALAN HENRIQUEZ

https://www.createspace.com/4245049

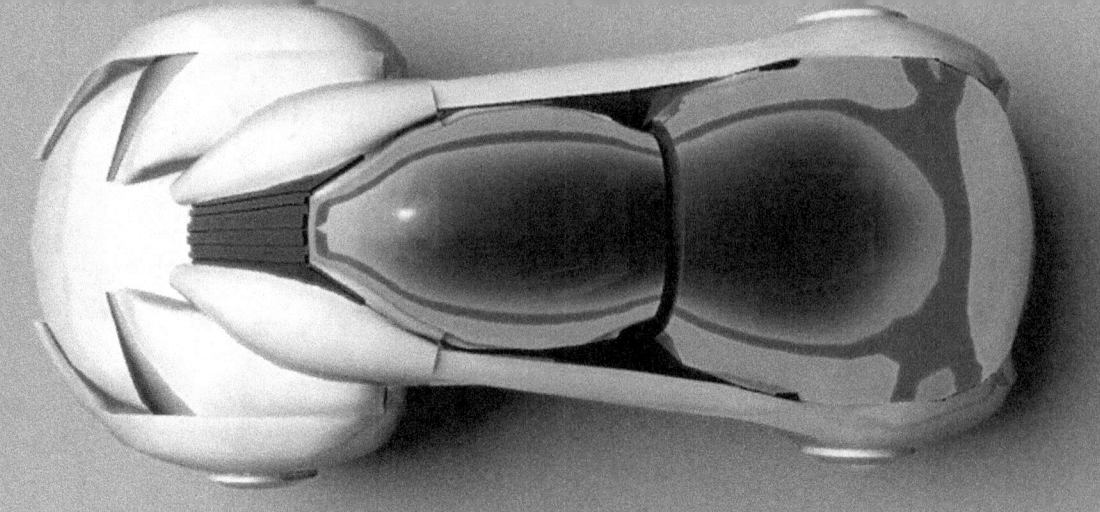

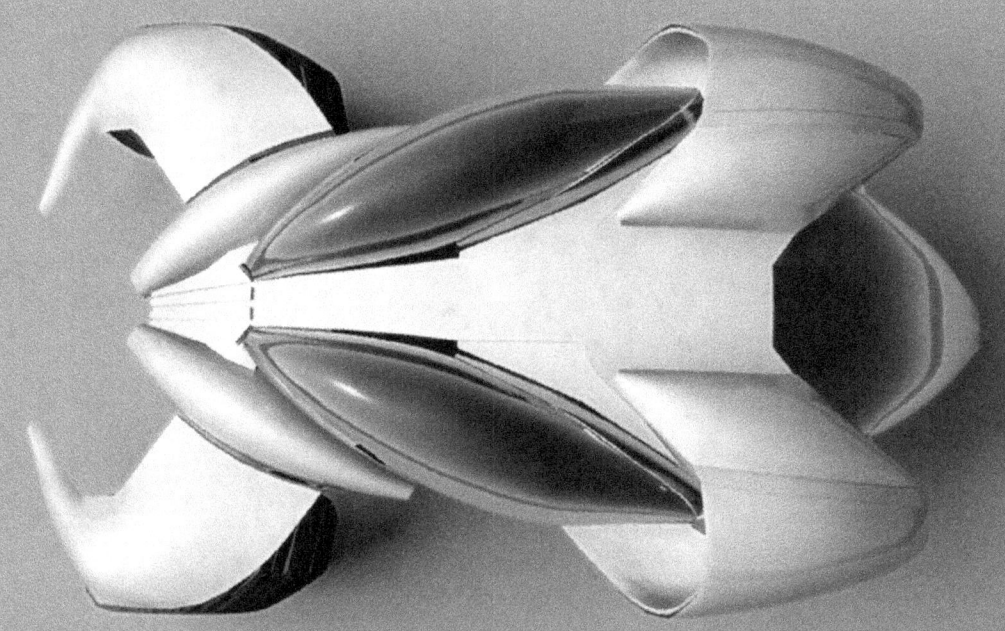

SUN CHARIOTS PROJECT
MARCO AURELIO GALAN HENRIQUEZ

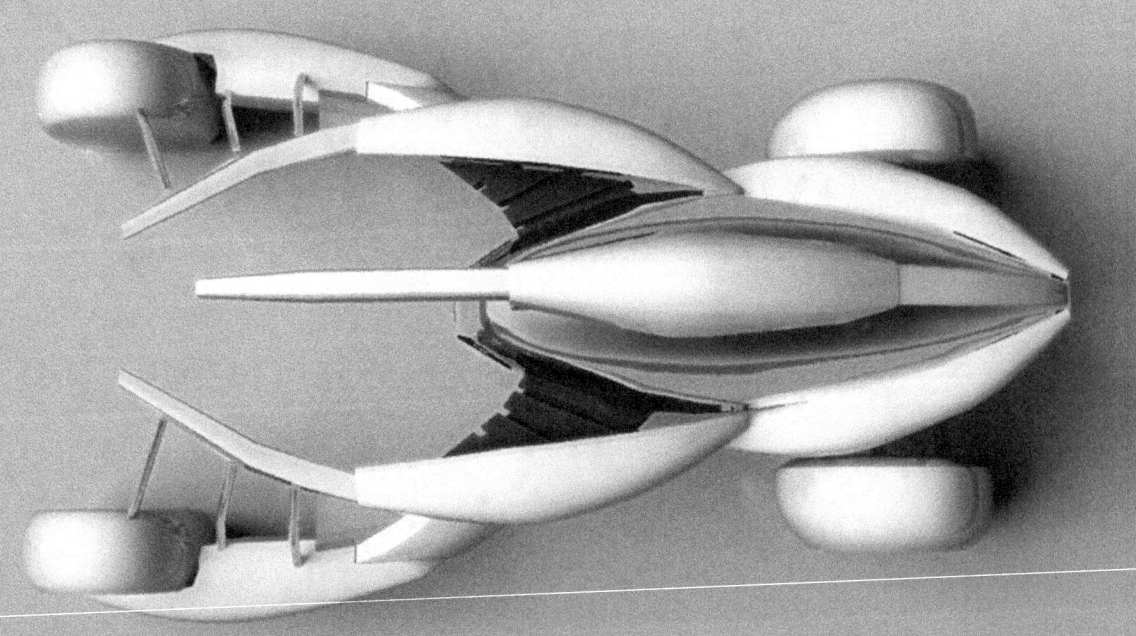

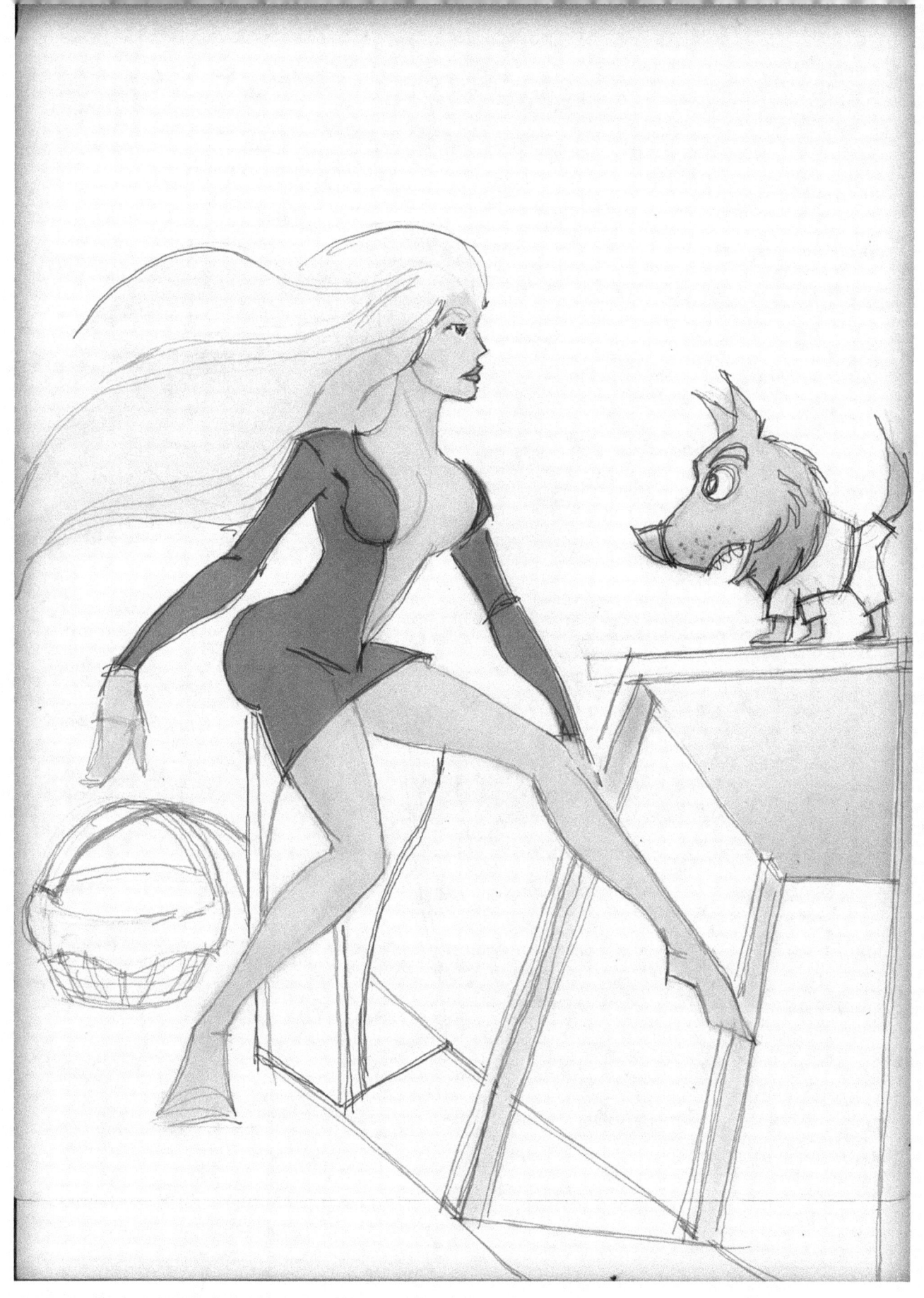

DECONSTRUCCIÓN DE
CUENTOS DE HADAS
MARCO AURELIO GALAN HENRIQUEZ

www.ingramcontent.com/pod-product-compliance
Lightning Source LLC
Chambersburg PA
CBHW081505170526
45166CB00008B/2560